# Building an Authoritari&

M000009389

Graeme Gill shows why post-Soviet Russia has failed to achieve the democratic outcome widely expected at the time of the fall of the Soviet Union, instead emerging as an authoritarian polity. He argues that the decisions of dominant elites have been central to the construction of an authoritarian polity, and explains how this occurred in four areas of regime-building: the relationship with the populace, the manipulation of the electoral system, the internal structure of the regime itself, and the way the political elite has been stabilized. Instead of the common "Yeltsin is a democrat, Putin an autocrat" paradigm, this book shows how Putin built upon the foundations Yeltsin had lain. It offers a new framework for the study of an authoritarian political system, and is therefore relevant not just to Russia but to many other authoritarian polities.

GRAEME GILL is Professor Emeritus in the Department of Government and International Relations at the University of Sydney. He specializes in Soviet and Russian politics and has published nineteen books and more than eighty papers in this area, including *Symbolism and Regime Change in Russia* (Cambridge University Press, 2013) and *Symbols and Legitimacy in Soviet Politics* (Cambridge University Press, 2011).

# Building an Authoritarian Polity

*Russia in Post-Soviet Times*

Graeme Gill

**CAMBRIDGE**
UNIVERSITY PRESS

# CAMBRIDGE
## UNIVERSITY PRESS

University Printing House, Cambridge CB2 8BS, United Kingdom

Cambridge University Press is part of the University of Cambridge.

It furthers the University's mission by disseminating knowledge in the pursuit of education, learning and research at the highest international levels of excellence.

www.cambridge.org
Information on this title: www.cambridge.org/9781107562424

© Graeme Gill 2015

First published 2015

Printed in the United States of America by Sheridan Books, Inc.

*A catalog record for this publication is available from the British Library*

ISBN 978-1-107-13008-1 Hardback
ISBN 978-1-107-56242-4 Paperback

# Contents

# Tables

# Preface

One of the constants of political life is change. In contemporary democracies, individual politicians need to remain alert to the emergence of new issues and new political forces, to the erosion of old loyalties, and to the impact of random and unprecedented events. The politician who tries to ignore such developments is a politician who is likely to have only a short career. At the broader systemic level, the political system too must remain flexible and able to adapt to changing circumstances. Such adaptation may be a result of conscious action by leading political figures, but it may also result simply from the political dynamic of the system itself. One of the strengths of democracy has been that the system has generally been able to adapt to new circumstances, although there have been some spectacular failures in this regard, with Weimar Germany a prominent example of this.

The challenge of change applies to all types of political systems, not just the democratic. But there is a fundamental difference in the situation facing the authoritarian polity compared with the democratic. While the latter gives free rein to autonomous political activity, and therefore to the capacity of political forces other than the regime to operate independently and thereby to help shape the political system itself, one of the essential characteristics of authoritarian rule is the restriction of autonomous political activity. The rulers of authoritarian regimes seek to prevent autonomous political forces from having any influence in the political system. By confining such forces to established regime-sponsored channels of political activity, authoritarian leaders seek to isolate the effect of oppositional activity and prevent it from playing a major part in the unrolling of political life. To the extent that this sort of neutering of potential opposition forces is successful, the authoritarian regime's position is strengthened. But this also underlines the fact that the major political player in an authoritarian system is the regime (or its leading actors) itself. The principal (but not only) influence upon the way in which the political system develops in an authoritarian polity is the regime and the decisions it makes about how to respond to both real and potential

challenges. The role the regime plays in shaping the contours of the political system is therefore generally much greater in authoritarian than in
democratic polities, where that role is shared with non-regime forces.

This role played by the regime means that a useful way of understanding authoritarian polities is to see them as being constantly under
construction. The most successful authoritarian regimes are those where
the leaders have been best able to adjust structures and processes of
rule to meet the challenges that arise. What this means is that as autocrats take measures to meet challenges, those measures will, they hope,
effectively continue to build the political system. Of course they may take
initiatives that are not prompted by the perceived need to meet a challenge, and these too can contribute to the building of the system (although
of course some initiatives may actually backfire and undermine that system). Whatever their motivation, the actions of authoritarian regimes are
central to the shaping of an authoritarian polity, and this process is one
that is likely to continue throughout the life of that polity. This notion of
the building of the system by its rulers provides a useful perspective to the
question of how to explain the longevity of some authoritarian regimes,
and it is particularly useful for an explanation of why post-Soviet Russia
has taken an authoritarian political trajectory. The utility of this approach
is demonstrated in this book.

The argument in this book has been taking shape for more than a
decade, principally in response to developments in Russia itself, but
also to the way in which both at the time and now, many in the West
have argued (put baldly) that Yeltsin's democracy has been displaced by
Putin's autocracy. I think this is a profound misunderstanding of what has
gone on and that the authoritarian trajectory widely attributed to Putin
was embarked upon under Yeltsin. Certainly Putin has extended and
altered some aspects of this, but the essential path was set in the 1990s.
This argument came under considerable attack in various international
fora in the late 1990s and early 2000s, and I want to thank those critics for
forcing me to think again and to sharpen my thoughts on this question.
Also important in helping me to crystallize my thoughts have been two
groups within the Department of Government and International Relations at the University of Sydney. The first is the authoritarian politics
research cluster. Through a number of meetings, the members of the
cluster – including Minglu Chen, Ben Goldsmith, Ryan Griffiths, Justin
Hastings, John Keane, Diarmuid Maguire, Lily Rahim, Jamie Reilly,
Fred Teiwes, and Yelena Zabortseva – forced me to rethink some of the
theory and to be clearer about what I was arguing. The second group is
the Electoral Integrity Project run by Pippa Norris. Although the focus
of this project is different from that of my own work, participation in the

seminars sharpened my appreciation of some issues, particularly those discussed in Chapter 3. Both groups have considerably improved this work, and for that I give them heartfelt thanks. Such thanks are also due to Yelena Zabortseva, whose diligent research assistance has contributed so much to this project, and to the Australian Research Council, who generously funded it. I would also like to acknowledge that some material in the book has already appeared in "The Stabilization of Authoritarian Rule in Russia?" in *Journal of Elections, Public Opinion and Parties* 25 (1), 2015, pp. 62–77, and in "The Decline of a Dominant Party and the Destabilization of Electoral Authoritarianism?" in *Post-Soviet Affairs* 28 (4), 2012, pp. 449–71. And finally, without the love and support of Heather, this, like everything else, would have been impossible.

# 1    Stability and authoritarian regimes

With the collapse of Soviet rule in 1991, Russia was widely seen both within the country and outside to be embarking on the road to a democratic future. The democratic mobilization and consequent partial opening of the political system in the last years of perestroika (especially 1988–91) encouraged many to believe that Russia would slough off its authoritarian past and proceed to build a democratic polity. However, such hopes were doomed to disappointment, as the potential for democratization was snuffed out and an authoritarian polity built. This book seeks to understand how an authoritarian polity could be built and become consolidated in Russia and the potential for democratic development thereby blunted.

The Russian experience of a potential opening to democracy being closed off by a reassertion of authoritarian rule was not unique. This was one possible trajectory of development for states that experienced political change during the so-called third wave of democratization during the last decades of the twentieth and first of the twenty-first century. Despite the characterization of these years as a period of democratization, the survival, resilience, and even emergence of authoritarian rule was a significant trend – as of 2013, some 54 percent of all regimes on the globe were adjudged not to be free[1] – and has led, belatedly, to an interest in the reasons for the survival of authoritarian regimes. This essentially means the question of the bases of stability of these regimes: why do they survive and how do they cope with challenges?

Attempts to explain authoritarian rule, including in Russia, have generally focused either on questions of legacy or path dependency, or on the primacy of the actions of particular actors.

---

[1] According to Freedom House, 46 percent of polities were adjudged to be "free," 30 percent "partly free," and 24 percent "not free." Freedom House, Freedom in the World 2013: Democratic Breakthroughs in the Balance, www.freedomhouse.org/report/freedom-world/freedom-world-2013#.U13eRMcwily, p. 4. Accessed December 20, 2013.

Two basic types of legacy explanations have been advanced to explain authoritarian stability: a focus on values, and a concentration upon the circumstances of the regime's birth. In both cases, the argument is that the regime is sustained by factors stemming from the past. This has been a common characteristic of analyses of Russian development.

The first type of explanation is about values. One of the enduring themes in the study of Russian politics has been the idea that that country is destined to have an authoritarian political system because of the values inherent in Russian popular culture. There has been a tendency to argue in circular fashion, that Russian history is overwhelmingly characterized by nondemocratic political systems, that this reflects the weakness of democratic values within the political culture, and that this means that a democratic outcome of political development is highly unlikely. Feeding into this line of argument is the view that traditional Russian conceptions of authority are highly authoritarian and paternalistic.

This sort of approach has been evident in a wide range of types of studies of Russia and its past.[2] It was reflected in works that sought to argue for a specific Russian "national character," in line with a common approach evident in the 1950s to the question of attitudinal differences between nations.[3] Others have sought to explain this perceived attitudinal pattern by references to assumed psychological traits of the Russian people.[4] There has been a tendency to attribute authoritarian values to Russian culture,[5] encapsulated by the so-called "Russian idea."[6] Closely related, history and the perceived pattern of Russian history have also

---

[2] For two overviews of some of this literature, see Nicolai N. Petro, *The Rebirth of Russian Democracy. An Interpretation of Political Culture* (Cambridge [Mass.]: Harvard University Press, 1995), Chapter 1; and Alexander Lukin, *Political Culture of Russian 'Democrats'* (Oxford: Oxford University Press, 2000), pp. 22–32.

[3] For example, see H.V. Dicks, "Some Notes on the Russian National Character," C.E. Black (ed.), *The Transformation of Russian Society* (Cambridge [Mass.]: Harvard University Press, 1960), pp. 558–73.

[4] For example, Geoffrey Gorer and John Rickman, *The People of Great Russia. A Psychological Study* (London: The Cresset Press, 1949); Geoffrey Gorer, "Some Aspects of the Psychology of the People of Great Russia," *The American Slavic and East European Review* 8 (3), 1949, pp. 155–66; and Margaret Mead, *Soviet Attitudes toward Authority. An Interdisciplinary Approach to Problems of Soviet Character* (New York: William Morrow, 1955).

[5] For example, Tibor Szamuely, *The Russian Tradition* (ed. Robert Conquest; London: Secker & Warburg, 1974). Also see James H. Billington, *The Icon and the Axe. An Interpretive History of Russian Culture* (New York: Alfred A. Knopf, 1966); D. Tomasic, *The Impact of Russian Culture on Soviet Communism* (Glencoe: The Free Press, 1953); and Nicholas P. Vakar, *The Taproot of Soviet Society. The Impact of Russia's Peasant Culture upon the Soviet State* (New York: Harper & Brothers, 1961).

[6] Nikolai Berdyaev, *The Russian Idea* (New York: The Macmillan Co., 1948).

been identified as a source of popular attitudes toward authority,[7] an approach that underpinned much of the "political culture" literature that emerged from the 1970s.

The essence of these sorts of studies was the argument that Russian history and culture were characterized by a model of authority in which supreme power was vested in an autocratic leader, be that a patriarchal father or the tsar, that such power was validated by a higher authority,[8] and that the populace owed total loyalty and obedience to this authority. All-powerful and all-wise, the authority figure was one to whom no opposition was possible. This was a model that saw initiative and innovation coming from the top; the people were the passive receptors of what the supreme authority figure deigned to pass down to them. Rather than being active participants in a dynamic process of political life, the populace was reduced in this conception to the passive receivers of wisdom from on high. This was clearly a highly authoritarian conception of power, and one which, in the eyes of observers at the time, was deeply unsympathetic to the values associated with democracy. It was, it was argued, this conception of authority that underpinned the tsarist political system, and that was carried forward into the Soviet era where the chief orientations of the regime reinforced this pattern.

The basic logic here appeared simple: an authoritarian political culture underpinned and was consistent with an authoritarian political system. Where popular values were overwhelmingly authoritarian in their orientation, they provided a buffer to nondemocratic rule because they portrayed that form of rule as the norm. In this sense, the regime gained popular legitimacy because its forms reflected predominant values. Such legitimacy would have been lacking had authoritarian political forms confronted a political culture dominated by ideas of democratic accountability and popular control because the modus operandi of the system would have been so at odds with popular values. This logic seems simple and compelling, but it does obscure some important qualifying factors.[9]

---

[7] For example, see Richard Pipes, *Russia under the Old Regime* (London: Weidenfeld & Nicolson, 1974); Stephen White, *Political Culture and Soviet Politics* (London: Macmillan, 1979); and Stephen White, "The USSR: Patterns of Autocracy and Industrialism," Archie Brown and Jack Gray (eds), *Political Culture and Political Change in Communist States* (London: Macmillan, 1977), pp. 25–65.

[8] On the association between God and tsar, see Billington (*Icon*), p. 35. Also M. Cherniavsky, *Tsar and People: Studies in Russian Myths* (New York: Random House, 1969), p. 35.

[9] For an excellent critique of the way the notion of political culture has been used in communist studies, see Mary McAuley, "Political Culture and Communist Studies: One Step Forward, Two Steps Back," Archie Brown (ed.), *Political Culture and Communist Studies* (Basingstoke: Macmillan, 1984), pp. 13–39.

One is the question of causality. Much of the literature on Russia's so-called authoritarian political culture assumes that culture shapes, perhaps even determines, the political forms that take hold in the society: Russia has an authoritarian political system because it has an authoritarian political culture. However, this seems to assume that the state and its political forms play no role in helping to shape the way that popular culture develops. Clearly what the state does and how it does it can have an impact on popular values. For example, the Soviet industrialization drive, which led to mass migration from the countryside into the cities, and the accompanying expansion of education is likely to have had a profound effect on popular values. Similarly, in Britain, the gradual expansion of the franchise from 1832 reinforced the strengthening of democratic values throughout British society in a way that might not have occurred so easily in the absence of such reforms. So values and structures interact in an important way, each shaping the other as they go. This means that a model of values determining structures is too simplistic and misunderstands the complex way in which these two interact. But once we accept that they interact, the danger is that the argument could become circular, the institutions are shaped by the institutions.[10]

There is also an assumption that values are unchanging, that rather than being something that is dynamic and in a process of continuing development, political culture is something that once established remains largely in its original form. This is, clearly, a view at odds with the reality. A society's values are in a constant state of change, and although this process may have accelerated and become more complex in recent decades, it has nevertheless been a characteristic of culture at all times. Even when regimes sought to restrict this process, as in Ming China and Tokugawa Japan, they achieved only limited success. Acknowledgement that a culture changes and may therefore be differentiated (i.e., some parts may have changed in ways that are different from and incompatible with other parts), makes it more difficult to draw a direct causal line between regime forms and cultural values.

The other factor that this logic obscures is the nature of the perceived values that constitute the political culture. Anyone trying to outline the contours of a particular culture must be selective in the choice of values they see as important. This means that values that are contrary to the presumed main thrust of the culture are excluded (or at least downplayed) in the analysis. For example, the view that Russian culture

---

[10] The danger of circularity is quite high as soon as scholars shift from an understanding of political culture as subjective values to a wider one including institutions and patterns of action. But the focus on subjectivism also has problems. See McAuley ("Political Culture") and Lukin (*Political Culture*), pp. 28–31.

was one that involved popular passivity seems to ignore the history of rural revolts and the revolutions of the twentieth century, while the presumed absence of notions of control over the rulers ignores the veche of medieval Novgorod[11] and the role of the zemskii sobor in 1613.[12] Or turning to the Soviet period, the perception of Soviet political culture as unrelievedly authoritarian needs to take into account things like the rhetorical dominance of "democracy" in official rhetoric, the practice of representation embodied in some of the lower level political institutions, and the upsurge of democratic activism between 1988 and 1991. These examples are not meant to deny the strength of authoritarian themes in historical Russian/Soviet culture, but to note that no culture is homogenous. Once this is accepted, it becomes increasingly tenuous to draw a direct and unambiguous causal link between values and institutions.

This does not mean that values do not have an influence on political institutions and the way they develop, nor that they have no relevance to the question of regime legitimacy. If there is a lack of fit between regime forms and popular perceptions, the buffer of popular support enjoyed by the regime is likely to be thin and the credit the regime enjoys with the populace limited. In contrast, when values and structures broadly align, popular attitudes to the regime are likely to be generally supportive and to allow the regime some leeway before disillusionment and opposition set in. But given the nature of value patterns, and the likelihood that in any particular national case there will be a diversity of values and attitudes, the precise relationship between political culture and regime will be complex. This is clearly the case with regard to post-Soviet Russia. It also means that, while values may help to shape regime outcomes and forms, they do not determine them.

The second type of legacy argument concerns the circumstances whereby the regime came into existence. This essentially amounts to an argument about the way in which the contours of politics in the new regime are shaped by the disposition of forces that brought about the regime change. In the Russian case, the key element about the replacement of the USSR by fifteen independent states of which Russia was one, is that this was a process governed by elites and one in which mass-based political actors played relatively little part.

The trigger for ultimate regime change was the process of reform set in train by Mikhail Gorbachev following his election as General Secretary in

---

[11] The assembly that was central to the running of the city before its incorporation into Muscovy in 1478.
[12] The assembly that elected Mikhail Romanov to the throne following the "time of troubles."

March 1985. This reform program,[13] popularly known as "perestroika," was something that for the first three and a half years (i.e., until the middle of 1988) comprised overwhelmingly measures introduced by Gorbachev and his supporters from the top. Hence the term used by one scholar, "revolution from above."[14] Although one aspect of this program, that of "democratization," did call upon the populace to become more active in political life – and over time this did become more radical in terms of the shift from simply criticizing malfeasance by officials to electing them in a competitive ballot[15] – this was to be at the behest of the political leadership and was to be strictly circumscribed within the boundaries specified. Thus, while increasingly there was recognition of the need for popular activism, this was still seen as being within parameters tightly defined by the leadership. The logic of this stage of perestroika still vested primacy within the top political leadership, with all others being supplementary to this. However, this began to change with the XIX Conference of the Communist Party in June–July 1988.

At this Conference, Gorbachev significantly radicalized the reform program, not only introducing a new structure of state legislative institutions and sidelining the party, but also shifting towards a competitive electoral process.[16] But also it was from this time that actors outside the political elite began independently to influence the reform process. Political parties began to emerge at this time,[17] although for the most part they remained weak and marginal to the mainstream of political life. What were to become more important were the popular fronts that emerged in most of the republics of the USSR from 1988 on. It was the activities of these groups that propelled the country on the trajectory to disintegration, with the main role in this being played by the fronts in the Baltic republics of Estonia, Latvia, and Lithuania.[18] These were popularly based movements, usually led by dissidents from the elite, that

---

[13] Although use of the term "program" gives too great a sense of coherence and considered thought to what was a much more disjointed set of measures which, over time, became increasingly radicalized.

[14] Gordon M. Hahn, *Russia's Revolution from Above 1985–2000: Reform, Transition, and Revolution in the Fall of the Soviet Communist Regime* (New Brunswick: Transaction Publishers, 2002).

[15] On this, see Stephen White, "'Democratisation' in the USSR," *Soviet Studies* 42 (1), 1990, pp. 3–24.

[16] On the Conference and its importance, see Graeme Gill and Roger Markwick, *Russia's Stillborn Democracy? From Gorbachev to Yeltsin* (Oxford: Oxford University Press, 2000), Chapter 3.

[17] On parties, see M. Steven Fish, *Democracy from Scratch. Opposition and Regime in the New Russian Revolution* (Princeton: Princeton University Press, 1995).

[18] On the role of the popular fronts, see Mark R. Beissinger, *Nationalist Mobilization and the Collapse of the Soviet State* (Cambridge: Cambridge University Press, 2002).

were able to mobilize sections of the populace into political activism, ultimately confronting the Moscow leadership and using this oppositionist stance to make major gains in the elections to the new central Congress of People's Deputies in 1989 and, more importantly, the republican elections of 1990. It was the capacity of the fronts in the Baltic states to win control of the republican governments that was the key factor in driving the union towards fragmentation along republican lines.

But while the Baltic popular fronts thereby played a key role in shaping the last years of Soviet political life, the corresponding front organization in the Russian Republic remained weak and politically marginal. It was never able to generate the sort of popular support based on opposition to Moscow that was evident in some other republics and was thereby never able to command a prominent place in shaping the course of Russian politics. More important in shaping such a course (and crucial for the union as a whole) was the split that occurred in the Communist elite. From the outset, members of the elite had held different views about the reforms, with no one sure of the consequences of what they were doing, but some unutterably opposed. By 1989, that elite was split in three ways. A group around Gorbachev sought to continue with a measured pace of reform, although in practice this involved some tacking back and forth, a process that ultimately led to the erosion of the numbers comprising this group. Another, more conservative group opposed the course of reform. Some of these believed that all sorts of change were wrong, others accepted that some change was needed but argued that the changes espoused by Gorbachev went too far too fast. Initially this group was personified by Yegor Ligachev,[19] but in the last years there was no single person who could act as its primary standard bearer. The third group was headed by Boris Yeltsin,[20] and believed that Gorbachev's reforms went neither far enough nor fast enough. Over time, the center around Gorbachev seems to have contracted while the two extremes expanded.

All three groups sought to court popular appeal, but only the third one around Yeltsin saw this as a major priority, and this was simply a recognition of their apparent weakness within the traditional Soviet structure. The conservatives sought to rely overwhelmingly upon the institutional structures of the Soviet regime (including the newly established in 1990 Communist Party of the RSFSR), although they did also seek to

---

[19] Ligachev was a leading party official, a CC Secretary 1983–90.
[20] Yeltsin was a leading party official until early 1988, a member of the CC Politburo (a candidate member) and Secretariat and head of the Moscow city party committee until his open clash with Gorbachev at the end of 1987. Then he was effectively an independent politician.

mobilize sections of the populace fearful about the impact of the reforms upon their lives. Gorbachev and supporters sought to shift the power from the old Soviet institutions to the newly created bodies, as well as appealing to that section of the population they believed supported the moderate path of reform they were pursuing. The group around Yeltsin sought to use his personal charisma to generate a wide wave of support and to thereby sweep into power in the republican organs of government in Russia. This strategy had some success in establishing a beachhead for the Democratic Russia party in the Soviet Congress of People's Deputies, but even more importantly gaining a significant position in the Russian Congress of People's Deputies. This facilitated Yeltsin's election by the Congress as chairman of the Russian Congress of People's Deputies in May–June 1990, followed in June 1991 by his popular election as President of Russia. Once he occupied the top position in the Russian government, he eschewed party building[21] and sought to rest his authority solely on his charismatic relationship with the people. He used this to oppose Gorbachev at every turn.[22]

While Yeltsin's appeal to charisma seemed to insert the populace into the political equation, it did so in only a subsidiary fashion. They were there only as support for an elite actor, and there was never any sense that Yeltsin was willing to foster the development of autonomous political activity that was likely to diverge from his own course of action. As the dynamic of the final eighteen months of the USSR played out, its focus remained the conflict between elites, with the mass of the populace playing a mainly observer role. The elite focus was clearly reflected in the attempted putsch of August 1991 and the means of the final dissolution of the USSR. The putsch was one set of elite actors (the conservatives) moving against another (Gorbachev et al.), and although a section of the populace was mobilized into the fray, significant in this was Yeltsin and his ability to generate that popular support. Thus, while the show of popular opposition to the putsch was crucial for its collapse, it remained secondary to the role of Yeltsin (and of Gorbachev). In terms of the final dissolution of the USSR, the elite focus is even more clear. Despite a majority of those who voted in March 1991[23] expressing a desire to

---

[21] Hence undercutting the development of Democratic Russia. See Geir Flikke, *The Failure of a Movement: The Rise and Decline of Democratic Russia 1989–1992* (Oslo: Faculty of Humanities, University of Oslo, 2006).

[22] On this, see M.K. Gorshkov, *Gorbachev–Yeltsin: 1500 dnei politicheskogo protivostoianiia* (Moscow: Terra, 1992) and Fedor Burlatsky, *Mikhail Gorbachev–Boris Yeltsin. Skhvatka* (Moscow: Sobranie, 2008).

[23] For the results of the referendum, see Richard Sakwa, *Russian Politics and Society* (London: Routledge, 1993, 1st edn.), p. 427.

see a renewed union continue, in early December the leaders of Russia, Belarus, and Ukraine met privately and disbanded the USSR. This was not something that the populace was given a say in, but was purely the result of elite action.

Overwhelmingly the course of politics in the Russian Republic in the 1985–91 period was structured by elite activity, with little scope available for organized popular involvement. Where the opportunity presented itself, people often did organize in the so-called informal groups, and later political parties and popular movements, but in Russia these remained largely sidelined. The elite sought to use these instrumentally, but without allowing them significant independent power. This means that genuine democratic forces, which were emerging at this time, had little scope for either popular involvement or for their own growth. The result is that when the new Russia emerged on January 1, 1992, democratic forces were very weak. The stability of the new regime in this argument thus rested on the weakness of potential popular mobilization and challenge to the regime stemming from the late-Soviet period.

As well as explanations focused upon a legacy of earlier development – values that have emerged over time or the elite dominance of politics stemming from the circumstances of regime change – there have also been explanations emphasizing the centrality of actors' actions. While such actions can contribute to the development of longer term structural factors, in the short term what political actors do has immediate effects in shaping the context of political life and regime development. A number of this type of explanation has been offered for the survival of authoritarian regimes, with most involving a combination of at least two of three elements:

- regime strength and capacity, or how regime elites go about building the regime;
- opposition strength and capacity, or how opposition forces seek to develop a viable opposition to the regime; and
- international influences, or how international actors attempt to affect the domestic political dynamic.

These three elements – what regimes do, what oppositions do, and what international actors do – interact with each other to shape the immediate process of regime building and survival. Different explanatory schema deploy these elements to varying degrees to offer sophisticated explanations for the survival of authoritarian regimes. The three main examples discussed below show how these different elements can be interwoven to produce a theoretically robust explanation of political change and its absence.

Valerie Bunce and Sharon Wolchik[24] have sought to explain why post-communist authoritarian leaders have been overthrown via the ballot box. Their analysis emphasizes the role of the opposition and of international influences. They reject the view that the strength of the regime, the position of civil society, economic performance (e.g., onset of economic difficulty, or increasing prosperity), political trends (e.g., recent crackdown on opposition), or US government support for the opposition can provide any real purchase in seeking to explain regime change or survival. Instead they emphasize the potential independent role of elections in bringing about regime change. But this can only occur, in Bunce and Wolchik's view, when the opposition adopts an innovative electoral strategy. This means that they are not concerned with the structural position of the opposition, with any attempt to evaluate the strength of the opposition, but with the electoral strategy it brings to the election.

Bunce and Wolchik are not completely clear about the components of the electoral strategy that has produced opposition success, but this so-called electoral model seems to involve[25]

- opposition unity; this means not only creation of a united bloc among established opposition forces, but the drawing into oppositional activity of civil society organizations.
- measures to improve the quality and transparency of electoral procedures; principal means are through a high level of election monitoring, the conduct of exit polls, and the holding of parallel independent vote tabulation.
- an ambitious and well-organized campaign that offers a real policy alternative to the government and focuses on increasing voter registration and turnout; this is where the activation of civil society is central.
- possession and projection of the conviction that real change is possible through the electoral process.

Bunce and Wolchik argue through their case studies that where this model was applied (Slovakia, Croatia, Serbia, Georgia, Ukraine, and Kyrgyzstan), authoritarian leaders were removed and where it was not (Armenia, Azerbaijan, and Belarus) those leaders remained in power.

This electoral model, argue Bunce and Wolchik, emerged in the Philippines in 1986 and traveled from Southeast Asia through Latin America (1988 Chilean referendum) to eastern Europe. It then moved through the successful countries, beginning in Slovakia in 1998 and (thus far) ending

---

[24] Valerie J. Bunce and Sharon L. Wolchik, *Defeating Authoritarian Leaders in Postcommunist Countries* (Cambridge: Cambridge University Press, 2011). Also Valerie J. Bunce and Sharon L. Wolchik, "Defeating Dictators. Electoral Change and Stability in Competitive Authoritarian Regimes," *World Politics* 62 (1), 2010, pp. 43–86.

[25] Bunce and Wolchik (*Defeating Authoritarian Leaders*), pp. 252–60.

in Kyrgyzstan in 2005. International diffusion of this electoral model is thus intrinsic to the authors' conception of the process of regime change. They argue that central to the adoption of this strategy by opposition forces in the respective countries was not just modeling of the success of others, but the conscious part played by pro-democracy activists mainly from the successful countries in the later ones. Such activists, often supported by Western governments and institutions (including NGOs), gave practical advice, and sometimes material resources, to their would-be emulators, and for Bunce and Wolchik this input was essential to success. These transnational networks of pro-democracy activists were more important to the outcome than simply assistance provided by the US.

This is a beguiling explanation because it emphasizes the capacity of the opposition to bring about change, and therefore assumes the primacy of human agency over structural conditions. It is also quite convincing because there is a logic to the argument that the better an opposition conducts itself during an election campaign, the more likely it is to have significant political effects. But as it stands, the argument is incomplete because it ignores the role played by the regime in this. The authors argue that "the regimes where challenges to authoritarian rule did not succeed tend to be stronger on the whole than the other regimes," but because there was significant variation in capacity, there was no consistent link between regime strength and electoral outcome.[26] It is not clear why differences in capacity should negate the basic picture that emerges, namely, that stronger regimes tended to survive. Part of the problem with the Bunce and Wolchik position is linked to the fact that they are looking at a particular type of regime, the mixed or competitive/electoral authoritarian regime where a "democratic" electoral process is used to stabilize a nondemocratic regime. As will be shown in Chapter 3, in such systems a regime uses a range of measures to create an electoral system in which any challenges can be rebuffed. This means that the regime creates the rules that structure the electoral process. In those cases where there was electoral turnover as a result of the application of the electoral model identified by Bunce and Wolchik, the ability of the opposition to implement that model was a result of the fact that the regime effectively allowed them to do so. Rather than crack down on the opposition and tighten electoral controls, the regime had enabled the opposition to utilize the electoral practices that brought about an effective challenge to the regime. This is reflected in the fact that the figures cited by Bunce and Wolchik (p. 217) seem to suggest that generally the more

---

[26] Bunce and Wolchik (*Defeating Authoritarian Leaders*), pp. 226–7. The variations in capacity are presented in Table 8.4, p. 225.

"democratic" countries were, the more likely they were to experience regime change.[27] That this was not universal[28] simply reflects the fact that the nature of the regime was not the only influential factor. So while the Bunce and Wolchik focus on the importance of electoral strategy does help to explain electoral outcomes, by neglecting the way in which the capacity to implement this strategy was dependent upon prior decisions by the regime with regard to the structuring of the electoral process, the explanation for regime change/non-change is only partial.

Another analysis based on a large number of case studies, by Steven Levitsky and Lucan A. Way,[29] emphasizes the importance principally of international influence, with regime strength and capacity a contingent factor. Their view is well summarized in the following:

Where linkage to the West was high, competitive authoritarian regimes democratized. Where linkage was low, regime outcomes hinged on incumbents' organizational power. Where state and governing party structures were well organized and cohesive, regimes remained stable and authoritarian; where they were underdeveloped or lacked cohesion, regimes were unstable, although they rarely democratized.[30]

Unlike Bunce and Wolchik, Levitsky and Way do not see elections as independent mechanisms of regime change. In their view, the key was international influence, of which they identify two types, leverage and linkage.[31] Leverage was defined as a government's vulnerability to external pressure to democratize, and this in turn was affected by the political and economic strength of the state, competing Western foreign policy objectives, and the influence of counter powers that sought to negate such Western influence. However, leverage alone was rarely, in Levitsky and Way's view, able to bring about regime change, principally because it focused on electoral matters and little else. Linkage was more complex, involving the density of ties and cross-border flows among the competitive authoritarian countries on the one hand, and on the other the US, pre-2004 EU members, and Western-dominated multilateral institutions. Six dimensions of linkage were seen to be of particular importance:

---

[27] This is in spite of their comment that "Variations in electoral outcomes do not seem to be explained by variations in how democratic mixed regimes are or, consequently, by the extent to which regimes narrow or widen opportunities for democratic change." Bunce and Wolchik (*Defeating Authoritarian Leaders*), p. 218.

[28] In four of the five cases of no change, according to the figures cited by Bunce and Wolchik, the country was less democratic than all of the cases where regime change occurred. Bunce and Wolchik (*Defeating Authoritarian Leaders*), p. 217.

[29] Steven Levitsky and Lucan A. Way, *Competitive Authoritarianism. Hybrid Regimes after the Cold War* (Cambridge: Cambridge University Press, 2010).

[30] Levitsky and Way (*Competitive Authoritarianism*), p. 5.

[31] Levitsky and Way (*Competitive Authoritarianism*), pp. 38–54.

- economic, comprising trade flows, investment, and credit.
- intergovernmental, including bilateral, diplomatic, and military ties and involvement in Western-led alliances, treaties, and international organizations.
- technocratic, meaning the education of the country's elite and/or professional ties to Western universities or Western-led multilateral institutions.
- social, involving people flows across borders, including tourism, immigration, refugee flows, and diaspora networks.
- information, including telecommunications, internet connections, and media penetration.
- civil society, or local ties to Western-based NGOs, international, religious, and party organizations, and other transnational networks.

Linkage was seen as a mechanism that could increase the costs to regimes of the abuse of democratic principles, it could strengthen domestic constituencies favoring democracy and its creation, and thereby weaken authoritarian regimes. So both leverage and linkage were about constricting the room for authoritarian regimes to function and thereby ultimately about bringing them down.

However, where levels of linkage were low, the domestic organization of power on the part of the authoritarian regime was central. According to Levitsky and Way, the role of the weakness or internal decay of states was often unrecognized in the literature, and that a well-organized and cohesive state or party structure could enable autocrats to defeat democrats. Two organizations are central, states and parties. Effective state and party organizations enhance elites' capacity to prevent defection, co-opt or repress opponents, blunt protests, and win elections. Where state and party are strong, powerful opposition can be overcome; where they are weak, relatively weak opposition can prevail. Central to this is coercive power, the ability to use force to consolidate themselves in power and overcome any challenges. State coercive capacity has two dimensions: scope and cohesion. Scope refers to the effective reach of the apparatus,[32] cohesion to the level of compliance within the state apparatus. A state apparatus with broad scope and a high level of cohesion was the key to regime survival. While fiscal health was important (i.e., the ability to pay functionaries), three chief sources of cohesion were identified: in ethnically divided societies, shared ethnic identity could be a

---

[32] Confusingly, they associate this with Michael Mann's notion of infrastructural power. Michael Mann, "The Autonomous Power of the State: Its Origins, Mechanism and Results," John A. Hall (ed.), *States in History* (Oxford: Basil Blackwell, 1986), pp. 109–36.

source of cohesion, with Malaysia cited as an example; shared ideology, as in Serbia; or solidarity forged through violent struggle or revolution, as in Zimbabwe. Coercion is where these twin characteristics of scope and cohesion come together; a regime must be able to wield the degree of coercion necessary to retain control, yet it is precisely high intensity coercion that can most strain the unity fundamental to regime cohesion. Party strength, measured in terms of scope and cohesion, was also important because of the role parties can play in the stabilization of such regimes. This is discussed in Chapter 4. Organizational power is strongest where both party and state are strong.[33] While Levitsky and Way do acknowledge that opposition capacity can be a factor,[34] this is clearly seen as subordinate to the organizational power of the regime.

This too is a persuasive argument. However, the primacy accorded to international influence, with state strength as only a contingent factor, risks underestimating the role played by the state. Vulnerability to international influence, be it of the linkage or leverage variety, is in part dependent upon the strength of the state and the skill with which its leaders handle international connections. A strong state, in terms of both of the Levitsky and Way criteria (scope and cohesion), will be much better placed to fend off or moderate international influences than a weaker state. While it may be that in the contemporary world no state can isolate itself from the international system without paying significant costs, not all states occupy the same location within that system. Weak states are clearly much more vulnerable to the international system than strong states, and therefore more likely to have to give way to external pressure than stronger and more confident states. And given the way in which authoritarian regimes are organized, generally with less independence for social forces in the society, an effective authoritarian regime will ensure that as much as possible, international connections will be mediated through regime structures. In this sense, rather than the state's organizational strength coming into play only when international linkages are weak, the nature of state organization will help to shape the role that international influences can play domestically. This is recognized in the third type of approach, that emphasizing regime strength and capacity.

An example of this sort of approach is provided by Lucan Way writing alone.[35] In seeking to answer why authoritarian regimes in Armenia,

---

[33] Levitsky and Way also allow for state economic control as a possible substitute for party and coercive organization. Levitsky and Way (*Competitive Authoritarianism*), pp. 66–7.

[34] Levitsky and Way (*Competitive Authoritarianism*), pp. 68–70.

[35] Lucan Way, "Resistance to Contagion: Sources of Authoritarian Stability in the Former Soviet Union," Valerie Bunce, Michael McFaul, and Kathryn Stoner-Weiss (eds), *Democracy and Authoritarianism in the Postcommunist World* (Cambridge: Cambridge University Press, 2010), pp. 229–52.

Belarus, Moldova, and Russia survived in the 1990s–2000s but Georgia, Ukraine, and Kyrgyzstan succumbed, he focuses upon state and party strength. He argues that autocrats were more likely to survive when they had at least one of what he calls "pillars of incumbent strength." These were

- "a single highly institutionalized ruling party backed by a nonmaterial source of cohesion such as a revolutionary tradition or highly salient ideology";
- "an extensive, well-funded, and cohesive coercive apparatus";
- "state discretionary control over the economy, generated either by the failure to privatize or by reliance on easily captured energy revenues."[36]

For Way, ruling parties helped to discourage elite defection by institutionalizing the distribution of patronage and helped pro-government deputies ride the coattails of popular incumbents and thereby gain a dominant place in the legislature. Nonmaterial sources of cohesion were important because they made the regime less vulnerable to economic crises or perceived swings in its popularity, both of which could affect patronage based upon material resources. A coercive apparatus was key to maintaining control.[37] Its effectiveness could be undermined by significant underfunding and/or large wage arrears, or strengthened by successful participation in national level coercive activity, such as a war. A powerful, cohesive coercive apparatus could strengthen state capacity. And finally, discretionary control over wealth gave the capacity to buy off opposition and consolidate loyalty, and starve the opposition of resources.[38] Any one of these three pillars, in Way's view, strengthened the regime against potential opposition action. Importantly, Way recognizes that state organizational power shapes opposition mobilization.

Way's focus on the characteristics of the regime acknowledges a key element in the explanation of the durability of authoritarian regimes. However, it is not clear that the argument that only one of the three pillars is sufficient to guarantee survival is correct. In particular, the third one, discretionary control over the economy, would appear by itself to be insufficient to ensure regime survival. Indeed, it is difficult to see how such control could be maintained without an effective state structure,

---

[36] Way ("Resistance"), p. 230.

[37] On Lukashenka in Belarus acting preemptively in this way, see Vitali Silitski, "Contagion Deterred: Preemptive Authoritarianism in the Former Soviet Union (the Case of Belarus)," Valerie Bunce, Michael McFaul, and Kathryn Stoner-Weiss (eds), *Democracy and Authoritarianism in the Postcommunist World* (Cambridge: Cambridge University Press, 2010), pp. 274–99.

[38] For an argument about the way that state control over the economy limits the personal economic autonomy that underpins political activism, see Kelly M. McMann, *Economic Autonomy and Democracy. Hybrid Regimes in Russia and Kyrgyzstan* (Cambridge: Cambridge University Press, 2006).

including a coercive apparatus. This may not have to be developed to the extent envisaged in Way's three pillars, but there would need to be at least some form of organizational control outside the economic sphere if such economic control were to be maintained.

Way's emphasis on parties is consistent with broader literature on the role of political parties in explaining authoritarian resilience. This began from Barbara Geddes' observation that regimes that had parties tended to be more long-lasting than those that did not, while holding regular elections also seemed to increase regime life.[39] Although there has been some criticism of Geddes' analysis,[40] there has been general acceptance of her basic point: party regimes tend to survive longer than those regimes without parties.[41] In attempting to explain this, many scholars have pointed to the role of the party in resolving elite tension and conflict. For example, Brownlee argues that ruling parties "bridle elite ambitions and bind together otherwise fractious coalitions,"[42] while Geddes argues *inter alia* that parties can enforce elite bargains to limit competition and can help deter potential challenges from within the elites; because of the party's continuing access to power and resources, party factions see themselves as being better off if they remain united in the party rather than split from it.[43] In this view, the role the party plays in managing elite relations is fundamental to the continuing stability and maintenance of authoritarian rule.

Another aspect of the role the party plays has been emphasized in discussion of the so-called competitive authoritarian, electoral authoritarian, or hybrid regimes.[44] These were regimes that combined democratic

---

[39] See Barbara Geddes, "What Do We Know about Democratization after Twenty Years?," *Annual Review of Political Science* 2, 1999, p. 131; and Barbara Geddes, *Paradigms and Sand Castles. Theory Building and Research Design in Comparative Politics* (Ann Arbor: University of Michigan Press, 2003), pp. 69–86.

[40] Benjamin Smith suggests that the longevity of the Soviet and Mexican cases may so distort the analysis of the length of party regimes that Geddes' general finding may be questionable. Benjamin Smith, "Life of the Party. The Origins of Regime Breakdown and Persistence under Single-Party Rule," *World Politics* 57 (3), 2005, p. 426. Jason Brownlee argues that elections are much less important as causal factors than Geddes suggests. Jason Brownlee, *Authoritarianism in an Age of Democratization* (Cambridge: Cambridge University Press, 2007), pp. 30–31.

[41] Although hereditary monarchies, which do not figure in Geddes' analysis, on average have longer life spans than party regimes.

[42] Brownlee (*Authoritarianism*), p. 30.

[43] Barbara Geddes, "Why Parties and Elections in Authoritarian Regimes?," unpublished, March 2006, pp. 5 and 9–11; and Brownlee (*Authoritarianism*), pp. 35–42.

[44] As well as Levitsky and Way (*Competitive Authoritarianism*), see Larry Diamond, "Thinking about Hybrid Regimes," *Journal of Democracy* 13 (2), 2002, pp. 21–35; Marina Ottaway, *Democracy Challenged. The Rise of Semi-Authoritarianism* (Washington, DC: Carnegie Endowment for International Peace, 2003); Andreas Schedler (ed.), *Electoral*

and nondemocratic elements in such a way that democratic procedures, most importantly elections, were used to stabilize nondemocratic rule. They had for the most part regular competitive elections, but in which the electoral contest was skewed in favor of the ruling party, making its defeat at the polls unlikely. However, what distinguished many of these regimes from earlier nondemocratic ones where more than one party participated in the election (including, for example, communist regimes in Poland and China) was that although the electoral playing field was structured in such a way as to favor the ruling party, the result of the election was not a foregone conclusion; opposition parties could at times defeat incumbents despite the barriers the former faced. Although the electoral process was unfair, electoral outcomes remained uncertain. Such regimes, it was argued, had initially been seen in terms of the democratization paradigm, as having stalled on the path from authoritarian rule to democracy, but, it was now argued, they should actually be seen as a regime type in their own right.[45] This sort of approach attributed to parties an important role in the functioning of the system: the ruling party was central to the use of the electoral mechanism to consolidate the regime's power. Without it, the electoral process could have no meaning. Thus in this view, the party's role in regime maintenance stemmed from its dominance of the electoral arena.

The focus on the party has been a major one in scholarship on nondemocratic systems, but in the attempt to explain authoritarian stability, the existing explanations have been too narrow. It is not only the party's role in moderating elite conflict or in winning elections that is important. In order to maximize the chances of the party contributing to regime maintenance and stability, the party must successfully fulfill more functions than these explanations allow. This will be discussed in greater detail in Chapter 4.

Another argument consistent with that of a strong state structure focuses on the power of the presidency. Building on substantial literature,[46] many have argued that presidential systems are more likely to lead to authoritarian outcomes than are parliamentary systems. This is because presidential systems are believed to vest undivided power in

*Authoritarianism. The Dynamics of Unfree Competition* (Boulder: Lynne Riener Publishers, 2006); and Andreas Schedler, *The Politics of Uncertainty. Sustaining and Subverting Electoral Authoritarianism* (Oxford: Oxford University Press, 2013).

[45] Levitsky and Way (*Competitive Authoritarianism*), pp. 3–4.

[46] For example, see Arend Lijphart (ed.), *Parliamentary versus Presidential Government* (Oxford: Oxford University Press, 1992); Juan J. Linz and Arturo Valenzuela (eds), *The Failure of Presidential Democracy: Comparative Perspectives* (Baltimore: The Johns Hopkins University Press, 1994); M. Shugart and A. Carey, *Presidents and Assemblies: Constitutional Design and Electoral Dynamics* (Cambridge: Cambridge University Press,

the leading office in the land, that this winner-take-all system discourages compromise and a willingness to be open to diversity of opinion, there is less capacity for the representation of different social interests, and that there is less institutional control over the chief executive than exists in a parliamentary system. All of these perceived problems with presidential rule have been identified in the Russian experience and the post-Soviet space more generally.[47]

## Building the authoritarian regime

While these institutional aspects of an authoritarian regime may help in explaining authoritarian resilience, the institutions themselves explain little without reference to how they relate to the actions and perceptions of political actors. For example, political actors who sought to build a democratic polity could overcome the assumed authoritarian tendencies in presidentialism. But where political actors are determined to build an authoritarian polity, those institutions can be used to facilitate achievement of that aim. This is clearly evident in the Russian case, where post-Soviet elites sought to build such a regime, and reflects the fact that the most important conjunctural factor in explaining authoritarian rule is the attempt to build an authoritarian polity by political elites. In doing this, they had to create a political structure designed to carry out the two tasks essential to the maintenance of authoritarian rule.

1992); and Alfred Stepan and Cindy Skach, "Constitutional Frameworks and Democratic Consolidation: Parliamentarianism and Presidentialism," *World Politics* 46, (1), 1993, pp. 1–22.

[47] For example, M. Steven Fish, *Democracy Derailed in Russia. The Failure of Open Politics* (Cambridge: Cambridge University Press, 2005), Chapter 7; Gerald M. Easter, "Preference for Presidentialism. Postcommunist Regime Change in Russia and the NIS," *World Politics* 49 (2), 1997, pp. 184–211; and Timothy Frye, "A Politics of Institutional Choice. Post-Communist Presidencies," *Comparative Political Studies* 30 (5), 1997, pp. 523–52. Another institutional choice that is believed to have an impact on regime trajectory is choice of electoral system, with majoritarian systems tending to reduce the number of political parties and deliver single-party governments while plurality or proportional systems ensure wider party representation and promote party fragmentation. The latter facilitates the representation of a wider range of views and therefore a more diffuse decision-making environment, the former the consolidation of rule and much narrower diversity of interests. For studies of Russia in this regard, see Robert G. Moser, *Unexpected Outcomes. Electoral Systems, Political Parties, and Representation in Russia* (Pittsburgh: University of Pittsburgh Press, 2001); Bryon Moraski, *Elections by Design. Parties and Patronage in Russia's Regions* (DeKalb: Northern Illinois University Press, 2006); and Erik S. Herron, *Elections and Democracy after Communism* (Basingstoke: Palgrave Macmillan, 2009).

First, the structuring of public political activity. The key to the designation of a regime as authoritarian, or nondemocratic, is that it is not responsible to the people over whom it rules. However, this does not mean that there are not pressures for involvement in political life by individuals, groups, and organizations outside the regime. In all sorts of political systems, such pressures exist, and they must be accommodated. Even in those regimes that in the past had been labeled "totalitarian," there was provision for the involvement in public politics of the citizenry as a whole. If no such provision is made, the result is likely to be widespread disillusionment and the generation of feelings of opposition. Alternatively, there could simply be a popular withdrawal from the regime and society, which could lead to the system becoming totally dysfunctional. Accordingly all regimes make some provision for participation on the part of non-regime actors – social movements, interest groups, professional associations, business – and although such provisions are often derided and described as purely ritualistic or tokenistic, as the role of elections in some regimes has shown, these can prove to have real political salience. But even when they do not take on this sort of political importance, such institutions are central to the regime's survival. If such institutions can act effectively, they can co-opt the society into the regime's structures, and thereby compromise its independence and consolidate the regime's foundations. If the regime can create structures that will capture social pressures for political involvement, and thereby direct them into safe, even regime-supporting, channels, it has gone a long way toward guaranteeing its longevity.

Second, the structuring of the way the regime actually works. All regimes, regardless of their aims – and these range from complete social and political transformation to simply remaining in power, perhaps in order to enable the enrichment of its members – seek to remain in power. This aim of remaining in power will be complicated if the regime's internal procedures lack routine and system; ambiguous lines of command, competing jurisdictions, and idiosyncratic procedures all contribute to a regime that works in a nonsystematic and ineffective fashion. Prospects for regime survival will be increased when domestic procedures are routinized. This removes the possibility of continuing disputes over non-substantive policy issues and should provide a mechanism for resolving those disputes that do arise. Ideally, such routinization should include questions of leadership succession, decision-making, policy debate, policy implementation, and ensuring the obedience (and loyalty) of lower level functionaries. This therefore involves the structuring of activity at both the levels of elite politics and of lower range administrative positions. The key question is the extent to which the administrative structure obeys decisions taken at the top, and the way in which unity is maintained among the central political elite.

The structuring of action in the public political and more restricted regime spheres of life is not a task that can be completed once and for all. Rather it is a continuing process of adjustment and institutional reform as new challenges emerge or existing institutions are deemed deficient. In this sense, the building of an authoritarian polity is a continuous process driven by the need to deal with potential challenges, such as economic downturn, internal/external violence and conflict, leadership succession, the enactment and implementation of policy. If it fails to respond to such challenges effectively, it may fall. This problem is exacerbated for authoritarian regimes by two things: deficiencies in information, and the uncertainty about whether there is a buffer of public support in the face of policy failure. The information deficit is a product of the way in which such regimes are constructed: restrictions on freedom of speech and public discourse mean the weakness or absence of channels of independent information flow from society to regime and the consequent difficulty for the regime of gaining accurate information about a wide range of questions. The uncertainty about levels of public support reflects the absence in such regimes of a mechanism for society to truly and openly express its feelings about the regime and its policies. In the absence of things like independent polling agencies, fair competitive elections, and a free media, the regime can never be sure about how the society feels about it, and it can therefore never be certain how much room it has for performance failure before its credit runs out.

These two dimensions of rule, the structuring of public political activity and of internal regime functioning, are central to regime stability and durability. If either of them is deficient in a major way, the prospects for regime stability and survival will be diminished. This does not mean that, for example, widespread opposition activity or the absence of a clear mechanism for leadership succession will necessarily cause the regime to fall. A range of other factors, including the strength of the opposition, may come into play. But if there are significant deficiencies in either of these dimensions of rule, and they are not addressed through a process of institutional reform, the long-term stability of the regime will be under question. This is not to deny that, as some of the authors discussed above suggest, international factors may be important, but those factors will be mediated through the dimensions of rule of which the regime consists.

The importance of these two dimensions of rule is clearly evident in the way in which Russia's post-Soviet leaders set about building an authoritarian polity.[48] It has been the way that these dimensions of rule have been shaped by elite political actors and the inability of other actors, either domestic or international, to deflect them from this that has determined the authoritarian trajectory of Russia's political development. Had the successive elites around Yeltsin and Putin sought to structure these two dimensions of rule in different ways, the political outcome may have been different. Instead they chose to build Russia as an authoritarian polity.

Following the fall of the USSR, the Yeltsin administration systematically sought to close down the channels for popular activism that had opened up during the Gorbachev period. This closure involved a combination of repressive action and attempts to impose a restrictive structure on emergent forms of autonomous activity. Within the regime, attempts were made intermittently to impose a structure that maximized the president's power and autonomy. In both spheres these efforts had mixed results. Yeltsin's successor, Vladimir Putin, both learning from Yeltsin's mistakes and building on the beginnings he made, strengthened the authoritarian elements of the polity and was able to construct a system that seemed significantly more stable and consolidated than that he had inherited. He brought greater routine and discipline to the structuring of both public political activity and elite political life. How this process of authoritarian consolidation was achieved is the focus of this book. Part I analyzes the structuring of public political activity. Chapter 2 will investigate how the incorporation of autonomous political activity moved from the less effective efforts of the Yeltsin years to a more consolidated system under Putin, even while new (and potentially dangerous) forms of mobilization appeared. Chapter 3 looks at the way in which electoral politics was tamed. Part II concerns the structuring of the regime internally. Chapter 4 focuses on the machinery of rule and the way in which this

---

[48] The emphasis given to decisions taken by the leaders in the construction of an authoritarian polity is consistent with that of Ostrow, Satarov, and Khakamada, who point to the centrality of decisions made by Yeltsin and his supporters on what they see as four crucial issues: the refusal to introduce major political reform as soon as the USSR collapsed, the form of the new Constitution, the subversion of political competition, and the refusal to allow the question of political succession to be resolved democratically. Joel M. Ostrow, Georgiy A. Satarov, and Irina M. Khakamada, *The Consolidation of Dictatorship in Russia. An Inside View of the Demise of Democracy* (Westport: Praeger, 2007). My analysis differs from this in assuming that there was never a democracy as such that could suffer demise; it is too simplistic to look solely at these four issues; and in seeing the current system as much less efficient than they saw it in 2007 to be.

was made significantly more consolidated and coherent under Putin than it had been under Yeltsin, while still retaining a level of ambiguity and uncertainty. Chapter 5 looks at the attempts to structure and stabilize elite politics. The Conclusion outlines the form of authoritarian polity that exists and suggests some tensions leading to possible future change. In this way, the book will lay out the way in which regime elites built an authoritarian polity in post-Soviet Russia.

*Part I*

# Structuring public political activity

# 2    Regime and society

An essential part of building an authoritarian polity is the structuring of public political activity in such a way as to prevent the emergence of an effective opposition that could challenge the regime. This first dimension of rule involves what in Russia has been called the "nonsystemic" (meaning non-electoral) opposition, and the "systemic" opposition, which involves the electoral process more narrowly. This chapter will focus on the way in which the restriction of the nonsystemic opposition began under Yeltsin, before becoming more systematic under Putin. Following discussion of mechanisms for the regulation of potential and real opposition activity, the focus will then shift to the arenas in which such mechanisms were deployed in Russia to block opportunities for opposition to mobilize against the regime.

The popular mobilization of 1988–91 provided a basis upon which many had hoped a new democratic political structure would be built. Not only did such activity create a rudimentary structure for political activism in the form of autonomous organizations, parties, and elected assemblies, but it also gave a sense of legitimacy to such activity that had been lacking during the Soviet period. That legitimacy was bolstered by the democratic rhetoric of the post-Soviet period. However, in retrospect, it is clear that the prospects for democracy were much less rosy than this might suggest. The emergent political parties were generally weak, had little effective organization or resources, and usually lacked a consistent ideology to provide a sense of unity and commitment. As Chapter 1 explains, the elite-centered nature of the transition meant there was little scope for meaningful participation in political life for those bodies, which might have encouraged their institutional development, while the absence of a clear commitment to an early election in the initial period of Russian independence meant that party development could not be stimulated by the need to organize for electoral competition. As Chapter 3 shows, the result was that democratic forces in the party arena remained weak and ill organized. Moreover, the apparent strength of popular mobilization evident in 1990–91 hid the fact that in Russia this was largely confined to Moscow and was generally unable to sustain itself in the face of serious economic downturn. With the end of the Soviet Union, the drive seemed to leach out of popular mobilization as people concentrated on their more immediate problems of daily survival. So the main domestic strands of a putative democratic movement inherited from the Soviet period were too weak to have a major impact on post-Soviet political life.

In this context of a weak democratic legacy, it may be thought that the West could have been influential in fostering such a development, and certainly attempts were made in this regard. At the grassroots, governmental, quasi-governmental and civil society organizations did direct significant assistance to civil society organizations in Russia, although this was generally limited to those believed to be ideologically sympathetic to the Western view.[1] Significant attempts were also made to help build up the private economic sector and to encourage national politics in a democratic direction. However, this soon became politicized, chiefly stimulated by Western support for Yeltsin in the clash with the parliament that extended through 1992 to reach its violent climax in October 1993. The rationale underpinning the aid was transparent: to prevent the return of the communists by helping Yeltsin to consolidate his rule. Accordingly, despite some international criticism of the way the 1993 (and later) elections were conducted (see Chapter 3), no serious pressure was applied to try to make the regime change its ways. And as it became clear that the Western approach was partisan – not just pro-Yeltsin but designed to further Western interests[2] – the generally favorable attitude to the West soured, thereby reducing Western capacity to influence events inside Russia. When Putin came to power and took a more assertive stance toward the West, including projecting a clear message rejecting Western "advice" and influence, the capacity of the West to exercise real influence in Russia was even more severely reduced. The West was therefore never able to exercise substantial influence in promoting the growth of would-be democracy or oppositional forces in Russia, and therefore could not compensate for the weakness of domestic democratic forces stemming from the Soviet experience.

This left the way relatively clear for the regime to dampen down potential challenges to its authority from within society at large. Successive presidential administrations consistently acted to constrain the

---

[1] Sarah L. Henderson, *Building Democracy in Contemporary Russia. Western Support for Grassroots Organizations* (Ithaca: Cornell University Press, 2003).

[2] On this see Janine R. Wedel, *Collision and Collusion. The Strange Case of Western Aid to Eastern Europe 1989–1998* (New York: St. Martin's Press, 1998).

activities of the so-called "nonsystemic" (non-electoral) opposition, to restrict oppositional activity to ensure that it did not challenge regime control or stability. In doing so, they utilized a range of measures commonly used by authoritarian regimes elsewhere to structure and control autonomous political activity.

In its most obvious form, the compression of opposition involves the prevention of opposition forces from mounting an effective challenge to the regime. If an opposition is able to mobilize effectively, it can pose a challenge to the regime, either by showing the hollowness of the mechanisms the regime has in place to provide for some form of participation, or by acting outside those mechanisms and thereby potentially bringing the whole structure into question. Mobilization in the streets is dangerous if not under regime control because it suggests that there is an independent sphere of political activity within which the people's real feelings about the regime may be aired. It can also be an important stage in the organization of opposition that, if achieved, may pose an enhanced threat to the regime and its tenure; protest can raise questions about the regime's invincibility and thereby puncture the view that opposition is useless. But to be effective, mobilization must overcome the collective action problem. The essence of this is that people are generally unwilling to act unless they know that other people (and hopefully large numbers of them) will join them in that action. If individuals and groups are dissuaded from acting by the belief that they may not be supported and will therefore be more vulnerable, opposition mobilization will be very difficult. Therefore overcoming the collective action problem is central to the prospects for opposition success and regime stability.

There are two principal reasons for the collective action problem. The first is fear of the consequences. Authoritarian regimes have generally been more willing than democratic ones to use force against their citizenry. This does not mean that such regimes rule only through reliance upon coercion, but that their use of coercion is less restrained by the presence of independent sources of power and opinion than in more democratic systems. In most such regimes, the more potent thing is not the actual use of force (because, in practice, this is often quite sparing), but the threat of its use. The presence of a major security apparatus added to a history of its use against oppositionist or dissident forces, is often sufficient to keep people in line under normal circumstances. Opponents do not mobilize because they know they may be beaten, locked up, or even killed. This sort of situation where people tailor their actions because of the expectation of retribution if they act out of line is consistent with the notion of "soft authoritarianism."

The second reason for the collective action problem is the perception that any action will be meaningless. Potential opponents believe that any action they take will not make a difference, that regardless of what they do the authoritarian rulers will remain in power and the system will not change. The most important factor in the way this perception arises and becomes embedded is how the regime structures political life and the avenues it provides for popular participation. In the twenty-first century, where "democracy" reigns as the hegemonic principle of regime form (even though it will mean many different things to different people), few regimes do not make some provision for popular involvement in political life. But within this context, the key to regime stability is embedding within the populace the perception that there are no alternatives to the way the regime is functioning. Going outside the regime is not an option. Another way of looking at this is in terms of the closure of political space for autonomous activity; the only way people can be politically active is through the institutions of the regime itself. This involves the perception that if people act outside the institutional structure of the system, regardless of what they do it will have no effect. If the regime can inject this feeling of inefficacy into the populace, it is well on the way to achieving the popular passivity that will help to sustain its rule. This will also prevent the emergence of the appearance of a credible alternative to the regime,[3] something without which potential mobilization is unlikely.

The most satisfactory way of handling opposition, at least from the regime's perspective, is to prevent such opposition from emerging in the first place, but it is impossible to do this and achieve complete success. Inevitably in any political system, oppositionist forces will form, and thereby create a policy problem for the regime and its leaders. A number of different strategies are available to regimes in such situations:

1. repression. Use of the coercive arms of the state to repress the opposition. This may involve the killing or incarceration of opponents, but it can also take less violent forms, like the banning of opposition organizations, the break-up of meetings, the harassment of activists, and the intimidation of participants and would-be participants.
2. marginalization. This may involve the use of regulations and the law to place barriers in the way of opposition forces and thereby reduce their impact, the construction of the public agenda such as to make

---

[3] An important element in this is that popular mobilization can facilitate elite splits by providing potential elite dissidents with another option to remain within politics outside of elite constraints.

the opposition appear irrelevant, or the closure of arenas wit'
the opposition could play a part.

3. co-optation. The inclusion of opposition elements witl.
   tem, but in a carefully circumscribed and limited way. This n..
   done either by incorporating whole organizations into the politicai
   system, or by giving particular leaders positions, thereby potentially
   cutting the head off the opposition. Another form of co-optation is
   the effective buying off of potential opposition through the provision
   of benefits or goods. The fostering of a thriving economy in which
   people can achieve their material desires is often seen as one form
   of this.

4. ignore the opposition. This involves refusing to recognize that the
   opposition has a valid part to play within the political system, doing
   nothing that might either encourage them or give them an opening
   to become politically active. This strategy is unlikely to work unless
   opposition forces are small and fractured and lack media access.

5. give concessions. It may be more effective to grant some of the opposition's demands, especially where these are essentially marginal to
   the regime's central interests and concerns.

Such strategies are analytically distinct but, in practice, can shade into
one another. Almost inevitably, regimes will seek to use a combination of
these strategies in their attempts to deal with opposition forces, and this
is what the Russian regime has done.

An opposition's ability to become a powerful force involves three elements: opportunity, vehicles, and capacity. Opportunity may be conceived as an opening within the political system that a potential opposition can use to transform that potentiality into reality. Such an opening
could take a variety of forms, for example, legal room for oppositional
activity, a split in the regime elite, or a perceived weakening of the regime
and its controls. Vehicles refers to the fact that in order to be effective, an opposition must be organized. The level of organization required
is not fixed and will change over time, but at least a modicum of this is
essential. Accordingly, an organization to sustain opposition activity must
either exist or be created. This role has usually been played by political
parties, but other organizational forms are possible. Capacity refers to the
resources available to the opposition to enable it to effectively mount an
oppositionist campaign. The resources are chiefly of two types: material
(usually finance but also such things as access to media and allies) and
leadership. Without both of these, oppositions are likely to struggle even
given favorable opportunity and vehicles. These three vectors, while in
principle distinct, may in practice overlap. All are essential to successful
opposition activity, and if a regime wants to compress opposition, it is in

these areas that they are likely to act. This is reflected in the means used to structure autonomous political activity in Russia.

### Protest in the streets

The formal legal structure in Russia was ambiguous in its approach to protest. The Constitution introduced in 1993 made provision for the protection of human rights and freedoms, and allowed the formation of social associations unless they sought the forcible alteration of the constitutional order or the integrity of the Federation, the undermining of state security, the creation of armed formations, or the fueling of social, racial, national, or religious strife. The Constitution also guaranteed the freedom and inviolability of the person and their private life (including both verbal and written correspondence and place of dwelling), with detention only possible as a result of judicial decision. It also guaranteed freedom of conscience, religion, thought, and speech, and the right of association in bodies designed to protect their members' interests. Article 31 gave citizens "the right to assemble peacefully without weapons and to hold meetings, rallies, and demonstrations, processions and pickets." The Constitution thus formally provided a legal infrastructure that could underpin protest activity; here was the opportunity for an opposition to function.

However, given that much of the actual working out in practice of these principles was governed by legislation and regulation rather than the constitutional provision, it was in the detail of these regulations that restrictions were embedded. This was particularly important with regard to freedom of assembly. Until the introduction of a new law in June 2004,[4] this was regulated by a Soviet-era law slightly amended. The new law made provision for the organizers of a protest action to notify the authorities of the details of the proposed action between fifteen and ten days before the action (three days for pickets[5]). Although this was a notification to the authorities rather than a request for permission, upon receipt of the notification, the authorities could change the location or timing of the event and call on the organizers to remedy any way in which any aspect of the event was contrary to the law (this meant effectively that the organizers were responsible for any infringements of the law that occurred during the protest). Such public actions could not take place in

---

[4] Federal'nyi zakon ot 10.06.2004 N54-F3 (red. ot 08.06.2012) "O sobraniiakh, mitingakh, demonstratsiiakh, shestviiakh i piketirovaniiakh," www.consultant.ru. Accessed October 10, 2012.

[5] Although single pickets did not require prior notification.

the vicinity of hazardous facilities, important railways, viaducts, pipelines, high voltage power lines, prisons, courts, presidential residences, border control zones, or cultural and historical monuments. The law imposed modest fines for illegal protests. However, it was through this notification process, and the effective power of local authorities to issue or withhold permits for protest activities, that the main legal restriction upon this sort of activity lay. Authorities could prevent a protest by declaring that it was near one of the designated places that was out of bounds for such activity, that the proposed location had already been booked by another group, or that it would cause unacceptable disruption to the course of ordinary life. In this event, the organizers could usually legally proceed with their protest, but only if it was held in another location. If they went ahead with it in the original location, it could be declared illegal; furthermore, if the numbers attending a mandated activity exceeded those projected by the organizers, the activity could also be declared illegal. In June 2012, the penalties for an unsanctioned meeting were increased one hundred and fifty fold. Thus, while the Constitution embedded rights of free assembly, the regulations provided scope for authorities to significantly impinge on that right in practice.

The early post-Soviet years were characterized by a high level of elite disunity as Yeltsin sought to overcome the opposition to his policies located in the old Soviet legislative organs. But while the roots of this conflict lay within the elite, its manifestations overflowed into the streets. The most extreme form of this came in autumn 1993 when Yeltsin's parliamentary opponents sought to mobilize their followers onto the streets and to seize the Moscow mayor's office and Ostankino television station. It was this that provided the rationale for Yeltsin to call on the military to close the parliament and arrest his opponents. The open clashes in the streets, both at the White House where the military shelled the premises of the parliament, and at Ostankino where supporters of both sides met in a brief clash, and Yeltsin's victory marked a clear message to would-be opponents about the willingness of the regime to use force when it felt threatened. This was clearly the most spectacular instance of the use of force against opponents in post-Soviet Russia, and may in part be responsible for ensuring that opposition groups stepped carefully in the future. In any case, this sort of conflict did not recur.

Indeed, levels of street protest during the 1990s were much lower than many, including members of the Russian elite, had expected. Strike activity and popular demonstrations had been instrumental in 1989–91 in bringing about the collapse of the USSR, and many people believed that this presaged a more active part in public affairs on the part of the Russian labor movement. In addition, the economic hardship that was brought on as a result of the policies of economic restructuring introduced by the Yeltsin administration was widely seen as likely to inflame public passions and to bring large numbers of protesters onto the streets. But despite what seemed a propitious opportunity for opposition to emerge, this did not eventuate. Scholars have sought to explain this passivity in a number of ways: the buffering effect of non-wage benefits and the shadow economy, the role of barter and wage substitutes, the absence of a feeling of efficacy on the part of potential protesters, the fact that many jobs gave little leverage or scope for effective action, the traditional passivity of Russians, a lack of understanding of the issues and of who was to blame, the weakness of potential organizational vehicles for protest, the lack of unity, and the absence of leadership have all been suggested as factors in the lower than expected levels of protest activity.[6] Regardless of the combination of factors that came into play at various times and in different parts of the country, the reality of the 1990s was a general passivity among the Russian populace.

The general passivity of the Russian populace does not mean that there was no protest activity during this time, but owing to the problems of data collection,[7] accurate estimation of its dimensions is well-nigh impossible. According to the most complete study of this,[8] the low levels of protest in the 1990s escalated to a peak in 1997–9 and then dropped back until they reemerged as a significant issue during Putin's second term (2004–8). In the first two-thirds of the 1990s, there was regular protest activity in the form of demonstrations organized by the communists, usually on May Day, the anniversary of the revolution and Lenin's birthday. These were generally small affairs with a large proportion of the protesters of advanced age, and they involved a march (sometimes to Lenin's Mausoleum) followed by speeches by party leaders. Some of the extreme nationalist groups also held rallies from time to time, but these too tended to be small, although the participants were often much younger than those attending the communist rallies. The regime generally ignored these.

Other protests took place, but these were, in Robertson's words, "primarily local in nature, based on narrowly conceived notions of identity,

---

[6] Debra Javeline, *Protest and the Politics of Blame: The Russian Response to Unpaid Wages* (Ann Arbor: University of Michigan Press, 2003), pp. 161–220; and Linda J. Cook, "Russian Labour," Graeme Gill and James Young (eds), *Routledge Handbook of Russian Politics and Society* (London: Routledge, 2012), pp. 320–22.

[7] See the discussion in Graeme B. Robertson, *The Politics of Protest in Hybrid Regimes. Managing Dissent in Post-Communist Russia* (Cambridge: Cambridge University Press, 2011), pp. 44–9 and Javeline (*Protest and the Politics of Blame*), pp. 45–50.

[8] Robertson (*Politics of Protest*).

and making demands that are largely material, exclusive, and conservative or defensive in nature."[9] Rather than being over matters of state or principle, such disputes were usually over bread and butter issues, including arrears in wages,[10] and of essentially local concern. As such, they often were not reported in the national press and made little impact on national politics. The decentralized and small-scale nature of much of this protest activity meant that the regime for the most part did not need to take any action with regard to it, although if Robertson is correct and much of this activity was actually stimulated by regional governors as a means of placing pressure on their masters in Moscow,[11] this sort of protest could be considered to have been co-opted right from the outset.

From the beginning of its rule, the Yeltsin administration was concerned about the continuing presence of communists and their capacity for ongoing opposition to the government and its plans. This concern was realized with the unrolling of the crisis between president and parliament. Part of this wariness related to the trade union movement, which moved into the post-Soviet period largely in the form it had had in the Soviet era: the principal organizational form, the Federation of Independent Trade Unions of Russia (FNPR) was the lineal descendant of the official Soviet union movement. It remained intact, with its membership, property, apparatus, role as major distributor of social security funds and social services, and as chief representative of labor still in place.[12] Given the acknowledged impact the economic reforms would have on the workforce and the role of strikes in eroding the position of Gorbachev in the last years of his rule, Yeltsin and those around him viewed the FNPR with considerable suspicion. The FNPR too was concerned about the attitude the government would take to it. The concern for the union was that, given the above considerations, the government might take action against it. This was an acute worry because, in practice, the rights and privileges enjoyed by the union were dependent upon government legislation and administrative practice.[13] Accordingly, initially the union sought to adopt a moderate stance. Although it did seek to press its concerns through strikes, pickets, and demonstrations in 1992–3, these were

[9] Robertson (*Politics of Protest*), p. 42.
[10] This question, and the popular response to it, is discussed in Javeline (*Protest and the Politics of Blame*).
[11] Robertson (*Politics of Protest*), pp. 7, 75–81, 105–7.
[12] Linda J. Cook, "Workers in the Russian Federation. Responses to the Post-Communist Transition," *Communist and Post-Communist Studies* 28 (1), 1995, p. 30.
[13] Sarah Ashwin and Simon Clark, *Russian Trade Unions and Industrial Relations in Transition* (Basingstoke: Palgrave Macmillan, 2003), p. 36.

generally poorly attended. Strike activity, or in some cases threatened strike activity, by pilots and air traffic controllers (February 1992), trolley, bus, and tram drivers (April 1992), coal miners and oil and gas workers (May 1992) were all met by government concessions, principally increased levels and payment of wages. Similarly strikes over wage arrears were held in late spring–summer 1992 and in summer and early autumn 1993, with the latter involving timber and agro-industrial workers, doctors, teachers, transport and communications workers, coal, oil, and gas workers, and some defense personnel. Such strikes were generally of short duration, sometimes organized by one of the new independent unions that had been emerging to challenge the FNPR since 1989, and were usually ended by the government meeting some of the workers' demands. Such activity was focused on immediate bread and butter issues rather than political opposition to the new regime.

The FNPR was clearly adopting a moderate, "loyal opposition," position. This is further reflected in its involvement in the government's notion of "social partnership." This was a scheme whereby representatives of government, business, and labor were to meet regularly to deal with questions of wages and disputes. The institutional format for this was the Tripartite Commission on Regulation of Social and Labour Relations established in January 1992. Of its fourteen labor representatives, FNPR had nine, Sotsprof (an organization of professional and skilled workers established in 1989) three, the Independent Miners' Union (established 1990) one, and the Independent Union of Civil Aviation Pilots (established 1990) one. Although relations between the different partners in the Commission fluctuated over time and the government frequently ignored it in practice,[14] this was clearly an attempt to co-opt the union movement and thereby prevent it from becoming a vehicle for political opposition. This attempt suffered an early setback when the FNPR came out in support of Yeltsin's parliamentary opponents, but the president quickly pulled them back into line. The government froze the FNPR's bank accounts, cut off the telephones, banned collection of union dues, stripped the union of its responsibilities for social insurance and health and safety, and threatened to confiscate the union's property. The FNPR quickly fell into line, replacing its leader with a more conciliatory one and again adopting a stance of seeking to achieve its aim of moderating the deleterious effects of economic reform through lobbying activity in the State Duma and criticism that could not be interpreted as taking a political stance against the regime. Certainly the FNPR continued to

---

[14] For a discussion of "social partnership," see Ashwin and Clark (*Russian Trade Unions*), Chapter 6.

be involved in some collective protest activity – there were strikes in the coal fields in the first half of 1994, demonstrations occurred in all years, including the so-called "Days of Action" launched by the FNPR (the first on November 30, 1995) and the regular demonstration on May Day – but in those cases where it was involved, it was under pressure from its members and its role seemed to be more half-hearted and ritualistic than one of full engagement.

A new Law on Trade Unions came into effect in January 1996 replacing the Soviet law of 1990. This reinforced the subjection of the unions to the state. It enabled the banning or suspension of a union for up to six months by the Supreme Court on the submission of the Procurator if the union violated the national (or a regional) Constitution or federal law. The effect of this was strengthened by a provision of the Civil Code (Part 1, Chapter 4, Article 61) that enabled a legal entity (including a trade union) to be liquidated as a juridical subject by decision of its members or by a court for various reasons, including systematically acting in violation of its established aims, acting without proper authority, or acting in violation of the law or other judicial acts. The vagueness and ambiguity of the bases upon which unions could be liquidated under the Civil Code increased their vulnerability to the state and constituted a clear threat in the event of undertaking activity to which the government objected. A strike could be declared illegal, and therefore trigger the provision making for liquidation of a union, if it was called without giving due and proper notice; was contrary to the principles established to govern conciliation, mediation, and arbitration; it presented a real threat to the constitutional order or the health of other people; it involved state officials including members of the armed forces, security services, and law enforcement organs; and the minimum necessary work was not being carried out. If a union continued a strike after that strike was declared illegal, not only did it run the risk of triggering the liquidation mechanism, but it had to pay from its own funds court-assessed losses incurred as a result of the strike. The FNPR was also reliant on the state for funds to run some of its activities, especially education and research.

Another measure that could be used against the unions was the anti-extremism legislation adopted by Yeltsin in 1992. This defined extremist activity in such a broad fashion that it called into question basic freedoms of speech, and gave the authorities the right to prosecute or ban any organization if a leading member made an extremist statement without explicitly labeling that a purely personal belief.[15] In practice, this law was little used. However, the line against extremism was hardened under

---

[15] Richard Sakwa, *Putin. Russia's Choice* (London: Routledge, 2008, 2nd edn.), p. 181.

Putin. In 2006 a new anti-terrorism law was introduced, shifting the focus away from acts of violence against civilians to acts designed to pressurize the state,[16] while from 2008 the definition of "extremism" remained ambiguous (e.g., "extremism under the guise of Islam") and gave the authorities significant scope to pick up opponents, dissidents, and those simply exercising the right of free speech.[17]

These sorts of measures appear to have contributed to the relative quiescence of organized labor during much of the 1990s. Although Graeme Robertson sees higher protest levels in the late 1990s with the economic crisis of 1997 as a trigger, it is not clear that these levels are much elevated compared with what went before.[18] Furthermore, he argues that during this time, higher levels of protest were to be found in some regions while in others levels were much lower. Such low levels continued into the first Putin presidential term. Nevertheless, the Putin administration took steps to guard against future protest by blocking the potential opportunity, vehicles, and capacity of opposition.

An early move in this regard was the introduction of a new labor code to replace the existing one, which dated from 1971.[19] Following concerted opposition (including demonstrations and picketing) to an initial government draft that would have severely reduced the rights and privileges of unions, a new draft was presented in mid 2001 that was supported by both the government and FNPR and hotly opposed by the independent unions. FNPR support reflects the fact that this seemed to consolidate its monopolistic position at the expense of the independent unions, but may also have been in response to threats from within the Presidential Apparatus to create a comprehensive new trade union federation to replace it.[20] Four elements in the new legislation disadvantaged the independent unions and consolidated the position of the FNPR: it was made more difficult to register a trade union, especially if it sought to break from an official union and establish an independent union; participation in negotiations for a collective agreement at the enterprise level was limited to unions that were part of an all-Russian union (which independent unions often were not); if more than one union was present in a factory, a joint negotiating team should be established, and if this could not be done, the

---

[16] Marie Mendras, *Russian Politics. The Paradox of a Weak State* (London: Hurst & Co., 2012), p. 269.

[17] Andrei Soldatov and Irina Borogan, *The New Nobility. The Restoration of Russia's Security State and the Enduring Legacy of the KGB* (New York: Public Affairs, 2010), Chapter 5.

[18] The most reliable data upon which he rests his analysis only dates from 1997.

[19] For a discussion of this, see Robertson (*Politics of Protest*), pp. 150–51; and Irina Olimpieva, "'Free' and 'Official' Labor Unions in Russia: Different Modes of Labor Interest Representation," *Russian Analytical Digest* 104, October 27, 2011, p. 4.

[20] Ashwin and Clark (*Russian Trade Unions*), pp. 71–2.

majority union will take responsibility for the negotiations (therefore an FNPR affiliate could exclude competitor unions simply by not talking to them); and by making the legality of a strike dependent upon a majority vote of a meeting attended by two-thirds of the labor force of the enterprise, it was difficult for any independent union which represented only a particular group within that labor force to gain the votes to make a strike legitimate. These measures effectively consolidated the dominant position of the FNPR within the enterprise and, in conjunction with the measures noted above from the Yeltsin era, virtually integrated the largest union into the official power structure. This sort of co-optation reestablished the union as a major mechanism of interest intermediation, just as it had been in Soviet times albeit with greater independence than its Soviet era predecessor had had, while at the same time marginalizing the independent unions.

During Putin's first term as president (2000–2004), protest remained a minor part of the political landscape. The communists and nationalist groups continued to hold small demonstrations from time to time, but these remained marginal to the course of political life and were largely ignored by the government. A change came about during Putin's second term (2004–8), prompted principally by the color revolutions in Ukraine, Georgia, and Kyrgyzstan.[21] These were events in which popular dissatisfaction with perceived fraudulent election results overflowed into street protest that led to the replacement of the incumbent leader. This development both gave encouragement to the nonsystemic opposition in Russia and seems to have caused consternation among those around Putin.[22]

[21] On these, see the following journal special issues: David Lane and Stephen White (eds), "Rethinking the Coloured Revolutions," *The Journal of Communist Studies and Transition Politics* 25 (2–3), 2009; and Evgeny Finkel and Yitzzhak M. Brudny (eds), "Reassessing Coloured Revolutions and Authoritarian Reactions," *Democratization* 19 (1), 2012. Kathryn Stoner-Weiss argues that Russia differed from the countries experiencing color revolution in five ways: the incumbent was very popular; the political elite was cohesive and the opposition weak and divided; there were few mechanisms of mass mobilization; the media was under greater state control; and there were only weak independent election-monitoring capabilities. Kathryn Stoner-Weiss, "Comparing Oranges and Apples: The Internal and External Dimensions of Russia's Turn Away from Democracy," Valerie Bunce, Michael McFaul, and Kathryn Stoner-Weiss (eds), *Democracy and Authoritarianism in the Postcommunist World* (Cambridge: Cambridge University Press, 2010), pp. 255–69.

[22] For an argument about the effect of this on the political elite, see Robert Horvath, *Putin's Preventive Counter-Revolution. Post-Soviet Authoritarianism and the Spectre of Velvet Revolution* (London: Routledge, 2013); Robert Horvath, "Putin's Preventive Counter-Revolution: Post-Soviet Authoritarianism and the Spectre of Velvet Revolution," *Europe-Asia Studies* 63 (1), 2011, pp. 1–25; and Peter J.S. Duncan, "Russia, the West and the 2007–2008 Electoral Cycle: Did the Kremlin Really Fear a 'Coloured Revolution'?," *Europe-Asia Studies* 65 (1), 2013, pp. 1–25. One echo of the effect of the color revolution is the practice of Russian Foreign Affairs officials to use the term "Maidanskaia vesna"

The result was from 2005 a new dynamic of protest activity and new forms of response by the authorities.

The first wave of protest brought large numbers of pensioners out onto the streets, protesting the government's decision to monetize many of the benefits that they received from the state. While the focus of this activity was similar to that which had preceded it, the bread and butter question of income and entitlements,[23] the constituency that was mobilized was new. These were not just the supporters of the communists, many of whom were of pensionable age and constituted much of the crowd that the communists were able to get at their demonstrations, but people whose political allegiances were spread across the board. This was not some marginal group who could easily be dismissed, but a section of the mainstream populace whose entitlements had broad-based popular support. The government's response was to concede to some of the protesters' demands.

Protest also developed around environmental issues. The environmental question has a long history of generating protest activity, stretching back into Soviet times and the protests surrounding the construction of industrial facilities on Lake Baikal and the plans to turn various north-flowing rivers southward, not to mention the Chernobyl nuclear accident in 1986.[24] Environmental concerns remained salient in the second half of the 2000s; for example, in March–April 2006 there were protests in Irkutsk against the proposal to construct an oil pipeline near Lake Baikal that resulted in a decision to alter the proposed route. The most prominent instance (in part because it was in the Moscow region) concerned plans to construct a new road through old growth forest at Khimki on the outskirts of Moscow. A local environmental protest group emerged and managed to gain national (and international) media exposure. Their activities, principally rallies and pickets, evoked a low grade forceful response from the authorities in the form of arrests of leading demonstrators. However, their activities did also lead to President Medvedev

(Maidan spring) to refer to events in Egypt in 2012–13. Maidan Square was the chief site of the Ukrainian orange revolution.

23  Protests over personal entitlements/conditions continued to occur. Perhaps the most dramatic instance of this was the protests in 2010 in Kaliningrad where people protested against the policies of the incumbent regional governor, Georgy Boos. Following this, President Medvedev declined to nominate him for a second term as governor. Most of these protests have been local in their focus. Cook ("Russian Labour"), p. 325. On the pensioners' protests, see Horvath (*Putin's Preventive Counter-Revolution*, 2013), pp. 48–56.

24  For a useful set of essays on these issues, see John Massey Stewart (ed.), *The Soviet Environment: Problems, Policies and Politics* (Cambridge: Cambridge University Press, 1992).

temporarily halting the construction work pending a reconsideration of the project, but this resulted in confirmation of the original decision and resumption of the project. Moscow has also seen frequent protests around the destruction of historic buildings in the capital, although such protest has often taken the form less of public demonstrations and more pressure through publicity by such groups as the Moscow Architecture Preservation Society.[25] Similarly in St. Petersburg there has been a significant level of protest, including public demonstrations over the proposal to build a skyscraper over 400 meters in height for the new Gazprom building in the heritage area of the city. In December 2010 it was announced that the building would be built outside the heritage area. There have at times also been protests about the proposed demolition of people's homes in various parts of Moscow, for example, South Butovo in mid 2006 and Rechnik in 2009–10, both of which resulted in slight changes in the plans.

Another form of protest that developed in Moscow in 2010[26] but which was more difficult to combat has been the so-called "blue bucket" protest. The origin of this lay in the way that official cars with flashing blue lights (migalki) simply ignored the standard traffic rules, disrupted ordinary traffic and often caused accidents as they transported their official passengers around Moscow. It was widely believed that many of the cars carrying such blue lights were not entitled to do so, and that influential people were abusing the system for their own convenience. The protest, directed at both the principle and its abuse, took the form of people driving around with blue buckets strapped to the roofs of their cars, a kind of passive protest. Generally the authorities have done little in response to this[27] except for the temporary arrest and fining of some drivers.

To all of these sorts of protests, the authorities have generally responded in a moderate fashion: perhaps minor penalties and some concessions. In the case of demonstrations and rallies, the authorities (usually at the local level in whom this power was vested), often used their power to deny permission to potential demonstrators to hold a rally in their location of choice; sometimes it was a blanket refusal (e.g., claiming it would lead to public disorder), at others permission was given for

[25] For details of its activities, see its website www.maps-moscow.com. Accessed February 10, 2013.
[26] For protest activity by car owners in St. Petersburg, see Markku Lonkila, "Driving at Democracy in Russia: Protest Activities of St. Petersburg Car Drivers' Associations," *Europe-Asia Studies* 63 (2), 2011, pp. 291–309.
[27] In April 2011 the Duma rejected a bill to limit the use of these blue lights to emergency situations.

the rally at another location, much less strategically situated and less accessible than the original location of choice. Such decisions constitute an attempt to marginalize the opposition, to close off the opportunity for opposition to develop, and to hinder the emergence of vehicles that the opposition might use. Infiltration of opposition groups was another tactic designed to disrupt opposition activities.[28] However, there has also been a greater willingness to use force in response to particular sorts of protests. This has usually taken the form of police action to break up the protest, sometimes following the rejection of an organization's application to conduct a demonstration in a particular place and the protesters ignoring of that decision and trying to go ahead with the protest. This was generally the pattern for the so-called Strategy-31 protests. This group was protesting against what it perceived to be the authorities' unwillingness to allow people to enjoy the rights to public gathering enshrined in Article 31 of the Constitution, from July 2009 seeking to hold a protest demonstration in Triumfal'naia Square in Moscow on the thirty-first of each month that had thirty-one days. Strategy-31 was a subgroup under the general opposition banner "Other Russia" (Drugaia Rossiia founded in July 2006), and included extreme nationalists like Eduard Limonov, founder of the National Bolshevik Party, and mainstream human rights organizations like Memorial and the Moscow Helsinki Group.[29] The Moscow authorities responded by refusing the marchers a permit to gather in their chosen location, usually on the grounds that some other group had organized to use that site for a demonstration at that time, and offered instead a permit for a gathering somewhere outside central Moscow. When the protesters tried to march to Triumfal'naia Square, they were usually harassed, there was sometimes physical intimidation by bystanders, and the leaders were often arrested. This pattern continued until the replacement of Moscow mayor Yury Luzhkov in October 2010 by Sergei Sobyanin, who stopped the municipal authorities from seeking to prevent this protest. This was effective, withdrawing the oxygen that had kept the protest alive.

Since November 2011 "Russian Marches" have been held by a coalition of ultra-nationalist groups in various cities of Russia, with the largest being in Moscow.[30] Comprising mainly youth and held on the official Day of National Unity, it was prohibited in 2006 and 2008 (and as a result occasioned clashes with police when the marchers sought to go ahead) and rival marches were organized in 2007 and 2009 in different parts of

---

[28] Soldatov and Borogan (*New Nobility*), pp. 49–62.
[29] See Horvath (*Putin's Preventive Counter-Revolution*, 2013), Chapter 5.
[30] Denis Zuev, "The Russian March: Investigating the Symbolic Dimension of Political Performance in Modern Russia," *Europe-Asia Studies* 65 (1), 2013, pp. 102–26.

Moscow. The marches generally have a strongly anti-immigration flavor, and have been characterized by significant disunity among the component groups. "Dissenters' Marches" (Marsh nesoglasnykh) were also held periodically from late 2006, seeking to express opposition to the regime and the course it was following. Such marches were usually both refused permits and police action was taken against them. Arrests were also made throughout this period of various people who were deemed to be engaged in unsanctioned protest activity, including protesters at the G8 summit in St. Petersburg in 2006 and human rights groups when they sought to mount public action. The latter, in particular, seem to have been especially vulnerable to violent attacks and beatings by gangs of youths, none of whom ever seem to have been apprehended by the police. All of these groups, which sought to protest against the authorities, have generally been met with a combination of repression and mobilization; the former in the form of harassment, arrest (either before a demonstration or at it), or beatings, and the latter by organizing counter-demonstrations at the same time and sometimes in the same location the opposition sought to use. The occupation of public space by pro-Kremlin forces added to the denial of access to such space on the part of the opposition was an important weapon against dissent.

Protest seemed to reach a new peak in the aftermath of the December 2011 Duma elections discussed in Chapter 3 with the "For Fair Elections" movement. The allegations of fraud surrounding the Duma election provoked major demonstrations in central Moscow on December 5, 10, 24, 2011, February 4, March 5, the week beginning May 6, June 12, and September 15, 2012. Initially the demands were for a new election, but by December 10 this had broadened to include annulment of the election results and a new election, sacking of the head of the election commission (Vladimir Churov), an official investigation into vote fraud, and new legislation on parties and elections. But what appeared to be becoming the real thrust of the demonstrations was encapsulated in the slogan carried by some of the demonstrators, "Russia without Putin." This demand was stimulated by the announcement in September that Putin rather than Medvedev would contest the forthcoming presidential election. The demonstrations thus soon turned into the sort of anti-regime protest that had typified the earlier color revolutions, a development given resonance by the way the protesters wore white ribbons to signify the demand for "clean elections." The format of the demonstrations (some of which were optimistically labeled the "march of millions") remained broadly consistent: a march to a designated location (usually Sakharov Prospekt or Bolotnaia Square) followed by addresses by a range of speakers. Following violence between police and protesters at the May demonstration (although arrests had occurred at earlier demonstrations), two other forms of protest (both short-lived) emerged. The first was a so-called "Test March" where prominent writers wearing white ribbons invited sympathizers to join them in a mass walk through Moscow streets. On May 13 a crowd of some 10,000 was able to peacefully make its way to the site of the other new form of protest, an "occupy"-style camp of protesters. This had been set up at Chistie Prudy soon after the May demonstration, but under police harassment and legal injunction, they were forced to move to Kudrinskaia Square and then to the Okudzhava statue (which became adorned with a white ribbon) on Novyi Arbat, losing significant numbers of protesters with each move. The protest crowd also differed from that of earlier protest activity, in that it seemed to be significantly younger and middle class,[31] with many using new forms of social media to maintain contact.[32]

The government's reaction to this unprecedented challenge was both multifaceted and quite sophisticated. Initially, the first protest on December 5 was given no publicity by the mainstream Russian media, consistent with the way protest had generally been treated in the past. However, from the December 10 demonstration, events in the streets of Moscow were given extensive domestic press coverage, although this was accompanied by attempts by the authorities to disrupt social networking media. The government was also quick to announce some measures that could be seen as concessions to the demonstrators' demands – web cameras to be in all polling stations, transparent ballot boxes, relaxation of the rules for registering parties, and restoration of the direct election of governors. Efforts were also devoted to mobilizing pro-government forces to offset the appearance of public opposition. From early in the protest cycle, pro-Putin rallies were organized at the same time as the opposition rallies, while pro-government civil society organizations (see next section were also mobilized onto the streets. In part this was carried out within a framework of presenting the demonstrators as the instruments of foreign powers, an image that held strong resonance with the concerns about the export of color revolution to Russia; Putin himself encouraged this

---

[31] For one survey of the protesters at the December 24 demonstration, see "Opros na prospekte Sakharova 24 dekiabria," www.levada.ru/print/26–12–2011/opros-na-prospekte-sakharova-24-dekabrya. Accessed January 2, 2012. Also see Leon Aron, "Russia's Protesters: The People, Ideals, and Prospects," *Russian Outlook* (Washington, DC: American Enterprise Institute for Public Policy Research, Summer 2012), pp. 1–13.

[32] On this, see Stephen White and Ian McAllister, "Did Russia (Nearly) Have a Facebook Revolution in 2011? Social Media's Challenge to Authoritarianism," *Politics* 34 (1), 2014, pp. 72–84; and Sarah Oates, *Revolution Stalled. The Political Limits of the Internet in the Post-Soviet Sphere* (Oxford: Oxford University Press, 2013), Chapter 7.

(see next section), and on March 15, 2012 (with a second part shown in early October 2012), the Gazprom-owned NTV showed a documentary entitled "The Anatomy of Protest" that claimed the demonstrators had been paid to attend. Generally the protests were peaceful, but that of May 6 saw clashes between protesters and police, with around 400 of the former being arrested, including three of the notional protest leaders, Aleksei Navalny, Sergei Udaltsov, and Boris Nemtsov; criminal charges were laid against some of the people arrested at that time, and threats were made to investigate Navalny's finances, culminating in his arraignment before a court in mid 2013 and his sentencing to a period of five years in jail (suspended, allowing him to compete in the election for Moscow mayor in September). On June 11, 2012, on the eve of the so-called "march of millions," early morning searches were made of the homes of some of the protest leaders, with some documents and computer materials confiscated. At around this time also, the government massively increased the fines for demonstrators participating in an unsanctioned rally from 2,000R to 300,000R[33] and strengthened the law regarding freedom of speech; slander was criminalized to be punished by large fines and prison terms. Measures were also taken against NGOs (see next section). In addition, the continuation of and publicity given to the anti-corruption campaign under way at that time could also be seen as a concession to the protesters, although its origins lay elsewhere. Similarly ambiguous, at least in its effect, was the decision of the Moscow Duma to set aside dedicated zones in Gorky and Sokol'niki parks for political events. Likened to Hyde Park, these were effectively fixed places for rallies, and required electronic registration (but not formal licensing by the authorities) three days before the event. Opposition speakers criticized these as too far from the city center and too small.

The increased resort to force[34] was most clearly reflected in the case of Pussy Riot, the punk band, some members of which entered Christ the Saviour Cathedral in February 2012 and sang an anti-Putin song. The three members of the band who took part were arrested, charged with "hooliganism," tried, and sentenced to two years in prison (one was released a few months after the verdict). This was the most public,

---

[33] This was on top of a December 2009 decision to increase the punishment for illegally interfering with the flow of traffic from 2,500R to 100,000R.

[34] On the role security services could play in preventing protest, see Paul D'Anieri, "Explaining the Success and Failure of Post-Communist Revolutions," *Communist and Post-Communist Studies* 39 (3), 2006, pp. 331–50. Enhanced pay raises were given to those working in the force structures over this period. See www.osw.waw.pl/en/publikacje/analyses/2012–02–01/a-significant-pay-increase-russian-army, February 1, 2012; http://pravo.ru/news/view/82532, February 12, 2013. Accessed February 28, 2013.

because of its wide international exposure, use of coercive force against the opposition, but such tactics had been used at a lower level for some years. As well as the breakup of meetings by police or thugs, the arrest of leaders and activists (sometimes only for short periods, sometimes with no penalty, sometimes with a fine) was common, sometimes at unsanctioned rallies but also often in a preemptive fashion before an authorized rally.[35] Prominent figures who had been in government but had subsequently flirted with the opposition – such as Boris Nemtsov and Mikhail Kasyanov – and others who had been prominent for other reasons and had associated themselves with the opposition (such as the former chess champion Garry Kasparov) often found themselves arrested or subject to formal investigation. Such treatment created a high level of uncertainty within society, something exacerbated by the unsolved killing of Nemtsov in February 2015. There were also instances of people being prevented from traveling to Moscow to attend opposition meetings. Attention was also turned to social media where the security services were accused of seeking to frame opposition figures by planting incriminating material on their sites.[36]

The challenge posed by the postelection demonstrations appeared to wither in the face of the state's response and the tactics of the protesters. The protesters' strategy of disjointed protests held, sometimes, at a number of months interval, meant that the protest movement could not build up any momentum. Also, despite the announcement in October 2012 that a Coordination Council of the opposition had been elected,[37] the lack of effective leadership in opposition ranks was clearly a hindrance to the development of a coherent opposition movement. So too was the diversity of views represented in opposition ranks, a particular problem when it became clear that the initial demands of the "For Fair Elections" movement were not going to be met. Another important factor has been the inability of this opposition to link up with other groups that sought to protest government actions on more bread and butter issues. Relevant here have been those involved in labor disputes, which have continued during this period,[38] but there were also other cases of

---

[35] For a report about a bill introduced into the Duma by a UR deputy in May 2014 imposing heavy penalties on those involved in meetings, marches, demonstrations, or picketing more than twice in a six-month period, see *Kommersant*, May 21, 2014.

[36] For example, http://agentura.ru/projects/identification/provocation/. Accessed March 16, 2013.

[37] ITAR-TASS 23 October 2012. For a positive evaluation of this by two of the organizers, see Fyodor Krashenninikov and Leonid Volkov, "Blue Skies, Clear Thinking: Russian Democracy in the Cloud," *Open Democracy*, November 16, 2012, www.opendemocracy .net. Accessed November 17, 2012.

[38] For some data, see Petr Bizyukov, "Labor Protests in Russia, 2008–2011," *Russian Analytical Digest* 104, October 27, 2011, pp. 6–9.

protest.[39] The inability of opposition groups to come together and cohere into a single movement has significantly hindered their ability to confront the government. Without an effective vehicle to sustain opposition activity and lacking the resources (both material and leadership) to develop the capacity needed successfully to challenge the authorities, the opportunity seemingly latent in the reaction to apparent electoral fraud and Putin's return, could not be translated into real political gains. Important in this also was the lack of a powerful infrastructure of civil society that could sustain an opposition.

## Civil society: non-government organizations

One of the principal sources of vehicles for the carriage of oppositional activity in most countries is civil society. This is where autonomous organization exists and where the development of social capacity that can underpin political activity takes place. However, despite the inclusion of a separate section on civil society in early drafts of the Constitution, when it was adopted that section had been excluded, ostensibly because of the perceived excessive length of the document as a whole. The effect of this was to weaken the legal position of civil society, although this was underpinned by the rights to free association embedded in the Constitution.

During the Yeltsin presidency, the approach to independent organization in the society, which for the most part took the form of NGOs, was one of benign neglect. Certainly there was rhetoric about extremist organizations, usually prompted by media reports about their activities or warnings about their increasing size and influence, but this rhetoric was rarely turned into action of any sort. NGOs were generally allowed to go their own ways, unless they breached the law. But in truth, during this period, NGOs were marginal to the main political scene. Although the new freedom for independent mobilization and organization that began under perestroika created opportunities for autonomous organization, and both during perestroika and after numerous such organizations were created, a vibrant civil society, in the sense of a public sphere within which such organizations competed in a marketplace of ideas, did not emerge. The civil society remained stunted,[40] composed of groups that were small in size, possessed few resources, lacked clear constituencies to sustain them, and exercised negligible influence on the Russian political scene. There were a few partial exceptions to this, such as the Soldiers'

---

[39] For some examples, see Robertson (*Politics of Protest*), pp. 183–8. One that gained significant publicity was a dispute in Pikalevo near St. Petersburg in mid 2009, which occasioned direct intervention by Putin.

[40] To use the term in Gill and Markwick (*Russia's*), p. 205.

Mothers group and Memorial, but their influence was very narrow and their successes limited. The Yeltsin regime could afford to ignore them because these groups were marginal to the main course of domestic politics.

The Putin regime has paid more attention to civil society. Like his predecessor, Putin has rhetorically noted the importance of civil society.[41] But he also seems to have better recognized the potential danger to a well-ordered state that a robust civil society could constitute. Accordingly measures were introduced to ensure that the activities of civil society actors were restrained within acceptable bounds. Regulations were introduced governing their activities. The new party law of 2001 discussed in Chapter 3 effectively denied NGOs the opportunity to participate in election campaigns, at least in the form of offering candidates for elections. New rules on NGOs came into effect in 2006, providing for the reregistration of such bodies, with a more rigorous set of provisions for achieving such registration, including greater financial accountability and openness; government officials had extensive powers to demand internal documents on the organization's day-to-day functioning and its financing.[42] In particular, the receipt of funds from abroad had to be reported, along with how those funds were spent,[43] a major constraint on many NGOs that sought to operate in the human rights area and which therefore saw as part of their raison d'etre to act to limit the state in some areas of its activity. This was followed by raids on prominent such NGOs, the British Council and Memorial in St. Petersburg, in 2007. Such activity reflected concern about the possibility of popular mobilization along the lines of the "color revolutions" and the role in them that foreign support had played, and it was consistent with the hostile stance taken by Putin in his 2004 address to the Federal Assembly where he said the priority of some NGOs was "receiving financing from influential foreign foundations" or "shady groups and commercial interests," and that they would do the bidding of such bodies rather than act in the interests of their constituents.[44] This view was also taken by

---

[41] For example, see V. Putin, "Kakuiu Rossiiu my stroim. Poslanie Prezidenta RF Vladimira Putina Federal'nomu Sobraniiu RF, 8 July 2000," *Ezhegodnye poslaniia prezidenta RF 1994–2005* (Novosibirsk: Sibirskoe universitetskoe izdatel'stvo, 2006), pp. 308–14.

[42] "On Introducing Amendments to Certain Legislative Acts of the Russian Federation," January 10, 2006, www.icnl.org in Horvath ("Putin's Preventive Counter-Revolution," 2011), p. 18.

[43] Along with mission statements, strategic plans and information on staffing. For one discussion see Horvath (*Putin's Preventive Counter-Revolution,* 2013), pp. 127–35.

[44] V. Putin, "Poslanie Prezidenta RF Vladimira Putina Federal'nomu Sobraniiu RF, 26 May 2004," *Ezhegodnye poslaniia prezidenta RF 1994–2005* (Novosibirsk: Sibirskoe universitetskoe izdatel'stvo, 2006), p. 392.

other leading figures in the regime[45] and created a significant edge in the public sphere by associating foreign links with anti-Russian intentions.

This was given legislative substance by the passage of a law in July 2012 requiring all NGOs engaged in "political" activities that received foreign funding to register as "foreign agents" and by a change to the criminal code that expanded the definition of "treason" to include "providing financial, technical, advisory and other assistance to a foreign state or international organisation . . . directed at Russia's security."[46] In October 2012 all USAid offices (USAid's chief function had been to direct funds to democracy-promoting activities) in Russia were closed while the following year many foreign organizations including the International Red Cross, World Wildlife Fund, and Ford Foundation lost their tax-exempt status; the election monitoring agency Golos was closed down in June 2013, although it soon reemerged; and in late 2014 Memorial came under pressure with moves to close it down. Also in 2013, "spontaneous" inspections of NGOs began to establish which could be classed as "foreign agents,"[47] while a mechanism for the funding of human rights organizations through presidential grants was created.[48] In May 2015, in a context of heightened rhetoric about foreign enemies in the wake of the Ukraine crisis, a law was passed enabling the government to ban "undesirable organizations" and to impose sanctions on citizens involved in their activities. These measures constituted an attempt at the repression and marginalization of opposition as well as the potential limitation of Western influence in Russian political life of the sort identified by Bunce and Wolchik as influential in the success of the color revolutions (see Chapter 1).

As well as more stringent regulation, the Putin regime also sought to co-opt these bodies. On November 21–22, 2001, the so-called Civic Forum convened in the Kremlin. This was a gathering of some 5,000 representatives of citizens' groups and NGOs addressed by Putin who discussed a series of issues deemed of importance to Russian society; corruption, educational reform, military reform, and the importance of

---

[45] For example, see Horvath ("Putin's Preventive Counter-Revolution," 2011), p. 18.

[46] www.omct.org/human-rights-defenders/urgent-interventions/russia/2012/10/d2204/. Accessed January 15, 2013. From December 2012, NGOs could be suspended if they were engaged in political activities and received financial support from US-based organizations or individuals.

[47] For the argument that the enforcement of this was moderated later in 2013, see Robert Orttung, "Kremlin Nationalism versus Russia's NGOs," *Russian Analytical Digest* 138, November 8, 2013, p. 10.

[48] For the argument that this would be done through an organization called Civil Dignity (which included the ombudsman and the Chair of the Presidential Council for Civil Society and Human Rights), and was therefore at arms length from the state, see the interview with Civil Dignity Chair, Ella Pamfilova, in *Novye Izvestiia*, November 7, 2013.

civil society were among the topics broached. This was the only time the Civic Forum actually met. However, on March 16, 2005, following the announcement in the September before, the Duma adopted legislation on the creation of a Public Chamber (Obshchestvennaia palata) to come into effect on July 1. This was to be an advisory body meeting at least twice a year in Moscow, although similar organizations were established in some regions, and its membership was largely shaped by the president. Forty-two members were to be handpicked by the president, forty-two were to be representatives of public organizations, and there were to be forty-two regional representatives. The president's forty-two members were to pick the next forty-two, and then that eighty-four were to choose the next forty-two, so the capacity to shape the membership of the Chamber lay directly with the president;[49] moreover, its staff and housekeeping functions were provided by the Presidential Administration. The Chamber seems to have been well received,[50] and was active in pursuing some issues that brought it into conflict with other bodies, including the State Duma (the law on the regulation of NGOs) and the Defense Ministry (the Sychev case on hazing in the military), thereby demonstrating a degree of independence.[51] The Chamber also generated a series of specialized commissions to work on different aspects of Russian life, to produce reports on them with recommendations for improvements. In early 2009 Duma rules were amended to make it compulsory to send all bills to the Public Chamber for comment before they were considered by the Assembly.[52] The Chamber has thus provided an arena within which representatives of civil society can participate in a structured fashion in the discussion of important issues, but this remains within the boundaries set by the president.

[49] For details of the initial membership, see Sakwa (*Putin*, 2nd edn.), p. 170. The mode of formation of the membership later changed. The president continued to nominate forty-two, with the others, in the words of one newspaper, "delegated to the Public Chamber by the general public." *Vedomosti* September 29, 2011.

[50] For example, only 19 percent of a 2005 survey in Novosibirsk saw this to be a means for the government to control NGOs. D. Javeline and S. Lindemann-Komarova, "A Balanced Assessment of Russian Civil Society," *Journal of International Affairs* 63 (2), 2010, p. 181.

[51] See the discussion in Alfred B. Evans Jr., "The First Steps of Russia's Public Chamber: Representation or Coordination?," *Demokratizatsiya* 16,(4), 2008, pp. 345–62.

[52] Paul Chaisty, "The Federal Assembly and the Power Vertical," Graeme Gill and James Young (eds), *Routledge Handbook of Russian Politics and Society* (London: Routledge, 2012), p. 98. Putin emphasized the importance of this pre-legislative examination of proposals in his 2013 address to the Federal Assembly. V.V. Putin, "Poslanie Prezidenta Federal'nomu Sobraniiu," December 12, 2013, www.kremlin.ru/news/19825. Accessed December 16, 2013.

President Medvedev also established in February 2009 (Presidential Decree #148) a Council for Civil Society Institutions and Human Rights, renamed in February 2011 the Council for Civil Society and Human Rights. The Council comprised thirty-six representatives of public organizations, including such prominent human rights figures as Mikhail Fedotov, Ella Pamfilova, and Ludmila Alekseeva, and was intended to make recommendations to the president about the strengthening of human rights protection. The Council under Fedotov was not unwilling to criticize the government, and in the wake of the December 2011 Duma elections and Putin's election and inauguration, a number of members resigned in protest. In November 2012 Putin replaced them with a larger number of people, in the process injecting a wider range of views on human rights into the Council, and thereby making the sort of consensus that underlay the earlier criticism more difficult to achieve.[53] Both bodies (the Public Chamber and the Council for Civil Society and Human Rights) seem to be clear cases of attempted co-optation, of the creation of organizations within which civil society organizations can find a place and through which their activities can be guided and restricted. The danger for a regime is that these bodies can take on a life of their own, but if the regime can maintain its control over their activities, they can also blunt potential independent initiatives coming from civil society.

As well as trying to co-opt civil society organizations through such bodies, the regime has also sought to marginalize them by generating groups and organizations of their own. The area in which the emergence of such ersatz social movements has been most marked has been among the youth. The aim has been to mobilize the youth into pro-Kremlin youth groups.[54] This has been seen as particularly important given the role of youth in the "color revolutions," and the development of opposition movements such as "Other Russia" and "Oborona."[55] Chief among these bodies have been Nashi and Molodaia Gvardiia (which had their origins, respectively, in Idushchie Vmeste that was created in 2000 to

---

[53] See the comments in ITAR-TASS, November 2, 2012.

[54] See Laura Petrone, "Pro-Kremlin Youth Movements in Russia and the Idea of Conservative Modernisation," *ISPI Analysis* (Istituto per gli Studi di Politica Internazionale), No. 46, April 2011.

[55] On "Drugaia Rossiia," see Richard Sakwa, *The Crisis of Russian Democracy. The Dual State, Factionalism and the Medvedev Succession* (Cambridge: Cambridge University Press, 2011), pp. 21–2 for its diverse membership. On the development of youth organizations, see Michael Schwirtz, "Russia's Political Youths," *Demokratizatsiya* 15 (1), 2007, pp. 73–84; and Robertson (*Politics of Protest*), pp. 183–188. Also Horvath (*Putin's Preventive Counter-Revolution*, 2013), pp. 68–81 and Chapter 7.

support Putin[56] and Molodezhnoe Edinstvo, the initial youth organization of United Russia), both of which were formed in 2005. Nashi, in
particular, was directly associated with Putin, playing an active part in the
2007–8 election cycle in supporting those associated with him. Molodaia
Gvardiia has been formally affiliated with United Russia. Nashi engaged
in a number of types of activity, including mass rallies, summer camps
for educational activities, intimidation of opposition groups (including
the British ambassador in 2006), and demonstrations and campaigning on particular issues.[57] Molodaia Gvardiia has been less engaged in
street activities than Nashi, and seems to expend most of its energies on
trying to build up United Russia. Both bodies identify themselves with
the Kremlin authorities and seek to advance their agendas, at the same
time marginalizing alternative movements that might have a less sympathetic attitude to the Kremlin and its plans than these bodies do. They
have clearly been attempts to crowd out of the public space alternative
independent movements and groups.

One of the characteristics of Nashi was that it vigorously emphasized
the importance of "Russia," its traditions, and unique nature. In this way
it fit in with a strong theme running through Putin's speeches,[58] the need
to strengthen Russia's state through means consistent with Russian tradition. The obverse side of this was a rejection of foreign influences and
especially the imposition of foreign models on Russia. Putin used this
perspective to criticize the notion of democracy that had prevailed under
Yeltsin and to advocate a form of "democracy" that was consistent with
Russian characteristics. This was given a programmatic form through
the generation by the then deputy head of the Presidential Administration (and principal patron of Nashi) Vladislav Surkov of the notion of
"sovereign democracy," and although this term was not used widely by
Putin, its essence remained at the heart of the narrative of a strong Russian state needing to face up to the challenges from without[59] that Putin
was presenting. It was reflected in his comments about NGOs receiving foreign funding in 2004 and his charge in December 2011 that the
protesters were in the pay of US Secretary of State Hillary Clinton, and in

---

[56] Robertson (*Politics of Protest*), p. 195.
[57] On Nashi, see Robertson (*Politics of Protest*), pp. 195–7; Evgeny Finkel and Yitzhak M.
Brudny, "Russia and the Colour Revolutions," *Democratization* 19 (1), 2012, pp. 18–
26; Horvath ("Putin's Preventive Counter-Revolution," 2011), pp. 15–18; and Horvath
(*Putin's Preventive Counter-Revolution*, 2013), pp. 99–118, 197–8.
[58] For a discussion of this, see Graeme Gill, *Symbolism and Regime Change in Russia*
(Cambridge: Cambridge University Press, 2013), Chapter 3. Also see section "The
populace" below.
[59] For a survey of Putin's views, see Gill (*Symbolism*), Chapter 3. On conspiracy theories,
Horvath (*Putin's Preventive Counter-Revolution*, 2013), pp. 90–99.

the 2006 legislation about receipt of foreign funds and the 2012 law that NGOs had to register as "foreign agents" if they received such funds.[60] This broad approach was effectively a way of demonizing NGOs with foreign connections, which tended to be the most critical of the regime, and of isolating the potential opposition both within the country and internationally. In January 2006 there were accusations of British spying, which fed into the debate about foreign funding of NGOs, quickly followed by the (temporary) closure of the Russian Research Center for Human Rights, an umbrella organization supporting pro-democracy and human rights NGOs.[61] This anti-foreign influence theme, which was significantly strengthened by the Ukraine crisis in 2014–15, was also reflected in the closure of the USAid offices and, in November 2012, the law that widened the definition of treason to include not only those who passed on state secrets, but those "providing consulting or other work to a foreign state or international organization" that works against Russian security interests.[62] This potentially opened the way for the arrest of anyone collaborating with an international organization, including NGOs, and represents a strong rebuff to the capacity of international actors to exercise influence in Russia.

The restrictions on civil society organizations limited the availability of organizational vehicles for potential protest activity and restricted possible capacity available to the nonsystemic opposition, while the construction of a framework of laws and regulations limiting autonomous political activity reduced the opportunity for popular mobilization. The fact that such laws and regulations were not applied consistently but on a selective basis did nothing to ameliorate their repressive effect. Limits on freedom of the media were also important constraints on the capacity of opposition to organize and spread its message.

## Media

Under Yeltsin, the media remained substantially independent of the government and reveled in the freer atmosphere than had prevailed under Soviet rule. However, the print media in particular found it difficult to survive in the new conditions of the free market where there were paper shortages, rising prices, and reduced purchasing power of consumers.

[60] Consistent with this was the provision that residents of Russia holding dual citizenship had formally to register with the authorities; failure to do so constituted a crime. *The Moscow Times*, May 30, 2014.
[61] Thomas Ambrosio, *Authoritarian Backlash. Russian Resistance to Democratization in the Former Soviet Union* (Farnham: Ashgate, 2009), pp. 50–51.
[62] *Moscow News*, November 1, 2012. The reference is to Law No. 190-FZ.

Apart from Yeltsin's banning of some outlets prior to the 1993 election (see Chapter 3), most press organs were not subject to stringent controls by the state. Indeed, some organs that showed a pro-government stance were able to benefit from state largesse in the form of subsidies. However the economic difficulties of the media – the weakness of the advertising market and declining readership were continuing problems for the print media – made the media vulnerable to takeover by the oligarchs (see below), some of whom viewed the media as potentially effective means through which to exert political influence. As well as taking over existing outlets, some oligarchs and others (especially Gazprom) established new media outlets, so that by the mid 1990s much of the media was widely seen as little more than mouthpieces of their owners. And such views had considerable validity; for example, the Gusinsky-owned NTV television station and the Berezovsky-owned *Nezavisimaia gazeta* newspaper were relentless advocates for the interests of their owners.

When Putin came to power, the vigorous freedom of the press inherited from Yeltsin was curtailed; by 2013 Reporters Without Borders ranked Russia 148 of 179 countries in terms of freedom of the press.[63] Restrictive reporting was imposed on the renewed Chechen conflict (although this was little different to the sorts of restraints imposed on Western reporters in war zones, but it was a sharp difference from the laissez-faire of the 1990s) and a number of prominent reporters including Radio Liberty's Andrei Babitsky, the environmental reporter Aleksandr Nikitin, and the popular Aleksandr Khinstein came under regime pressure. The killing of journalists, which had occurred under Yeltsin, continued, with the most high profile case that of Anna Politkovskaia in 2006, often with no one charged for the crime.[64] The bringing to heel of the oligarchs saw the last of the independent national television stations, NTV, taken over by the government-aligned Gazprom through its new media arm, Gazprom Media. This entity also absorbed the radio station Ekho Moskvy and the newspapers *Segodnia* and *Izvestiia*. In August 2005 *Nezavisimaia gazeta* was bought by an assistant to German Gref, minister for trade and economic development and former head of a think tank close to Putin, while *Kommersant* was taken over by Alisher Usmanov, who headed a

---

[63] Robert W. Orttung and Christopher Walker, "Putin and Russia's Crippled Media," *Russian Analytical Digest* 123, February 21, 2013, p. 2.

[64] In the first twenty years following the fall of the USSR, 341 reporters have been killed. Russian Journalists' Union, cited in Orttung and Walker ("Putin"), p. 3. Reporters were not the only ones to lose their lives. For example, the lawyers Sergei Magnitsky, who died in prison for lack of medical care in 2009, and Stanislav Markelov, who was assassinated on the street in 2009, and human rights activists including the head of the Memorial office in Grozny, Natalia Estemirova in 2009. Also see the discussion in Ostrow, Satarov, and Khakamada (*The Consolidation*), pp. 114–17.

fully owned subsidiary of Gazprom, Gazprominvestkholding. By 2006, all of the main national television channels (Channel One, Russian TV, TV-tsentr, and NTV) were under Kremlin control. In 2012 the state owned "either directly or through proxies, all six national television networks, two national radio networks, two of the 14 national newspapers, more than 60 percent of the roughly 45,000 registered local newspapers and periodicals, and two national news agencies."[65] Furthermore, the state owned 80 percent of presses and 90 percent of television and radio transmitters.[66] Most of the regional media remained largely under the control of the governors. In November 2011 a law came into force enabling the monitoring of the content of all mass media,[67] a measure which potentially tightened central control, while from July 2012 radio stations with more than 48 percent foreign ownership were prohibited from broadcasting, and in September 2014 a law limiting foreign media ownership to 20 percent passed the Duma.[68] Even before this, editors were complaining about the need for self-censorship,[69] a practice that can only have been strengthened by the re-criminalization of libel in July 2012 (it had been decriminalized in 2011). And in December 2013, the replacement of RIANovosti by a new body, Rossiia Segodnia was announced. The task of the new body seemed to be more to project good news about Russia than to present hard news.[70] Notwithstanding these developments, the media has not been a mere cipher of the government. Independent outlets exist, but they are mainly in niche markets, have limited public exposure, and often engage in their own forms of self-censorship; the death of leading critics of the regime, including Politkovskaia, Litvinov, Markelov, and Nemtsov seems to act as an effective inducement for journalists to moderate their criticism regardless of what outlet they work for. Most of the media does not vigorously criticize the regime.

The internet has been a new source of media over which the authorities have sought to exercise increasing control.[71] This has taken the form of legislative measures designed to limit the content and enhance

---

[65] Freedom House, cited by Orttung and Walker ("Putin"), p. 2. A new public television station was proposed to be established at the beginning of 2013, but most of its funding was still to come from the federal government. *Rossiiskaia gazeta*, April 19, 2012; and *Moscow News*, April 18, 2012.

[66] Sakwa (*Putin*, 2nd edn.), p. 154.      [67] *Nezavisimaia gazeta*, September 5, 2011.

[68] www.rt.com, September 26, 2014. Accessed September 28, 2014.

[69] Orttung and Walker ("Putin"), p. 2.

[70] Steven Lee Myers, "Without Notice, Putin Dissolves a News Agency," *The New York Times*, December 9, 2013.

[71] Oates (*Revolution Stalled*), Chapter 4.

surveillance capacities, active use of the medium to project their message and discredit their critics, and individual cases of the prosecution of critics, with such targeting meant to provide a lesson for all. From 2008 the numbers convicted for using the internet to foster extremist views have begun to rise as the authorities have sought a higher degree of regulation of this form of expression.[72] Attention has been focused in particular on VKontakte, the Russian counterpart to Facebook, significant in the light of the role of social media in the color revolutions (especially Ukraine), the "Arab spring," and the 2011–12 protests. In September 2011 Prosecutor-General Yury Chaika proposed an initiative to establish control over social networks on the internet, citing the August riots in London and other British cities,[73] and in mid 2012 a law was adopted enabling government agencies to order internet companies to block material deemed illegal (although this initially seems to have been interpreted in terms of child pornography, suicide, and drug taking).[74] The law is wide ranging in its effect, allowing the closure of an entire site even if only one page is offensive. An official (closed) register of web sites containing banned material has been established, and because of the vagueness and ambiguity of the guidelines, this provides a potential weapon for use against protesters seeking to use social media as a tool for organization. And in May 2014, measures were taken to equate sites with a high volume of traffic with newspapers, thereby making them responsible for the accuracy of the material they published, and to register bloggers. Nevertheless state control over the internet has remained much weaker than it has in places like China.

Thus, media freedom has been hedged since the collapse of the USSR, with the limits becoming much narrower after 2000 than they had been before.

## Economic actors

A major element in the capacity of opposition to mount a realistic challenge to a regime is access to material resources, and this is usually seen

[72] Natalia Yudina, "RuNet, Hate Crime and Soft Targets: How Russia Enforces Its Anti-extremism Law," *Open Democracy*, October 30, 2012, www.opendemocracy.net. Accessed November 1, 2012. The number of convictions remains low, with fifty-two (the highest number up to that point) in 2011. Yudina ("RuNet"), p. 1.

[73] Irina Borogan and Andrei Soldatov, "The Kremlin versus the Bloggers: The Battle for Cyberspace," *Open Democracy*, March 27, 2012, www.opendemocracy.net. Accessed March 28, 2012.

[74] *Moscow News*, November 2, 2012.

principally in terms of economic resources. In principle, where the state plays a large role in the economy, the availability of economic resources for opposition use is more limited.[75] By establishing control over the economy, a regime can both limit the development of alternative centers of power based upon economic resources and restrict the flow of such resources into opposition hands. However, when the Yeltsin government came to power, rather than maximizing state control, it was committed to passing economic resources into private hands.

The post-Soviet Yeltsin regime was in power at the same time that the legal private economic sector was coming into existence. With the overwhelming bulk of economic institutions and resources in the hands of the state during Soviet times, the new government saw one of its primary tasks to be the establishment of a private economic sector, with the result that that sector came into existence profoundly affected by state action. While some resources had been appropriated through the process of so-called "spontaneous privatization," which began during the Soviet era,[76] the privatization of most of the economy formally took place under the auspices of official government programs. In the early years, this process led on most occasions to the acquisition of economic resources by insiders, those who had connections into the hierarchical structures of the Soviet regime. This was the so-called "nomenklatura privatization,"[77] and its essence was that the "new" owners of private economic capital possessed close links into the bureaucratic structures of the state inherited from the Soviet Union. In this way there was a linkage between private capital and bureaucratic officials from the outset. Business has played little role in the formal political process; while some businessmen have been members of the Duma, some agents of business have been in the Presidential Administration, business lobby groups have enjoyed significant access into the government, while some of Yeltsin's ministers were recognized as the representatives of particular economic sectors, and a plethora of interest associations have arisen to look after

---

[75] The degree of state economic control is seen by Way as an important factor in the ability of post-cold war autocrats to sideline the opposition. Lucan Way, "The Sources of Authoritarian Control after the Cold War: East Africa and the Former Soviet Union," *Post-Soviet Affairs* 28 (4), 2012, pp. 424–48.

[76] For a discussion of the development of a new business class, see Graeme Gill, *Bourgeoisie, State, and Democracy. Russia, Britain, France, Germany, and the USA* (Oxford: Oxford University Press, 2008), Chapter 3.

[77] On this, see Ol'ga Kryshtanovskaia, "Transformatsiia staroi nomenklatury v novuiu rossiiskuiu elitu," *Obshchestvennye nauki i sovremennost'* 1, 1995, pp. 51–65; and David Lane and Cameron Ross, *The Transition from Communism to Capitalism. Ruling Elites from Gorbachev to Yeltsin* (Basingstoke: Macmillan, 1999), Chapter 9.

business interests, business has not been a major actor in the formal political sphere.[78]

Of greater importance has been the more informal relationship between big business and political elites. Just as elsewhere in the economy, big business was formed substantially under the influence of the state, with the loans for shares scheme of 1995–6 being the most egregious instance of this.[79] It was popularly believed, with considerable justification, that big business was able to establish itself only by engaging in if not illegal at least unethical practices; only by stealing the resources that formally belonged to the people at large could the sorts of fortunes that grew up develop so quickly. But what made this especially distasteful to many people was the influence that some of these people, called "oligarchs,"[80] seemed to wield in governmental circles. One basis of their power was the process of privatization noted above, which favored those in the politico-administrative structure who were able to make use of the official resources available to them to accumulate often large-scale holdings in the economy. With the contacts they retained in the politico-administrative structure, these people were often able to expand both their holdings (e.g., the development of "authorized banks," which were able to use state funds without cost for short-term speculative investment) and their influence within the government. The biggest of these, including some of the oligarchs, even came to act in lieu of the state; for example, Gazprom effectively absorbed many companies' tax arrears by providing them with cheap gas on credit. Such services were in return for the state allowing such actors free rein in expanding their wealth.

These sorts of contacts into the politico-administrative structure were also present at the highest levels of the state. Much has been made of the role of "the family" under Yeltsin, that informal cabal of people around the president who were believed to exercise significant influence upon him. Among these were the oligarchs Boris Berezovsky and, latterly, Roman Abramovich. While it is impossible to determine the influence the oligarchs exercised during the Yeltsin regime, notwithstanding boasts about "seven bankers" running the country,[81] individually these people could wield significant economic power and, at times, political influence.

---

[78]  Gill (*Bourgeoisie*), Chapter 5.
[79]  On loans for shares, see Chrystia Freeland, *Sale of the Century. The Inside Story of the Second Russian Revolution* (London: Little, Brown and Company, 2000).
[80]  On these oligarchs, see H.-H. Schröder, "El'tsin and the Oligarchs: The Role of Financial Groups in Russian Politics between 1993 and July 1998," *Europe-Asia Studies* 51 (6), 1999, pp. 957–88; and Stephen Fortescue, *Russia's Oil Barons and Metal Magnates. Oligarchs and the State in Transition* (Basingstoke: Palgrave Macmillan, 2006).
[81]  Boris Berezovsky cited in *The Financial Times*, November 1, 1996.

But it is clear that their influence rested as much upon personal contacts as any structural location, and this meant that their position was
vulnerable to personnel change.

When Putin came to power, and with the position of some of the oligarchs weakened by the 1998 financial crisis, he was able to establish a
new relationship with the oligarchs. Declaring a policy of "equi-distance"
from all and a desire to "eliminate the oligarchs as a class,"[82] Putin established a new set of ground rules for the oligarchs. He promised not to
question any of the gains they had made from privatization as long as
they remained out of politics and paid their taxes.[83] To back this up,
in the summer of 2000 a number of companies were accused of irregularities during privatization or were investigated by the tax police.[84]
But most striking was the way the regime went after the oligarchs who
seemed to ignore Putin's injunction and sought to continue to exercise
political influence, Vladimir Gusinsky, Boris Berezovsky, and Mikhail
Khodorkovsky. Gusinsky's NTV network had supported Fatherland-All
Russia in the 1999 election and had been hostile to the prosecution of
the second Chechen War. In May 2000, tax and security police raided
Gusinsky's Media-Most office and in June Gusinsky was arrested and
held for a short period. While being held, he agreed to surrender control
over NTV in return for the cancellation of all debts he owed to Gazprom
(which at that time was 40 percent state owned) and the dropping of
criminal charges against him. However, once released, Gusinsky repudi-
ated this deal. Increased pressure was placed upon him and NTV, leading
to Gusinsky fleeing abroad and Gazprom taking over NTV. The action
against Gusinsky was widely seen within business circles as an attack
upon them generally, and although some leading businessmen wrote a
letter of protest,[85] there was no concerted opposition to this move.

Berezovsky had tried to continue to exercise significant influence at the
top of the Russian state following Putin's election, had been critical of
some of Putin's policies, and had tried to establish a political movement
in opposition to Putin. Pressure was brought to bear on a number of his

[82]  His comments are in *Izvestiia*, February 25, 2000; and *Segodnia*, March 20, 2000.
[83]  Later added to this list was that business should assist the government in the achievement
      of so-called national aims, defined in terms of business' social responsibility. *Vedomosti*,
      November 17, 2004. For the argument that there was little commitment to this bargain,
      at least on the part of Putin, see William Tompson, "Putin and the 'Oligarchs': A Two-
      Sided Commitment Problem," Alex Pravda (ed.), *Leading Russia. Putin in Perspective*
      (Oxford: Oxford University Press, 2005), pp. 179–202.
[84]  These included Gazprom, Norilsk Nickel, Lukoil, and Avtovaz.
[85]  A.A. Mukhin, *Biznes-elita i gosudarstvennaia vlast': Kto vladeet Rossiei na rubezhe vekov?*
      (Moscow: Tsentr politicheskoi informatsii, 2001), p. 59.

companies,[86] in particular, the television station ORT and Aeroflot, and in November 2000 he fled abroad, whence he adopted an unremittingly anti-Putin position. In doing so, he lost control over all the companies he had hitherto headed, with those companies reverting to the state (ORT) or being closed down (TV6). But the most striking case was that of Mikhail Khodorkovsky, reputedly at that time the richest man in Russia and controlling the Yukos oil company. Khodorkovsky had been providing financial support to a range of opposition parties (including Yabloko, the Union of Rightist Forces, and the Communist Party), was reportedly planning to run against Putin in the forthcoming presidential poll, and was believed to have been gathering a core of loyal deputies in the Duma. In July 2003, the head of the holding company that held 61 percent of the shares of Yukos (Platon Lebedev) was arrested, and in October Khodorkovsky (who was chairman of Yukos) was taken into custody. Financial pressure was brought to bear on Yukos, which was accused of fraud, embezzlement, and failure to pay tax. Khodorkovsky was put on trial and sentenced to nine, later reduced to eight, years in prison (in 2010, a new trial on similar charges led to a further prison term), and Yukos was broken up and taken over by companies closely linked to the state.[87] These actions against prominent businessmen[88] were selective, in that all wealthy businessmen would have acted much as these three did in the 1990s, and therefore could have been subject to similar charges, and clearly signaled that the state was in control, and that while big business might seek to press its interests on the government, ultimately they were dependent upon the continued good favor of the president and those around him. It was the political elite that was in control, and that elite was willing to use force and its threat to ensure continuing conformity.

This change had been facilitated by a dramatic improvement in the fiscal position of the central state apparatus following tax changes introduced in 2000 and the economic boom following the crisis of 1998. As well as introducing a flat tax rate of 13 percent, which encouraged tax payers to meet their obligations and resulted in increased tax revenues, the tax system was restructured to shift funds from the regions to the center;

---

[86] Given Berezovsky's former closeness to the Yeltsin "family," this move marked Putin's severing of links with the old cabal.

[87] On Khodorkovsky, see Richard Sakwa, *The Quality of Freedom. Khodorkovsky, Putin, and the Yukos Affair* (Oxford: Oxford University Press, 2009) and Richard Sakwa, *Putin and the Oligarch. The Khodorkovsky–Yukos Affair* (London: I.B. Tauris, 2014).

[88] Others to come under some pressure, but at a very much lower level of intensity than Gusinsky, Berezovsky, and Khodorkovsky, included Oleg Deripaska, Roman Abramovich, and Vladimir Potanin.

proceeds from the goods and services tax, income tax, excise and customs duties, and natural resource taxes now also flowed into the central treasury, and with the economic boom at this time (growth rates averaged 7 percent over Putin's first two presidential terms[89]) increasing this inflow, the central state apparatus became fiscally much more soundly based. This meant that the sort of reliance on economic oligarchs present under Yeltsin disappeared under Putin, thereby strengthening the position of the political elite.

Putin's taming of the Yeltsin-era oligarchs fed through to the behavior of leading businessmen during the Putin period. Putin took an active interest in both who came to head leading companies and what those companies did. While his role in the former was generally behind the scenes and difficult to discern, he was clearly a major factor in shaping the identity of the post-Yeltsin oligarchs, with people who had links with him rising to leading places in major companies and those who were deemed to oppose him removed.[90] Under Putin, most of the major companies coordinated their policies with the interests of the state, while the businessmen thus involved – including Abramovich, Deripaska, Fridman, Potanin, Vekselberg, Alekperov, and Usmanov – were often referred to as "state oligarchs."[91]

At the same time that Putin was asserting political control in this way, he also promoted the expansion of the state's role in the economy. By the end of Yeltsin's rule, following successive waves of privatization, the state retained only the least profitable oil company Rosneft, natural resource monopolies, enterprises comprising the military–industrial complex, and some smaller enterprises, which were loss-making but were socially important.[92] Low level officials usually represented the government on the boards of these companies. Yeltsin's emphasis on the primacy of the private sector changed under Putin, when the principle became that the state should have a dominant role in the key strategic sectors of the economy – fuel and energy, military–industrial complex and transport and communications. This did not mean that all of those sectors should be renationalized, but that the state should own sufficient capacity

---

[89] Stephen White, *Understanding Russian Politics* (Cambridge: Cambridge University Press, 2011), p. 143.

[90] Karen Dawisha, *Putin's Kleptocracy. Who Owns Russia?* (New York: Simon & Schuster, 2014); Anne Applebaum, "How He and His Cronies Stole Russia," *The New York Review of Books*, December 18, 2014, pp. 26–30.

[91] Sakwa (*Crisis*), p. 135. Although compare this with the list on p. 338.

[92] Olga Kryshtanovskaya and Stephen White, "The Formation of Russia's Network Directorate," Vadim Kononenko and Arkady Moshes (eds), *Russia as a Network State. What Works in Russia When State Institutions Do Not?* (Basingstoke: Palgrave Macmillan, 2011), p. 28.

in each sector to be able to set the tone for that sector,[93] and in some sectors state control increased; the share of state-controlled companies in oil production increased from 24 percent in 2003 to 37 percent in 2007.[94] While this aim was facilitated by the resources boom and the consequent greater role in the economy played by such companies as Gazprom and Rosneft, this was reflected in the increased role played by the state in determining who could be involved in resources projects, especially in relation to foreign investment,[95] but also in the insertion into the boards of major companies of leading state officials. Rather than low level officials occupying seats on these boards, the government came now to be represented in the most important companies by leading political figures, including government ministers and many of Putin's close associates.[96]

Throughout the Putin period, many of the largest companies in which the government had major shares, including the monopolies Gazprom and UES, were sometimes forced to act in violation of market principles; for example, these two companies had to supply domestic customers with energy at below market prices, while the state cooperated with them in expanding and exploiting foreign markets. This symbiotic relationship between companies and state locked the two together in an alliance from which both could benefit. This development constitutes a structural basis upon which the political elite was able to tie big business to itself, and thereby ensure that independent centers of economic power did not develop in such a way as to challenge their political control, and although in 2011 Medvedev tried to bring about the withdrawal of many of these people from their corporate positions, this had little effect. The substantial state involvement in the economy, both formal and at a more informal level through personal connections, limited the scope for the mobilization of large economic resources behind opposition actors, while the co-optation of big business denied this as a major support for opposition. A combination of threat of repression or marginalization of potential business opponents and the opportunities that existed to

[93] For the list of 1,063 "strategic enterprises" in which the state intended to maintain decisive control over ownership and management, see the August 2004 presidential decree, Ukaz prezidenta rossiiskoi federatsii, "Ob utverzhdenii perechnia strategicheskikh predpriiatii i strategicheskikh aktsionernykh obshchestv," 4/8/04, No. 1009, http://document .kremlin.ru/doc.asp?ID=0237999. Accessed September 9, 2004.

[94] Sakwa (Crisis), p. 146. On state corporations, see pp. 153–9. For more figures, see David Lane, "Divisions within the Russian Political Elites," Russian Analytical Digest 124, March 18, 2013, p. 3.

[95] A law of May 5, 2007, barred foreign investment in forty-two strategic industries. Sakwa (Crisis), p. 152.

[96] For a partial list, see Kryshtanovskaya and White ("The Formation"), p. 31. There were also informal links with family members of government officials sometimes holding such positions. Sakwa (Crisis), p. 172.

become wealthy through official connections combined to keep business generally away from significant involvement in opposition activities.

## The populace

The opportunity for protest relies upon people being willing to overcome the collective action problem and to protest, and the regime has sought to blunt that willingness through a combination of denying the opportunity for protest, hamstringing potential vehicles for protest, and limiting the capacity. It has not done this through a major effort at popular mobilization along Soviet lines. There has not been a range of organizations whose task it has been to attract large numbers of members of the public into continuing organizational activity around the regime's goals. Certainly there have been attempts at election time to mobilize the voters and ensure an acceptable turnout, but during ordinary times of the year, the people are left largely to their own devices. Like classic authoritarian regimes,[97] the Russian has not sought the continuing mobilization of its populace. It has been more content with pacification reflected in a high level of apathy.

Such an outcome is often thought to be associated with policies that bring economic prosperity. This was certainly not the case under Yeltsin, when economic conditions were those of prolonged economic depression. But as noted above even under such circumstances, there was not widespread popular mobilization. The sort of apathy that appeared evident was attributed to a variety of factors: exhaustion following the mobilization of the perestroika years, the struggle to survive in the economic difficulties, and disappointment with the outcome of regime change. Most of the people seemed more intent on getting on with their own lives than becoming involved in politics. This trend continued under Putin, even when economic conditions had improved for many people. With the high growth rates between the economic setbacks of 1998 and 2008, the lives of millions of Russians improved significantly, especially in the big towns. This success was widely attributed to Putin and the policies that he followed, even if in fact it was probably more due to the rising prices of energy exports than to policies unique to Putin. Putin promoted this sort of performance legitimacy by directly associating himself and his regime with the economic successes. In addition, he openly eschewed

---

[97] For the classic definition, see Juan J. Linz, "An Authoritarian Regime: Spain," Erik Allardt and Stein Rokkan (eds), *Mass Politics. Studies in Political Sociology* (New York: The Free Press, 1970), pp. 251–83.

some policies that could have led to conflict in the society. His early statements about there being no redistribution of property, even if uttered in
a contingent form and with an underlying threat, was a signal of social
reconciliation. His acceptance of the Soviet era as a legitimate stage in
Russian history, even if it did have some negative sides to it, was also a
very different approach to the anti-communism of Yeltsin, and emphasized reconciliation of the society as a whole.

At no time has the regime sought to develop a coherent ideology to
legitimate itself and to mobilize the populace. An ideology is a coherent
body of values, assumptions, principles, and arguments that purports to
explain the course of historical development, and includes both an assessment of the deficiencies of the past and some idea about what needs to
be done to address these and to move on into the bright future.[98] Perhaps not surprisingly, Yeltsin eschewed the idea of having an ideology as
such because he associated this with the communist era, although he did
at times articulate views that constituted potential nuclei of a more formalized ideology, and he did in 1996 briefly favor the development of a
"new national ideology" termed the "Russian idea."[99] The heart of those
views[100] was a combination of vigorous anti-communism and criticism
of the Soviet past[101] and a commitment to "democracy" and a market
economy. Initially, up until about the end of 1993, he emphasized the
importance of universal values (like democracy and market economics),
counterposing these to more nativistic values arising from Russian traditions, but in the second half of the decade the focus on universalism
disappeared. This sort of combination – anti-communism, democracy,
and market economics – was not one that was likely to gain broad assent,
given the continuing support for the communists reflected in the polls
and the way in which democracy and the market came to be associated
with the crime and economic dislocation of the 1990s. So not only was
there no coherent ideological message emanating from the regime, but
the message that did come out was not likely to be very appealing to the
populace.

---

[98]  For a discussion of this and related concepts, see Graeme Gill, *Symbols and Legitimacy
    in Soviet Politics* (Cambridge: Cambridge University Press, 2011), p. 2.
[99]  For discussions of this, see Kathleen E. Smith, *Mythmaking in the New Russia. Politics
    and Memory during the Yeltsin Era* (Ithaca: Cornell University Press, 2002), Chapter 8;
    and Timothy J. Colton, *Yeltsin. A Life* (New York: Basic Books, 2008), pp. 389–90.
[100] For a more extended discussion of the development of the views of Yeltsin, Putin, and
    Medvedev, see Gill (*Symbolism*), Chapter 3.
[101] For example, see his speech on the anniversary of the revolution in 1997, BBC News
    Monitoring, November 7, 1997, http://news.bbc.co.uk/1/hi/world/monitoring/24845
    .stm. Accessed November 10, 1997.

When Putin first came to power, he emphasized the importance of Russia pursuing its own path of development and "the primordial, traditional values of Russians," focusing in particular on patriotism, the greatness of Russia (derzhavnost'), statism or a strong Russian state, and social solidarity.[102] These themes remained prominent in Putin's speeches throughout the first eight years he was president. In particular, he emphasized the need for a strong state as a means of restoring Russia as both a healthy society domestically and a great power internationally. While he recognized the importance of civil society, he argued that a strong civil society could come about only with a strong state. Particularly towards the end of his first tenure as president, Putin emphasized Russia's cultural uniqueness and the spiritual unity of the people, a unity that was predicated upon respect for Russian language, cultural values, and historical experience.[103] The reverse side of this was the argument that Russia did not need advice and lectures from outside and the creation of a sense that Russia was faced by external enemies whose influence domestically needed to be expunged.

With Putin's second ascension to the presidency, these themes were again present, but there seems to have been a sharpening of nuance, perhaps reflecting the nationalist riots in Manezh Square in December 2010 and Biriulevo in October 2013, the protest activity following the 2011 Duma election, and the continuing perception of the presence of international enemies of Russia. Putin's earlier emphasis on Russian values and identity again came to the fore. During the presidential election campaign, when Putin discussed the "national question,"[104] he mounted a strong argument that historically Russia had been a polyethnic civilization, but that this was bound together by the "Russian cultural core." The civilizational identity of Russian society "is based on preserving the Russian dominant cultural idea whose bearers are not only ethnic Russians, but also all bearers of that identity regardless of nationality." People could retain their faith and ethnic affiliation, but they were above all citizens of Russia. This primacy of Russians and Russian culture in the development of Russian society was confirmed in his prime ministerial

---

[102] These are spelled out explicitly in Vladimir V. Putin, "Rossiia na rubezhe tysiacheletii," *Nezavisimaia gazeta*, December 30, 1999. They are also redolent of the sorts of values emphasized in the political culture school discussed in Chapter 1.

[103] Vladimir Putin, "Poslanie Federal'nomu sobraniiu Rossiiskoi federatsii," April 26, 2007, http://archive.kremlin.ru/appears/2007/04/26/1156_type63372type63374type 82634_125339.shtml. Accessed April 29, 2007. Medvedev picked up many of these themes, but there was a difference of nuance in that he gave priority to civil society over the state.

[104] V.V. Putin, "Rossiia: natsional'nyi vopros," *Nezavisimaia gazeta*, January 23, 2012.

report on the activities of the government in 2011,[105] and in his report to the Federal Assembly in December 2012.[106] In the latter, he bemoaned the "deficit of spiritual values" and declared that in the need to rectify this, Russia needed to be guided by the values of Russian culture and its continuous thousand-year history. Russia was a multiethnic nation bound together by the Russian people, language, and culture. This spiritual unity was essential, and all forms of nationalism and chauvinism would be opposed. Democracy was declared to be essential, but echoing the position he had adopted during his first two terms, this had to be democracy in accord with Russian tradition. In this, Putin was clearly appealing to the sort of civilizational nationalism that is such a strong theme in Russian public life,[107] and seemed to be trying to merge ethnic Russian nationalism with civic Russian nationalism.

But there was also a sharper edge to some of his comments, which fed into a theme that seems to have become more prominent since the Manezh riot, that of anti-immigrant sentiment.[108] There had been an undertone of this in Russian public life since before the collapse of the USSR, but for most of the independence period, the more extreme sentiments were voiced by those on the margins of political life: Zhirinovsky, the National Bolsheviks, and other nationalist groups. However, this seems to have become more mainstream with, for example, both Sobyanin and Navalny taking a line critical of migration into Moscow during the 2013 mayoral election campaign.[109] The annual Russian Marches are another reflection of this, as is the fact that in an October 2013 opinion poll, two-thirds of Russians were found to support the

[105] "Predsedatel' Pravitel'stva Rossiiskoi Federatsii V.V.Putin vystupil v Gosudarstvennoi Dume s otchetom o deiatel'nosti Pravitel'stva Rossiiskoi Federatsii za 2011," April 11, 2012, http://premier.gov.ru/events/news/18671/. Accessed April 12, 2012.

[106] "Poslanie Prezidenta Federal'nomu Sobraniiu," December 12, 2012, http://kremlin.ru/transcript/17118. Accessed December 16, 2012. Also see his speech to Valdai in September 2013, http://valdaiclub.com.politics/62880.html. Accessed October 5, 2013.

[107] Luke March, "Nationalism for Export? The Domestic and Foreign Policy Implications of the New 'Russian Idea'," *Europe-Asia Studies* 64 (3), 2012, pp. 412–16.

[108] For some data on anti-immigrant violence, see Marlene Laruelle, "Anti-Migrant Riots in Russia: the Mobilizing Potential of Xenophobia," *Russian Analytical Digest* 141, December 23, 2013, pp. 2–4.

[109] See the comments by Moscow Mayor Sergei Sobyanin about the problems posed by migrants in Moscow. *Vlast'* 41, October 21, 2013, pp. 9–16 and *Komsomol'skaia Pravda*, November 20, 2013. The Patriarch has explicitly warned about migration, http://interfax-religion.ru/print.php?act=news&id=532555. Accessed November 15, 2013. For the argument that the appeal to traditional values was being used against sexual minorities, see Cai Wilkinson, "Putting Traditional Values into Practice: Russia's Anti-Gay Laws," *Russian Analytical Digest* 138, November 8, 2013, pp. 5–7.

idea of "Russia for Russians."[110] Putin has fueled this sentiment. In his address to the Federal Assembly in December 2013,[111] he confirmed the importance of traditional values and a conservative outlook, and noted the role played by Russian culture, history, and language in the development of the Russian Federation.[112] He declared that inter-ethnic tensions were not provoked by people from particular nationalities but by people devoid of culture and respect for traditions, by people who represent a form of amoral internationalism, "including rowdy, insolent people who come from some of the southern regions of Russia, corrupt law enforcement officials who cover for an ethnic mafia, and so-called 'Russian nationalists' and different types of separatists who are ready to turn any common tragedy into an excuse for vandalism and bloody rampage." But later in the speech he also said that labor migration could lead to ethnic conflict and needed to be more tightly regulated. Thus, while at one level Putin appealed to civic nationalism and eschewed crude nationalism and xenophobia,[113] his references to labor migration and the possible link with conflict is effectively an appeal to the anti-immigrant sentiment that generally before he had eschewed. This is in part an attempt to prevent that nationalism that had been an ideological prop to the regime from being taken over by extreme nationalists, as it had been under Yeltsin.

Consistent with this view of the centrality of Russian traditions has been the Putin-inspired attempt to rewrite the school history curriculum to present a more coherent narrative. Initiated in 2007 and revived in 2013,[114] the attempt at curriculum revision has been widely interpreted as seeking to impose an official version of the country's past, and one

[110] The high level of support for this sentiment has been evident for some time: 7/02, 55%; 8/06, 54%; 10/08, 57%; 11/11, 59%; 11/12, 56%; 10/13, 66%; http://levada.ru/print/05–11–2013/rossiyane-o-migratsii-i-mezhnatsionalnoi-napryazhennosti. Accessed December 10, 2013. The same source saw a jump from 64 percent in November 2012 to 73 percent in November 2013 of those who believed that illegal immigrants from the "near abroad" should be expelled from Russia. For some other poll figures, see "Russian Public Opinion on Migrants," *Russian Analytical Digest* 141, December 23, 2013, pp. 8–12.

[111] V.V. Putin, "Poslanie Prezidenta Federal'nomu Sobraniiu," December 12, 2013, www.kremlin.ru/news/19825. Accessed December 23, 2013.

[112] He also confirmed this in his press conference in December 2013. "Press konferentsiia Vladimira Putina," December 19, 2013, http://kremlin.ru/news/19859. Accessed December 23, 2013. He also said that he was not opposed to Western values, but to attempts to impose those values on others, and he spoke of Russian "cultural space" and "language space."

[113] For example, see his comments on the Day of Internal Affairs Staff reported on the news channel Rossia 24 on November 10, 2013. BBC Monitoring, November 10, 2013.

[114] Respectively, Gill (*Symbolism*), pp. 164–71 and Chapter 5 more generally; and Gabriela Baczynska, "Putin Accused of Soviet Tactics in Drafting New History Book," Reuters, November 18, 2013.

that whitewashes the negative aspects of it. While such criticism has in many instances been excessive, the desire to have a view of the past that celebrates Russian achievements is clearly consistent with the primacy accorded to Russian culture, language, and its past.

The position Putin espoused did not constitute an ideology, but it did represent an interpretation of Russian reality that had distinct political implications. By emphasizing spiritual unity based upon Russian tradition, he was effectively declaring opposition to be un-Russian, at odds with the unity stemming from Russian history and culture. While this seemed to apply specifically to actions by non-ethnic Russians, it could also apply to activity of the sort represented by the postelection protests. This was an appeal to Russian nationalism, and although unlike some others[115] he did not call for Russians to be given a special place in society, this was clearly a position that implied primacy for one group and played on popular suspicion about migrants in Russian society. This flirting with nationalism did not constitute an ideology, but its message is designed to appeal to the Russian majority and thereby garner support for the regime.

So although the regime did not seek to mobilize people through either organizational or ideational means, under Putin it did seek symbolically to encapsulate them within a framework that was rooted in the regime and its performance. The message was clear, if understated: under Putin, society was advancing, life was improving, and the country was being healed by its adherence to traditional Russian values. In this sense, the regime sought to root itself in an existential conception of the relationship between regime and society. The latter could prosper and grow stronger only while the former was in charge. Furthermore, the regime projected the image that the only acceptable behavior was that conducted in regime-sanctioned ways. This combination of messages, added to the weakness of the opposition, seems to have been sufficient to persuade the mass of the population to deny support to the opposition. The inability to mobilize large numbers remains a weakness of the opposition, and it is one that in part reflects the success of government policies designed to achieve precisely that aim. This is reflected in opinion poll data.

Opinion poll data under Putin reflect a situation in which the populace generally seems to accept that there is little alternative to acting except through the institutional structures of the regime. Since the collapse of the Soviet Union, democracy has been a prominent element in the regime's

---

[115] For example, Patriarch Kirill's comments following the Biriulevo events in October 2013. Interfax, October 31, 2013, http://interfax-religion.ru/print.php?act=news&id=53255. Accessed November 15, 2013.

Table 2.1. *Do you think Russia needs democracy? (in %)*[116]

|  | 6/2005 | 12/2006 | 12/2007 | 6/2008 | 6/2009 | 12/2009 | 10/2011 | 7/2012 |
|---|---|---|---|---|---|---|---|---|
| Yes | 66 | 55 | 67 | 62 | 57 | 57 | 61 | 63 |
| No | 21 | 27 | 17 | 20 | 26 | 23 | 25 | 24 |
| Don't know | 13 | 18 | 17 | 18 | 17 | 20 | 14 | 13 |

Table 2.2. *What type of state would you like Russia to be in the future? (in %)*[117]

|  | 1999 | 2008 | 2011 | 2012 |
|---|---|---|---|---|
| Socialist state like USSR | 15 | 17 | 23 | 21 |
| A state like Western states with a democratic government and a market economy | 35 | 32 | 30 | 31 |
| A state with a special system and a unique course of development | 45 | 39 | 36 | 41 |
| Difficult to answer | 6 | 11 | 12 | 7 |

discourse, albeit an element that has had a variety of meanings,[118] and its popular reception has been similarly ambiguous. Nevertheless, public opinion runs strongly in favor of "democracy," as Table 2.1 illustrates.

Although about a quarter of respondents believe Russia does not need democracy, around two-thirds believe Russia does need democracy.[119] However, when asked about what they would like Russia to be like in the future, the response has been as noted above (Table 2.2).

Only a third of respondents favor a Western-style democracy, significantly outnumbered by those supporting a system that is unique to Russia, reflecting its historical and cultural characteristics. If the Soviet

[116] Levada Analytical Center, *Russian Public Opinion 2012–2013. Annual* (Moscow: Levada Center, 2013), p. 26, www.levada.ru. Accessed June 3, 2015.
[117] Levada Analytical Center, *Russian Public Opinion 2010–2011. Annual* (Moscow: Levada Center, 2012), p. 22.
[118] On this, see the discussion in Gill (*Symbolism*), Chapter 3. Russians have generally favored democracy in principle while being critical of how it has worked in practice in Russia. Mendras (*Russian Politics*), p. 198.
[119] For a discussion that cites a lower approval rating for democracy, see Stephen Whitefield, "Russian Citizens and Russian Democracy: Perceptions of State Governance and Democratic Practice, 1993–2007," *Post-Soviet Affairs* 25 (2), 2009, pp. 93–117. For evidence of strong public support for individual elements of democracy, see Timothy J. Colton and Michel McFaul, "Are Russians Undemocratic?," *Post-Soviet Affairs* 18 (2), 2002, pp. 91–121.

Table 2.3. *What kind of democracy does Russia need? (in %)*[120]

|  | 2005 | 2006 | 2007 | 2008 | 2009 | 2010 | 2011 |
|---|---|---|---|---|---|---|---|
| Like in developed countries of Europe and America | 24 | 18 | 22 | 20 | 23 | 23 | 23 |
| Like was in the Soviet Union | 16 | 13 | 10 | 13 | 14 | 16 | 17 |
| A special kind, which suits national traditions and specifics of Russia | 45 | 48 | 47 | 45 | 43 | 45 | 44 |
| Does not need democracy | 6 | 10 | 7 | 8 | 7 | 7 | 7 |
| Difficult to answer | 9 | 11 | 14 | 15 | 13 | 10 | 10 |

experience was also to be interpreted in this light, the number approaches two-thirds. Such a view favoring a uniquely Russian system accords with Putin's emphasis upon the need for a strong state consistent with Russia's cultural traditions, which he has counterposed to the "Western model" of democracy.[121] Such a system, consistent with Russia's "cultural traditions," is often seen in terms of a special, Russian, form of democracy (Table 2.3).

This preference for a "Russian style" system rather than Western democracy seems also to be reflected in the willingness of Russians to accept "a strong and authoritative leader, a 'strong hand'" (Table 2.4).

The notion of the "strong hand," support for which was higher in 2011 than it was soon after the collapse of the USSR, sits uncomfortably with a commitment to democracy, at least as understood in the West,[122] but is consistent with the earlier finding that Russia needs a system in accord with its traditions. This is also consistent with the view that, if there was to be a choice, it was more important for Russia to have a strong state

[120] Levada (*Russian Public Opinion 2010–2011*), p. 28. For figures showing a breakdown on this question by age, see Iurii Levada, "Segodniashnii vybor: urovni i ramki," *Vestnik obshchestvennogo mneniia. Dannye. Analiz. Diskussi* 2 (76), Mart-aprel' 2005, p. 34.

[121] For example, see Vladimir Putin, "Poslanie Federal'nomu Sobraniiu Rossiiskoi Federatstii," April 25, 2005, http://archive.kremlin.ru/appears/2005/04/25/1223_type63372type63374type82634_87049.shtml. Accessed April 29, 2009.

[122] For the argument that the Russian preference is for a strong hand, but its wielder to be elected in a free and fair election, see Henry E. Hale, "The Myth of Mass Russian Support for Autocracy: Public Opinion Foundations of a Hybrid Regime," *Europe-Asia Studies* 63 (8), 2011, pp. 1357–75; and Henry E. Hale, "Trends in Russian Views on Democracy 2008–12: Has There Been a Russian Democratic Awakening?," *Russian Analytical Digest* 117, September 19, 2012, pp. 9–11. This is consistent with the notion of "delegative democracy" popularized in Guillermo O'Donnell, "Delegative Democracy," *Journal of Democracy* 5 (1), 1994, pp. 55–69.

Table 2.4. *Can there be situations in the country where the people need a strong and authoritative leader, a "strong hand"? (in %)*[123]

|  | 1989 | 1994 | 1995 | 1996 | 2006 | 2007 | 2008 | 2009 | 2010 | 2011 |
|---|---|---|---|---|---|---|---|---|---|---|
| All the time | 25 | 35 | 33 | 37 | 42 | 45 | 43 | 40 | 44 | 42 |
| Sometimes | 16 | 23 | 27 | 32 | 31 | 29 | 29 | 31 | 33 | 29 |
| Never | 44 | 23 | 24 | 18 | 20 | 18 | 18 | 25 | 19 | 22 |
| Difficult to answer | 16 | 18 | 15 | 13 | 8 | 8 | 10 | 5 | 5 | 8 |

Table 2.5. *And what, in your opinion, is more important for Russia right now, to have a strong state or to be a democratic country? (in %)*[124]

|  | 2008 | 2012 |
|---|---|---|
| Strong state | 43 | 41 |
| Equally important | 43 | 42 |
| Democracy | 10 | 11 |
| No answer | 4 | 5 |

than a democracy, although clearly many thought the two were equally important (Table 2.5).

Thus, while there is widespread public support for "democracy,"[125] there seems to be a larger constituency that is sympathetic to the argument that what Russia needs is a political system that accords with its traditions. While it is not clear exactly what traditions are envisaged here, those who have argued on this basis (including Putin) have

---

[123] Levada (*Russian Public Opinion 2010–2011*), p. 56. When asked what would be better, centralized power in the country or power shared between various structures keeping each other in check, in February 2010, 45 percent preferred the former and 42 percent the latter. Levada (*Russian Public Opinion 2010–2011*), p. 30. An undated poll suggested that 51 percent of people preferred a leader with a strong hand to direct the work of state organs compared with 39 percent who wanted a leader who strictly observes the constitution and works together with all social and political groups. Ellen Carnaghan, "Popular Support for Democracy and Autocracy in Russia," *Russian Analytical Digest* 117, September 19, 2012, p. 6.

[124] Hale ("Trends in Russian Views"), p. 13.

[125] For an argument about the pro-democratic disposition in Russian public opinion, see Colton and McFaul ("Are Russians Undemocratic?"), pp. 91–121. For a discussion of some of the problems involved in survey research on democracy in Russia, along with the conclusion that while Russians may be more supportive of democracy than is generally assumed, they are unwilling to do much to advance it, see Carnaghan ("Popular Support"), pp. 2–4.

Table 2.6. *Do you think you can influence the political processes in Russia? (in %)*[126]

|                    | 2008 | 2010 | 2011 |
|--------------------|------|------|------|
| Definitely yes     | 1    | 3    | 3    |
| Yes, rather than no | 7   | 7    | 11   |
| No, rather than yes | 36  | 30   | 34   |
| Definitely no      | 51   | 54   | 48   |
| Difficult to answer | 5   | 6    | 4    |

usually had in mind idealized images of traditional Russian folkways and an organic society, which is very far removed from the procedural principles of Western democracy. This constitutes a vision in which many of the classic features of democracy as known in the West are absent, and constitutes a solid social base for a nondemocratic form of rule. This means that despite the high general approval levels of "democracy," these do not represent a clear and unambiguous commitment to the sorts of procedural principles normally associated with a democratic political system.

Generally, Russians have evinced little trust in their governmental authorities,[127] and therefore little real connection with those authorities. But more important for the current argument, they believe overwhelmingly that they have little influence in the political process (Table 2.6).

Nor do they believe they can exercise much control over the authorities (Table 2.7).

This is also reflected in their view that politicians do not care about the voters: in 2011, 82 percent in a sample agreed that "Politicians just need to be elected and do not care about doing anything for the voters" while only 9 percent disagreed;[128] in 2010, 65 percent believed that the "Majority of politicians are in politics for personal gain only."[129]

The image that emerges from the figures in Tables 2.1–2.7 is one of the widespread lack of popular efficacy. People do not feel able to exercise much influence over their rulers in practice, while the ambiguous nature

---

[126] Levada (*Russian Public Opinion 2010–2011*), p. 41. Also see p. 49.
[127] For some figures on this, see Stephen White, "Ten Years On, What Do the Russians Think?," *The Journal of Communist Studies and Transition Politics* 18 (1), 2002, p. 42.
[128] Levada (*Russian Public Opinion 2010–2011*), p. 42.
[129] A further 22 percent partly agreed and partly disagreed. Levada (*Russian Public Opinion 2010–2011*), p. 44. Also see p. 48. For a similarly negative view of the role played by politicians, see the findings in *Izmeneniia politicheskikh nastroenii rossiian posle prezidentskikh vyborov. Doklad ekspertov Tsentra strategicheskikh razrabotok Komitety grazhdanskikh initsiativ*, Moscow, October 23, 2012, p. 36.

Table 2.7. *To what extent does the Russian public control the authorities? (in %)*[130]

|                        | 2001 | 2006 | 2010 | 2011 |
|------------------------|------|------|------|------|
| To a very large extent | 2    | 3    | 1    | 1    |
| To a fairly large extent | 9  | 6    | 8    | 10   |
| To a fairly small extent | 34 | 32   | 39   | 42   |
| Does not control at all | 48  | 51   | 41   | 39   |
| Difficult to answer    | 7    | 8    | 11   | 11   |

Table 2.8. *Do you think that regular elections can make the authorities do what the general public needs? (in %)*[131]

|                         | 3/2010 | 3/2011 | 11/2011 |
|-------------------------|--------|--------|---------|
| To a considerable degree | 6     | 3      | 8       |
| To a certain extent     | 31     | 29     | 35      |
| Not so much             | 29     | 30     | 30      |
| Absolutely not          | 26     | 31     | 22      |
| Difficult to answer     | 9      | 7      | 5       |

of the attachment to democracy means that the principle of popular control that is at the heart of such a notion remains weak in Russian public life. This widespread perception of limited ability to influence political life is a stark expression of the lack of efficacy felt by Russian voters.

Elections are seen by some as a means of influencing the authorities (Table 2.8).

While around a third of Russians see elections as a means of getting politicians to pay some attention to their needs, over half believed elections had little effect in this regard. Throughout much of the 2000s the largest category of those who said they would not vote said this was because their vote meant nothing – 24 percent in November 2003, 31 percent in November 2007, and 36 percent in November 2011.[132]

The existing institutions and the way they are currently working are not seen by much of the populace as a viable means of influence over their

[130] Levada (*Russian Public Opinion 2010–2011*), p. 46.
[131] Levada (*Russian Public Opinion 2010–2011*), p. 51.
[132] L.D. Gudkov, B.V. Dubin, N.A. Zorkaia, and M.A. Plotko, *Rossiiskie parlamentskie vybory: elektoral'nyi protsess pri avtoritarnom rezhime* (Moscow: Analiticheskii tsentr Iuriia Levady, 2012), p. 14.

Table 2.9. *Do you think people like you can influence the situation in the country by taking part in rallies, protests, and strikes? (in %)*[133]

|                    | 1/2001 | 4/2010 | 4/2011 | 10/2011 | 6/2012 |
|--------------------|--------|--------|--------|---------|--------|
| Definitely yes     | 5      | 4      | 3      | 4       | 4      |
| Most likely, yes   | 19     | 18     | 18     | 15      | 14     |
| Most likely, no    | 41     | 36     | 40     | 40      | 35     |
| Definitely no      | 30     | 32     | 32     | 34      | 35     |
| Difficult to answer| 5      | 9      | 7      | 8       | 12     |

rulers. In this sort of situation, where the populace believes it has little influence over the political process, politicians are not greatly concerned for their interests, and the existing institutions do not provide effective means for popular control or influence, it may be that nonsystemic forms of political activity might be seen as potential ways of exercising popular influence. While a majority of citizens generally see rallies and demonstrations as standard means of democratic activity that should not be banned by the authorities,[134] most also believed they were not an effective means for exercising political influence, including following the 2011–12 protests (Table 2.9).

In relation to the 2011–12 protests specifically, a majority believed that they had had no positive results (Table 2.10).

With this sort of direct action seen by a strong majority of respondents as unlikely to be an effective means of exercising influence on the political leadership, it is not surprising that 95 percent of people in April 2011 said that they had not participated in mass protests (picket lines, rallies, marches, or demonstrations) or strikes in the last twelve months.[135] In April 2010, 61 percent and in October 2011, 65 percent said that they

[133] Levada (*Russian Public Opinion 2010–2011*), p. 93 and for the 2012 figure, www.levada .ru/05-0702012/mitingi-oppozitsii-chast-1. Accessed January 7, 2013. Although when asked in December 2011 what the authorities were likely to do in the event of escalating protests, 40 percent said they would seek a compromise with the protesters; the remainder thought the authorities would seek to divide the protesters (20 percent), brutally suppress the protests (18 percent), or did not know. Levada (*Russian Public Opinion 2010–2011*), p. 198. For an argument that between 1992 and 2006 there was "relatively strong" consistency between public opinion and government policy, which suggests that the government has been sensitive to public opinion, see Cale Horne, "The Consistency of Policy with Opinion in the Russian Federation, 1992–2006," *Journal of Elections, Public Opinion and Parties* 22 (3), 2012, pp. 214–44.

[134] Levada (*Russian Public Opinion 2010–2011*), p. 93. Also p. 200.

[135] Levada (*Russian Public Opinion 2010–2011*), p. 94.

Table 2.10. *Do you think that the
protest actions have had any positive
results, have changed the situation for
the better in the country? (in %)*[136]

|                          | 3/2012 | 6/2012 |
|--------------------------|--------|--------|
| Definitely yes           | 5      | 7      |
| More inclined to say yes | 22     | 21     |
| More inclined to say no  | 32     | 45     |
| Definitely no            | 22     | 14     |
| Difficult to answer      | 19     | 13     |

Table 2.11. *If mass protests against electoral violations and falsification
were to be held in your city or district, would you be willing to participate?
(in %)*[137]

|                     | 12/2011 | 1/2012 | 2/2012 | 3/2012 | 6/2012 | 7/2012 | 8/2012 |
|---------------------|---------|--------|--------|--------|--------|--------|--------|
| Definitely yes      | 4       | 3      | 3      | 2      | 3      | 5      | 2      |
| Probably            | 11      | 10     | 10     | 6      | 11     | 14     | 11     |
| Probably not        | 30      | 31     | 30     | 30     | 28     | 30     | 31     |
| Definitely not      | 47      | 47     | 49     | 48     | 47     | 44     | 49     |
| Difficult to answer | 9       | 9      | 9      | 14     | 10     | 7      | 7      |

had never attended, and under no circumstances would attend, a political gathering or rally,[138] and these figures seem to have strengthened
following the beginning of the 2011–12 protests (Table 2.11).

By late 2013, 78 percent said they would not take part in protest
activity in their town or district.[139] Moreover, in a poll repeated over a
number of years, the numbers saying they were prepared to attend a rally
supporting the government's policies were greater than those prepared
to attend a rally opposing those policies (Table 2.12).

The attitude to protest reflected in Tables 2.9–2.11 suggests that
protest activity is not seen as a particularly useful way of seeking to

---

[136] http://levada.ru/05–07–2012/mitingi-oppozitsii-chast-1. Accessed August 2, 2012.
[137] www.levada.ru/28–08–2012/deistviya-vlasti-v-otnoshenii-oppozitsii-i-protestnye-
nastroeniya in Ben Aris, "Russia's Reaction to the Magnitsky Act and Relations with
the West," *Russian Analytical Digest* 120, November 23, 2012, p. 6.
[138] Levada (*Russian Public Opinion 2010–2011*), p. 42.
[139] www.levada.ru/13-11-2013/protestnye-nastroeniya-rossiyam. Accessed December 15,
2013.

Table 2.12. *If there is a mass demonstration taking place in your city on May 1, would you like to participate in the demonstration in support of/to protest against the president's and government's policy? (in %)*[140]

|         | 4/2004 | 4/2006 | 4/2008 | 4/2009 | 4/2010 | 4/2011 |
|---------|--------|--------|--------|--------|--------|--------|
| Support | 23     | 20     | 21     | 17     | 26     | 17     |
| Protest | 10     | 12     | 10     | 11     | 11     | 11     |

influence the authorities, and while the figures in Table 2.12 are quite small, they suggest that for those willing to participate in a demonstration, more see this as a form of traditional mobilization (as in Soviet times) than they do as a means of protest. Combined with the conclusion that the existing institutions are not effective vehicles for the exercise of popular control, this reflects a culture in which there is no real sense of popular efficacy.

The absence of a sense of efficacy is said to be central to popular apathy and a lack of willingness to become involved in political life.[141] A culture of political inefficacy seems to reign whereby people believe it is not worthwhile to become involved in protest activity. While such involvement could be dangerous, given the occasional use of force against the protesters, more important is the belief that the authorities will not take any notice of such activity. This sense of a lack of efficacy has not been dispelled by the protests linked to the 2011–12 electoral cycle. While it is not clear from the figures, this culture is probably strongest in the countryside and small towns and cities, and weakest in the major cities. This would be one factor in the much larger protests being found in Moscow than elsewhere. It is the strength of this culture that is the strongest buttress of the Russian authoritarian regime.

To the extent that this sense of a lack of efficacy pervades the broad population as a whole, it reflects the regime's success in projecting the view that currently there is no alternative to the existing system and to acting through it. While this perception remains, it constitutes a significant buffer for the regime because it represents a broad consensus around acceptance of the regime. The basis of this acceptance may be,

---

[140] Levada (*Russian Public Opinion 2010–2011*), p. 93.

[141] The original, classic, statement is in Gabriel A. Almond and Sidney Verba, *The Civic Culture. Political Attitudes and Democracy in Five Nations* (Boston: Little, Brown and Company, 1965), but the point has been made widely with regard to all sorts of cultures by later scholars.

for some, actual positive support for the regime and what it is doing, but for others it is likely to be more an acknowledgement that the regime is there and must be dealt with in a matter of fact way. This sort of approach, where the populace is not constantly mobilized into political activity, but remains essentially passive and uninvolved in political life, suits the regime because it leaves it relatively unencumbered by the need either to continually interact with the people or be too concerned about their expectations. Effectively it means the existence of two spheres of life that rarely meet: the popular and the governmental. While these remain relatively autonomous, meeting mainly through the ritualized electoral process, the regime would appear to be relatively immune from popular discontent. However, if the 2011–12 protests were to constitute a new means for these two spheres to interact in a more sustained fashion, the relative autonomy would break down and regime stability would be called into question, but there is no evidence that that is happening.

In its approach to the nonsystemic opposition, the regime has thus sought to structure the opportunities for political action in such a way as to block the emergence of opportunity, vehicles, and capacity for opposition to form. This has been more systematic under Putin than under Yeltsin, although paradoxically it has also been under Putin that protest reached its highest levels. Throughout the post-Soviet period, repression has been used on a selective basis to dissuade future oppositionist activity and break that which did emerge: the arrest of activists and leaders, the killing of critics, bashing of protesters and critics, and legislative restrictions. Although it is not clear that the agents of the state were directly involved in all the cases of assault, the political leadership did help to create the atmosphere within which they could take place, often with no one held responsible. Repression, or the threat of it, has underpinned all other aspects of the regime's program. But the regime has also worked assiduously at marginalizing and co-opting the opposition and, where these could not work, giving partial concessions (such as the Public Chamber, Council for Civil Society and Human Rights, and the post-December 2011 protest changes to the electoral and party laws). The broad strategy has generally been successful; even the partial concessions have had little effect on the way the political system functions. Even when protest has been at its highest levels, from the mid 2000s, the opposition has been unable to mount a sustained campaign. Protest has generally been tightly focused upon particular issues with no effective organizational umbrella emerging to provide a means of knitting these successive actions together into a coherent movement. The lack of a leadership able to project a message that could unite people across issues reinforced the organizational vacuum, which was further bolstered by the absence of a culture encouraging widespread political involvement. While the weaknesses of the opposition were a result of a range of factors, important was the effect of the government's policies designed directly to compress opposition. The drive to structure and thereby contain autonomous political activity on the part of the populace has therefore been largely successful, with this becoming more systematic and effective under Putin than it had been under Yeltsin.

# 3    The party system and electoral politics

Central to the first dimension of rule identified in Chapter 1, the structuring of public political activity, is the design of an electoral system that provides an element of competition while ensuring the regime remains relatively unchallenged. Under Yeltsin, steps were taken in this direction, but it was not until Putin came to power that the electoral system seemed, at least until 2011, to function smoothly for the regime. After briefly surveying the role and means of structuring the electoral system, this chapter explains how the Yeltsin and Putin administrations sought to constrain electoral challenge and how this was more successful under the latter than the former.

A central aspect of the regime's perceived need to constrain political activity was how to handle the political parties that had emerged during the latter stages of the perestroika period and those that developed after 1991. Given the rhetorical commitment shared by all of the elite to "democracy," even if this was interpreted in different ways by different sections of that elite, there was general agreement that the post-Soviet system had to include elections within which those parties could participate. The problem that this posed for that section of the elite that was unwilling to countenance the challenge to their positions that a genuinely democratic structure would have involved was how to structure electoral competition in such a way as to be able to retain a claim to democracy while blunting the potential challenge that could emanate through this. The result was an electoral system commonly identified as electoral or competitive authoritarian.[1] Where this sort of electoral system is working properly, regular elections are held, competition exists, but the ruling party is not really challenged. This use of democratic processes without democratic substance creates a whole dynamic of politics that differs from both classic authoritarian and democratic polities.

---

[1] For the term and an influential analysis, see Levitsky and Way (*Competitive Authoritarianism*). For the distinction between hegemonic and competitive electoral authoritarian regimes, see Schedler (*Politics of Uncertainty*), pp. 105–7.

Elections that feature competition but are structured in such a way that they are unlikely to be the means for a change of rulers can be seen to fulfill five principal functions:[2]

1. establishment of a regularized method to share power among ruling party politicians. Elections constitute a mechanism for rewarding party members' loyalty with office.
2. by disseminating a public image of the invincibility of the ruling party, reflected in high turnouts and huge margins, elections can convey the message that opposition is pointless because it can never succeed. Such an image can discourage both division within the ruling party and the development of opposition outside it.
3. elections can provide information to the ruling party about supporters and opponents of the regime.
4. an election can be a means of selective co-optation of the opposition. Involvement of the opposition in the political processes of the regime can be a means of persuading that opposition to invest in the existing institutions rather than challenge them from outside.
5. victory in elections can be a mode of legitimation, especially at the international level.

While these functions can also apply to fully competitive and fair elections, they are particularly important for those regimes where elections are not fair and therefore where there is likely to be embedded discontent within the political system.

In electoral authoritarian regimes, elections are not fair because of the huge advantages enjoyed by the rulers over the opposition. There are two main aspects of the electoral process that have been used to favor the authorities, the structural tilting of that process in favor of the authorities, and fraudulent manipulation of the voting and vote counting. A number of different ways have been used to structure the process to the disadvantage of opposition forces:[3]

---

[2] This extends the discussion in Beatriz Magaloni, *Voting for Autocracy. Hegemonic Party Survival and Its Demise in Mexico* (Cambridge: Cambridge University Press, 2006), pp. 8–10.

[3] Some of these are discussed in Ottaway (*Democracy Challenged*), pp. 139–42. Also see William Case, "Manipulative Skills: How Do Rulers Control the Electoral Arena?," Andreas Schedler (ed.), *Electoral Authoritarianism. The Dynamics of Unfree Competition* (Boulder: Lynne Riener Publishers, 2006), pp. 95–112. For a distinction between the manipulation of electoral institutions, of vote choice, and of the act of voting, see Sarah Birch, *Electoral Malpractice* (Oxford: Oxford University Press, 2011), esp. Chapters 4–6. Also interesting are Andrew Wilson, *Virtual Politics. Faking Democracy in the Post-Soviet World* (New Haven: Yale University Press, 2005) and E. Malkin and E. Suchkov, *Politicheskie tekhnologii* (Moscow: Russkaia Panorama, 2008).

(a) selective enforcement of the law and regulations. Potential candidates are barred from participating through the design or manipulation of electoral regulations, including the use of legal pretexts to close down opposition bodies, critical media outlets, competitor parties, and independent observers.

(b) manipulation of the constitution and/or political institutions to disadvantage opposition forces. Many authoritarian regimes stick rigorously to the constitution and the law, but they also change these documents quite frequently so that their normative authority is undercut by regime action.

(c) opposition parties and candidates are unable to run effective campaigns as a result of repression, harassment, legal controls, or sabotage. For example, prohibitions on ethnic or religious parties or on foreign sources of funding may be applied in ways prejudicial to opposition interests, power may be cut off to opposition meetings and rallies and would-be candidates, or their supporters physically assaulted.

(d) manipulation of information through media control. Biased coverage in the state media and harassment of independent media. This involves not just the denial of the opposition's capacity to air its views, but the conscious distortion of those views and the bias in favor of the authorities, both in terms of the level of coverage and its nature.

(e) limits on participation through such measures as complex voter registration procedures, demands for documents that large sections of the electorate may not possess (e.g., passports or identity cards, which can often be lacking in rural areas), and the location of polling stations a long way from certain, especially opposition-supporting, areas.

(f) use of state resources to fund authorities' election campaigns and the denial of such funds to opposition forces, either at the same level as that given to the authorities or in total. The massive imbalance in resources that can result from control over the state by the authorities may be reflected not just in funds, but also in the allegiance and loyalty of state officials who manage the election at the local level.

(g) creation of virtual opposition parties to leach votes away from the opposition.

Fraud may also be used to alter election results.[4] Examples of this include ballot box stuffing, reallocation of votes during the counting, multiple

---

[4] For discussions of electoral fraud, see Fish (*Democracy Derailed*), Chapter 3; and Mikhail Myagkov, Peter C. Ordeshook, and Dimitri Shakin, *The Forensics of Election Fraud. Russia and Ukraine* (Cambridge: Cambridge University Press, 2009), pp. 119–25.

voting, demands by authorities (e.g., employers) that people vote in certain ways and enforcement of this through a form of open voting (e.g., voters must show their marked ballot to someone involved in the scam). While low level fraud is probably present in all elections to some degree, if an electoral authoritarian system is working effectively, the regime should not need to rely on such measures. Provided the sorts of measures for tilting the system outlined above are working, fraudulent manipulation of the vote should be unnecessary; or at least they should not need to be so great as to make a substantial difference to the election outcome. Where these mechanics do not work effectively, the regime may experience a serious rebuff at the election and even in some cases (e.g., Mexico 2000) be defeated.

These characteristics of a competitive authoritarian electoral system manifested themselves in Russia from the time of the first post-Soviet election in 1993.

## Yeltsin and electoral manipulation

When Yeltsin found himself in power in an independent Russia following the collapse of the Soviet Union, he had no clear plans for the building of a new political system. He seems to have assumed that a charismatic presidency would be the key institution in the new structure, and apart from rejecting any notion of a ruling or dominant party in the mold of the former CPSU, he seems to have had little real idea about the forms the new system might take. His ideas, and those of the people around him, developed in the cauldron of the conflict with the parliament that consumed 1992 and most of 1993.

While there were many potential lessons that could be drawn from the conflict with the parliament, one that had clear implications for system development was that the parliament could act as an alternative center of power to the presidency and could even challenge the presidency. Yeltsin realized this political reality, but his response to it was to prove inadequate to the challenge it posed. His response was essentially twofold, constitutional engineering and electoral manipulation.

Two aspects of the constitutional settlement that Yeltsin imposed following the dissolution of the parliament in October 1993 are relevant. The first was the powers of the new parliament. From Yeltsin's perspective, ratification of a new constitution and election of a new parliament had to be rushed through to provide some fig leaf of legitimacy for his action in dissolving the old, Soviet parliament. Discussion had been proceeding for some time about the form the constitution should take, but agreement between presidential and parliamentary representatives had been impossible to obtain. Accordingly the draft that was put before the people on December 12, 1993, was one that emanated from Yeltsin's office[5] and which accorded greater power to the president than to parliament. The latter was to consist of two houses, the State Duma and the Federation Council. The former was to have 450 members, the latter 178, being two representatives from each of the 89 subjects of the federation, with one of those representatives coming from the executive and one from the legislative branch of the regional administration. In terms of the distribution of power, the new Constitution introduced a republic with a strong presidency and a much weaker parliament, although the powers of this body were not as puny as some have supposed. The Constitution bolstered the president against opposition from within the parliament. The president was popularly elected rather than being chosen by the parliament, and although the latter had the power to impeach the president, this was a prolonged and difficult process: it required a two-thirds vote of the members of both houses plus confirmation by, respectively, the Supreme Court and the Constitutional Court of the correctness of the charges and the validity of the procedure. The president appointed the government, which was thereby responsible to him rather than the parliament, and only the prime minister had to be ratified by the State Duma (lower house). If the Duma refused to ratify the president's nominee on three occasions, it was sent to election. Similarly, if the Duma repeated a vote of no confidence in the government within three months, the president could dissolve the Duma and send it to new elections. Certainly the parliament had the responsibility for passing (and therefore also the power to refuse to pass) government legislation including the budget, but every law it passed was subject to presidential veto (which could only be overridden by a two-thirds vote of both houses). So the president, who had the formal power to determine the basic guidelines of domestic and foreign policy, and his government not only were more powerful than the parliament, but the executive was also placed in a position that minimized the possibility of successful challenge by the parliament.[6] In addition, the president himself was given safeguards against challenge from within that executive. The post of vice-president, from where Yeltsin had been

[5] For a discussion of changes introduced by Yeltsin's office to remove parliamentary checks on president and government, see Ostrow, Satarov, and Khakamada (*The Consolidation*), pp. 44–9.

[6] On the poor coordination of the parties in the committee system in the chamber reducing the scope for the Duma to exercise an effective check on executive power, see Joel M. Ostrow, "Procedural Breakdown and Deadlock in the Russian State Duma: The Problems of an Unlimited Dual-Channel Institutional Design," *Europe-Asia Studies* 50 (5), 1998, pp. 793–816.

challenged by his deputy Aleksandr Rutskoi in 1992–3, was abolished, while the person authorized to take over from the president if the latter was unable to perform his functions, the prime minister, was appointed and dismissed by the president himself.

The second aspect of the constitutional settlement concerned the formal structuring of the electoral process. The law governing the 1993 election was enacted by presidential decree.[7] There had been considerable disagreement among Yeltsin's advisers about the nature of the electoral law.[8] They were all intent on creating a system that would maximize the pro-Yeltsin, what they saw as the "reformist," vote rather than a system that was fair to all. Some argued for a single member district (SMD) system whereby a deputy would be elected on the basis of a simple plurality (i.e., no runoff elections if the leading candidate did not get 50 percent of the vote) from a territorial constituency because they believed that such an electoral system would increase the reformist vote by creating a stark choice and because, following Duverger, they believed this would produce a two-party system. Others argued for a proportional representation (PR) system whereby candidates would be elected on the basis of a central party list in accord with the proportion of the national vote the party achieved, principally because they believed that communists (and therefore opponents) remained in positions that would enable them to dominate any local candidate selection process, and because they did not believe that reformers could organize constituency-based parties in time. Ultimately they adopted an amalgam of the two systems: half the 450 members would be chosen by the SMD system and half by PR, with a 5 percent threshold (i.e., parties would not gain any seats under PR unless they gained at least 5 percent of the national vote). This mixed voting system was clearly a compromise and did not assist in the development of a viable party system. With few resources and little time before the election, this system meant that if parties wanted to be successful they had to try to create both a powerful central party machine to exploit the PR system as well as an extensive network of party organizations to maximize support through the SMD aspect of the electoral system. None were able to deal with these twin demands. Furthermore, in order to be registered

---

[7] No attention was given to the Federation Council, and although these members were elected in open competition in1993, most had no party affiliation and came out of regional administrations.

[8] For discussion, see Iu.M. Baturin et al., *Epokha Yeltsina. Ocherki politicheskoi istorii* (Moscow: Vagrius, 2001), Part 3, Chapter 1; and Thomas F. Remington and Stephen S. Smith, "Political Goals, Institutional Context, and the Choice of an Electoral System: The Russian Parliamentary Election Law," *American Journal of Political Science* 40 (4), 1996, pp. 1253–79.

to put forward candidates, parties had to collect 100,000 signatures with no more than 15,000 from any one of Russia's 89 regions, again a considerable hurdle in the circumstances of 1993.[9] Required turnout for the validity of the election was a low 25 percent.

The Yeltsin team sought to bolster the effect of this constitutional engineering through manipulation of the electoral process itself. Yeltsin sought to skew the electoral choice available to voters. Following the closure of the parliament, Yeltsin banned fifteen newspapers on the grounds that they had contributed to mass disorder in Moscow (in other words, they had supported the parliament against him), and suspended sixteen parties on the grounds that they had been involved in these events. Importantly one of these parties was the Communist Party of the Russian Federation, although the ban on this party was removed in time for it to participate in the election.[10] Over thirty parties/electoral associations attempted to gather the 100,000 signatures needed, of which twenty-one claimed to have been successful. Some of those that did not get sufficient signatures claimed official harassment, such as the intimidation of those doing the collecting and the seizure of lists of signatures.[11] Of the twenty-one successful parties, eight were denied registration, leaving thirteen to compete in the election. Restrictions were also placed on the campaign, principally in the form of media bias against the communists.[12] Also the draft of the Constitution upon which people were meant to pass judgment in the referendum held jointly with the election was not released for public discussion until November 10, a bare month before the ballot, and Yeltsin warned the leaders of the thirteen blocs not to attack the draft Constitution, the president or each other, or they would lose the free time they had been allocated on the state media.[13]

[9] Independent candidates not nominated by a registered party required the signatures of 1 percent of the constituency electorate (some 4,000–5,000) in order to stand.

[10] Yeltsin had suspended the RCP on August 23, 1991, and on November 6, 1991, banned both the CPSU and the RCP in Russia. These moves were strictly illegal, and in early 1992 party supporters took the question to the Constitutional Court. Yeltsin's supporters countercharged that the party had been an extra-constitutional body that had acted illegally rather than a real political party. The Court refused to rule on the constitutionality of the party during the Soviet period, but ruled that Yeltsin's ban was legal at the national level but not the local level. This effectively relegalized the communist party.

[11] See Sakwa (*Russian Politics*, 2002, 3rd edn.), p. 146.

[12] The KPRF received only 0.4 percent of time on the radio and 1.4 percent on television in editorial programs compared with 37.1 percent and 29.1 percent for Russia's Choice. European Institute for the Media [EIM], "The Russian Parliamentary Elections: Monitoring of the Election Coverage in the Russian Mass Media. Final Report," February 1, 1994, pp. 30, 38, 117–22.

[13] EIM (1994), pp. 33–4.

When the voting was completed, eight parties won both list and SMD seats,[14] with no party gaining a majority; independents gained more than half the SMD seats. However, there was considerable controversy over the vote counting. A commission on electoral fraud reporting in May 1994[15] argued that regional administrations exaggerated voter turnout in order to achieve the 50 percent requirement needed for adoption of the constitution, and that in the single-member districts some 9.2 million ballots were falsified, about 17 percent of valid votes cast, mainly in the sense that they were allocated to parties for whom the elector had not voted (the LDPR was said to be a major beneficiary of this practice). Turning to the referendum on the constitution, it had been officially claimed that on a turnout of 54.8 percent of voters, 58.4 percent approved of the constitution, but the commission on electoral fraud later suggested that only 46.1 percent of the electorate had actually participated, meaning that while the election itself was legitimate, the constitution had not been formally adopted. This was ignored. So while the 1993 election was basically free, it was not fair. The circumstances of its calling, the restrictions placed on participation by opposition forces, and the manipulation of the voting all rendered it devoid of basic fairness.[16]

This combination of framing the electoral process and manipulating its operation was repeated in each of the elections held during the 1990s. A new election law was introduced for the 1995 Duma election. Under the new law of June 1995, the number of party leaders from Moscow who could appear on a party list for the PR section of the election was reduced to twelve, while only parties or movements registered six months before the poll were allowed to participate in the election campaign. The number of signatures required for registration of parties was doubled to 200,000 with no more than 7 percent from any one of the federal subjects; a candidate standing in a single-member district still required the signatures of 1 percent of the electorate. There was considerable debate over the 5 percent threshold, but ultimately it was retained. It was made illegal to offer inducements to potential supporters (in October 1995 the going rate for a registration signature was said to be 2,000 roubles[17]) and to contribute to the nomination of more than one list of candidates. The law also imposed campaign spending limits on parties and candidates.

---

[14] For the results, see White (*Understanding*), p. 32.    [15] *Izvestiia*, May 4, 1994.
[16] On the individual campaigns 1993–2003, see Wilson (*Virtual Politics*), Chapters 4, 5, and 7.
[17] *Izvestiia*, October 18, 1995. This was about US50c.

Despite the larger number of signatures required to participate in the election, sixty-nine parties/associations signaled their intention to collect the required signatures, of which forty-three submitted documentation with such signatures. The Central Electoral Commission refused to register some of these, including Democratic Russia, Yabloko, and Derzhava, because of claimed deficiencies in the documentation, but the Supreme Court ruled that some of these (including Democratic Russia and Yabloko) should be reinstated; in the end, forty-three parties and movements participated in the election. The proliferation of parties compared with 1993 reflected not just the greater opportunity for party formation that the longer timetable involved, but the weakness of the party system itself. Already it had developed the characteristics of what Vladimir Gel'man has termed "feckless" pluralism,[18] meaning fragmentation, electoral volatility, and a large role played by non-party actors. Only the KPRF had a developed infrastructure of party organizations across the country; the other parties were for the most part small groupings around prominent individuals, highly subject to splits[19] and with little in the way of machinery to provide any real substance to the party itself. In this sort of situation, the people around Yeltsin tried to build a two-party system. If successful this would not only have provided some stability to the political system but, and this was clearly a high priority, by creating two moderate parties, the extremes (which is where they believed Yeltsin's opposition was to be found) would be pushed to the margins. Accordingly two parties were created. The first, Our Home is Russia (NDR), was headed by Prime Minister Viktor Chernomyrdin and was designed to take up the center-right ground on the political spectrum. This was envisaged as a so-called "party of power," a party that represented the interests and views of the Kremlin, which would achieve a dominating position within the political system, and rested heavily on state officials for membership and state resources for sustenance.[20] It was meant to take the place of Russia's Choice, headed by Yegor Gaidar,

---

[18] Vladimir Gel'man, "From 'Feckless Pluralism' to 'Dominant Party Politics'. The Transformation of Russia's Party System," *Democratization* 13 (4), 2006, pp. 545–61.

[19] Party leaders' access to free air time encouraged some, especially in the "democratic camp," to split from larger entities and create their own party, thereby gaining access to that free air time. They assumed this would assist their election.

[20] On the notion of a party of power, see Hans Oversloot and Reuben Verheul, "The Party of Power in Russian Politics," *Acta Politica* 35 (2), 2000, pp. 123–45; Regina Smyth, "Building State Capacity from the Inside Out: Parties of Power and the Success of the President's Reform Agenda in Russia," *Politics and Society* 30 (4), 2002, pp. 555–78; and Zoe Knox, Peter Lentini, and Brad Williams, "Parties of Power and Russian Politics: a Victory of the State over Civil Society?," *Problems of Post-Communism* 53 (1), 2006, pp. 3–14.

which had gained representation in 1993, but had failed to really act as a major force subsequently. The second party, which was to take up the center left, was titled Ivan Rybkin's Electoral Bloc. Rybkin had been speaker in the Duma and a member of the KPRF ally, the Agrarian Party, so he had appeared to be a promising prospect for capturing the center-left vote. However, his party failed miserably in the election, capturing only 1.12 percent of the vote and three SMD seats, thereby dooming the attempt to create a centrist two-party system to failure.

The election does not appear to have been characterized by the same levels of vote manipulation as in 1993, although there were still claims that this did take place. But more important in rendering claims about the fairness of the ballot suspect was a combination of the media campaign and use of state resources. In the lead-up to the election, polls suggested the growing strength of the communist vote and a steep decline in support for Yeltsin. As a result of growing concern about the possibility of a communist victory, as the election approached, media coverage on the part of the major national newspapers and television stations became increasingly biased against the communists and in favor of NDR.[21] In addition, NDR used its close links with the state, and therefore its access to state resources, to run its campaign in a way that would have been impossible without access to state coffers. Even though some of the other parties may have exceeded the spending limits, none did so to the extent of NDR and its government supporters.[22]

The disappointing result in the 1995 legislative election (see below) reinforced the concerns that had been growing in those around Yeltsin about the outcome of the forthcoming presidential election scheduled for mid 1996, with increased pressure being brought to bear on Yeltsin to postpone the election.[23] Despite some wavering, Yeltsin resisted such pressure and the election went ahead as scheduled. The election, for the first time, made plain the advantages of incumbency. Yeltsin combined the resources of rich and influential business backers (the role of the

[21] NDR received 24.7 percent of all editorial time on television, with the second most going to Russia's Democratic Choice 12.8 percent compared with the communists' 5.9 percent. On radio NDR had a little more than 25 percent, Russia's Democratic Choice 23.8 percent, and the communists 2.7 percent. EIM, "Monitoring the Media Coverage of the 1995 Russian Parliamentary Election. Final Report," February 15, 1996, pp. 34–5. For the understated conclusion "that the media devoted more, and more positive, time/space to the incumbent, centrist, and reform-oriented parties and candidates, while treating the communists and extreme nationalists more scarcely and more negatively," see p. 89.

[22] For some figures see EIM (1995 Election), pp. 32–3.

[23] On this see Gill and Markwick (*Russia's*), pp. 189–90; David Remnick, "The War for the Kremlin," *New Yorker*, July 22, 1996, pp. 47–8; and Ostrow, Satarov, and Khakamada (*The Consolidation*), pp. 61–5.

oligarchs in this was crucial[24]) with those of the state treasury to spend his way back into power; it has been estimated that he may have spent $500 million on his campaign, compared with the $3 million allowed by the law,[25] while his campaign spent between 30 and 150 times the amount spent by the opposition.[26] Not only did this buy a lot of advertising, but it also enabled him to travel around the country doling out largesse to local officials and voters as a means of building up his support. Moreover if much of the media had been anti-communist in 1995, this reached a new level in the lead-up to voting in 1996.[27] Leading business and media owners had become increasingly nervous about the possibility of communist victory in the presidential election, and in February a group of them met and agreed to throw their weight behind Yeltsin.[28] As a result, much of the media coverage was unremittingly hostile to the communists, emphasizing the malign features of the communist period (much was made of the terror and the camps on the television just prior to election day) and linking this to the KPRF candidate Gennady Ziuganov.[29] The media, and its manipulation, was also important in the period between the first ballot and the runoff necessitated by the fact that no one received a majority in the first ballot. At the end of the campaign before the first ballot, Yeltsin was exhausted as a result of the vibrant campaign he had run. Just after the vote, he suffered a heart attack and was absent from the hustings in the two and a half weeks between the first ballot and the runoff vote. Nothing was made of this by the media, who thus colluded with those around the president to keep his true health status a secret from the electorate. These factors were not the only reasons for Yeltsin's success: he ran an excellent campaign; his lackluster opponent was unable to extend communist voting support beyond its established

---

[24] On the oligarchs and their support for Yeltsin, see Freeland (*Sale*); for their open letter, see *Nezavisimaia gazeta*, April 27, 1996. On FIG support for Yeltsin, see Henry E. Hale, *Why Not Parties in Russia? Democracy, Federalism, and the State* (Cambridge: Cambridge University Press 2006), pp. 163–6.

[25] White (*Understanding*), p. 92.

[26] Michael McFaul, *Russia's 1996 Presidential Election: The End of Polarized Politics* (Stanford: Hoover Institution Press, 1997), p. 13.

[27] For example, see the discussion in Rick Simon, "Media, Myth and Reality in Russia's State-Managed Democracy," *Parliamentary Affairs* 57 (1), 2004, pp. 177–8. Two of the leading television stations were in state hands (ORT and RTR) while a third, NTV, was so close to the government that its director, Igor Malashenko, became media director for the Yeltsin campaign. Levitsky and Way (*Competitive Authoritarianism*), p. 194.

[28] On this decision, see Gill and Markwick (*Russia's*), p. 190; and Freeland (*Sale*), Chapter 9.

[29] On the strong pro-Yeltsin bias, see EIM, "Monitoring the Media Coverage of the 1996 Russian Presidential Election," September 30, 1996, pp. 32–3. For figures showing the amount and nature (positive/negative) of exposure of the different candidates, see pp. 35–41. Also Ostrow, Satarov, and Khakamada (*The Consolidation*), pp. 69–72.

heartland; Yeltsin sacked some of his more unpopular advisers; and prior to the runoff he was able to co-opt the third place getter in the initial poll, Aleksandr Lebed, and thereby win over part of his vote. Nevertheless, the manipulation of the electoral process was sufficient to both win him the election and ensure that it could not be classed as fair.

Despite the best efforts of those around Yeltsin, the results of the 1993 and 1995–6 elections were disappointing. In 1993 the explicitly pro-Yeltsin parties (Russia's Choice and Party of Russian Unity and Concord) polled only 22.2 percent of the vote while the avowedly opposition parties (LDPR, KPRF, and the Agrarian Party) polled 43.3 percent. The 1995 election was a clear victory for the anti-Yeltsin forces. Only four parties crossed the 5 percent threshold, meaning that 49.5 percent of voters did not gain representation through the PR system, and of those four parties the largest by far were the KPRF and LDPR; the party of power, NDR, received only 10.1 percent of the vote.[30] The communists were the biggest single group in the Duma.[31] The strength of the opposition profile in both Dumas meant that the parliament remained a major thorn in Yeltsin's side. The government had difficulty getting legislation adopted, forcing Yeltsin to rely overwhelmingly on presidential decrees to enact the measures he supported, but the Duma frequently took up positions on issues directly at odds with those of the president, and even sought on a number of occasions to impeach the president. Thus, while Yeltsin and those around him sought to structure the electoral process to their advantage, they were unable to achieve the sort of control over the opposition that would transform the Duma into a tame assembly.

The failure of Yeltsin's strategy for dealing with the question of the parliament was a function of two interrelated factors, the absence of a single party that could dominate the political scene and carry Yeltsin's banner, and the polarized nature of politics. Attempts were made during the early and mid 1990s to develop a party of power that would unite the pro-Yeltsin forces and gain a dominant position within the system, in the form of Russia's Choice in 1993 and Our Home is Russia in 1995. However, the ability of both parties to develop as a true party of the president was undercut by Yeltsin's refusal to become the leader of either party. This may have been driven by two sorts of concerns on the part of Yeltsin different from the public rationalization, that he wished to be a president for all Russians and therefore should not associate

---

[30] White (*Understanding*), p. 32.
[31] From this time, the Federation Council was formed of the Governors and the heads of the regional parliaments, that is, the incumbents of the regional offices became ex officio members of the Council.

himself with one party. First, such a party may become so powerful and so authoritative that it could challenge the power and position of the leader, especially if it was deemed to be successful. Second, such a party could throw up an alternative leader who could use the party to move against the current party leader. In the position Yeltsin found himself in, further sources of challenge were something he could do without. This concern that a party could be the source of challenge to the president may have been a factor in the failure to develop a genuine party of power, with the failure of the president to trust it reflected in the limited patronage the party enjoyed from the presidential apparatus. Thus, while Yeltsin may have wished that the party could dominate within the Duma, he was unwilling to invest the sort of resources that might have made that possible. Furthermore, given the polarization of politics during this period, any party that was associated with Yeltsin and his policies was bound to be at one end of the political spectrum. It could not straddle the center of that spectrum and thereby drive opposition parties to the margins, and therefore unless electoral manipulation was undertaken on a much greater scale than it had been hitherto, a party of power was bound to fail under Yeltsin.

Significantly, throughout the 1990s, while Yeltsin and those around him worked to manipulate the electoral process to their advantage, there was little effective pressure from outside either to limit their actions or to build up the opposition. Certainly there were some attempts by Western governments and NGOs to foster the development of political parties and civil society more generally,[32] but these sorts of activities were both limited and disjointed and had little practical effect. Given the role of Western advisers and assistance in the economic sphere and the pro-Western orientation of Yeltsin's early foreign policy, there seemed to be significant scope for both leverage and linkage of the sorts discussed in Chapter 1. However, such opportunities did not translate into effective influence. Three factors seem to have been relevant to this. First, the West was compromised because it supported Yeltsin blindly against what it perceived to be an overwhelmingly communist opposition. Thus, the short-term tactic of supporting Yeltsin in his struggle with the communists overrode any long-term aim of bolstering the development of democratic institutions and processes. Second, attempts to foster the opposition were politically shaped in that Western actors sought principally to strengthen what they perceived to be liberal, pro-Western forces. However, the liberals suffered from an extreme variant of the "feckless pluralism" that infected the system as a whole; they were small, argumentative, and fissiparous,

---

[32] For example, Henderson (*Building Democracy*).

and therefore not good candidates as a major opposition force. Third, too many of the Western groups active in Russia were more concerned for their own interests than they were in fostering Russian democracy.[33] In the absence of concerted external pressure, Yeltsin was able to structure the electoral system in his own interests, but because scope remained for the opposition to continue to gain a substantial position through the electoral process, he was unable to create a stable system.

By the late 1990s, the failure of Yeltsin's strategy of relying upon a charismatic presidency bolstered by electoral manipulation was evident to those around the president, and steps were taken to address it in the context of the coming succession. The roots of an alternative strategy were found in the last twelve months of the Yeltsin presidency.

### Putin's strategy

In the period before the next scheduled elections, parliamentary in December 1999 and presidential in June 2000, a major question exercising the minds of the political elite was that of the succession. The Constitution mandated a maximum of two consecutive terms of office for a president, and Yeltsin was currently in his second term. This meant that unless the Constitution was changed, or ignored, Yeltsin could not stand for president again in 2000. And it is clear that at no stage did this course of action seem viable. Therefore, Yeltsin and those around him needed to identify a safe successor and find a way of finessing that person's entry into the presidency. This question was not resolved until late 1999 and Vladimir Putin's appointment as prime minister, with Yeltsin's subsequent endorsement of him as his successor. Because of the timetable, this question was also bound up with the parliamentary election at the end of 1999.

Another new electoral law was approved in June 1999. In an attempt to do something about the unbalanced representation arising from the fact that only four parties crossed the threshold in 1995, the new law provided for parties that had gained less than 5 percent of the vote to be included in the PR allocation of seats if the parties that exceeded the threshold together had less than half the party list vote. And if one party gained more than 50 percent of the vote and no others reached the 5 percent threshold, the second largest party would be included in the seat allocation. The law also allowed parties and candidates to gain registration by paying a deposit instead of collecting signatures, and candidates were compelled to declare any court sentences they had not discharged, as well as their

---

[33] For example, Wedel (*Collision*).

income and property. In the event, the provisions regarding the threshold had no impact on the election and its outcome.

The economic collapse of 1998 and the revolving door of prime ministers in 1998–9 (see Chapter 4), which appeared to suggest substantial government instability, seemed to many observers to imply that Yeltsin and those around him would have significant difficulty in getting their man, whoever it was to be, into office with a not too oppositional parliament. The danger seemed to be compounded by the emergence in August 1999 of a new potential "party of power," this time not based in the Kremlin, but among the governors and especially the office of Moscow mayor Yury Luzhkov, Fatherland-All Russia (OVR). This body, which also had former prime minister Yevgeny Primakov as part of its leadership, seemed to present a viable alternative to the continuation of Yeltsinism without Yeltsin. It seemed to promise competence, an ability to get things done, and a wide geographical base. However, Yeltsin's appointment of Putin as prime minister on August 9, 1999, was a masterstroke. Little known before then, Putin gave the impression of steely-eyed competence and an ability to get things done. He was not linked in the public eye with the corruption claims that had been swirling around Yeltsin and his group for some time, nor did he carry the political baggage of either Luzhkov or Primakov. His popularity soared, in part because of sympathetic, even at times enthusiastic, press coverage. The position of Yeltsin–Putin was, in retrospect, strengthened by the creation of a new Kremlin-based party of power, Unity, in September 1999. Such a party was needed if the Kremlin hoped to withstand the challenge posed by OVR. Unity was unlike any of the other parties. It was little more than a creation from above in the Kremlin, and it offered no independent policy positions except for support for the positions of Putin. It attracted, or perhaps co-opted, a strong list of candidates, and by tying themselves directly to Putin's rising star, they went into the election giving voters the appearance of a choice for a new future, but one which neither involved a restoration of communism nor a simple continuation of Yeltsin.

The emergence of Unity was a significant development because it marked the creation of a party of power which, in its transformed state of United Russia (UR – see below), was to dominate Russian party politics for more than a decade. While its ability to do this was related to the continuing capacity of the authorities to structure the electoral process in their favor, what was new and central to the party's success was the decline in political polarization accompanying the rise of Putin. The extreme positions adopted by the different political forces in the 1990s meant that the then parties of power appeared partisan in the conflict and therefore unable to appeal across political boundaries. Putin's shift towards the center, including his appropriation of some of the ground of the communists and nationalists, plus the focus of the new party of power upon him, broadened the potential constituency compared with that of its forebears. It was able to dominate the center, expanding to displace its opponents on both left and right, and thereby locate itself squarely in the electoral mainstream.

Thirty-five parties or electoral blocs sought registration for the 1999 election, and twenty-six successfully gained registration.[34] The campaign was overshadowed by the coming presidential election, with the parliamentary vote being seen in many circles as effectively a primary for the presidential poll. When the votes were counted, the KPRF had won both the largest percentage of votes and number of SMD seats,[35] but Unity, which had been in existence for only three months and had no policies except support for Putin, came second with just under a quarter of the votes. Six parties crossed the threshold, representing almost 81.5 percent of the votes cast. The success of Unity was in part a function of the support of the executive branch of government and its use of state resources on a large scale to underpin the campaign. But it also reflected Putin's popularity, which was itself mediated through the media, which gave significant positive support to the Kremlin team,[36] and by the vigorous media campaign mounted against OVR and its leaders Luzhkov and Primakov, which helped to destroy their standing as viable national leaders in this campaign.[37] The destruction of OVR at this time was a classic case of the Kremlin using its resources to destroy a potential challenger through a direct assault upon it.

As the focus now shifted to the presidential election, Yeltsin took further action to ensure that Putin would succeed him. By Yeltsin resigning at the end of December, Prime Minister Putin automatically became acting president, thereby gaining all of the advantages of incumbency

---

[34] On the deregistration of some candidates, see OSCE Office for Democratic Institutions and Human Rights, "Russian Federation. Elections to the State Duma 19 December 1999. Final Report," February 13, 2000, pp. 14–15. (henceforth, OSCE)

[35] White (*Understanding*), p. 32.

[36] EIM, "Monitoring the Media Coverage of the 1999 Russian Parliamentary Election. Preliminary Findings," March 2000, p. 2. Also see the comments in OSCE, 2000, pp. 12–13. See the discussion in Stephen White, Sarah Oates, and Ian McAllister, "Media Effects and Russian Elections, 1999–2000," *British Journal of Political Science* 35 (2), 2005, pp. 191–208. While NTV actually supported OVR, the state-owned television stations, which were the only ones with national coverage, supported Unity. See Sarah Oates, "Television, Voters, and the Development of the 'Broadcast Party'," Vicki L. Hesli and William M. Reisinger (eds), *The 1999–2000 Elections in Russia: Their Impact and Legacy* (New York: Cambridge University Press, 2003), pp. 29–50.

[37] On the rise and fall of OVR, see Hale (*Why Not Parties*), pp. 216–231.

in the election that was to come. In addition, this act moved the election forward from June to March, because according to the Constitution the election had to be held within three months of the president leaving office. Not only had Putin's opponents to contend with an extremely popular candidate[38] enjoying the advantages (including the resources and largesse) of incumbency, but they also had less time in which to turn around the popular perception of Putin. Furthermore, a number of potential candidates – Luzhkov, Primakov, and Yavlinsky – had been weakened by their parties' poor showings in the 1999 parliamentary poll. In the campaign Putin presented himself as a statesman, above the hurly burly of politics, refusing to offer an explicit election program[39] and presenting himself as someone offering both stability and improvement. Promoted by a sympathetic media[40] (although during 1999 the Gusinsky-owned NTV vigorously attacked Putin) and reinforced in some parts of the country by a certain level of both administrative pressure by officials and election fraud,[41] it was no wonder that Putin defeated his 10 rivals. Reflective of his dominance of the campaign was the fact that, for the first time in independent Russia's history, the presidential poll did not require a runoff because the winner exceeded 50 percent of the vote in the first round (Yeltsin had achieved a first round victory in the election in June

[38] Putin's popularity, especially given his very low approval rating when he was appointed prime minister (probably in part reflecting his low popular recognition), reflects in particular the way the media was used by those around Yeltsin and Putin to promote him. He was shown as young, fit, and healthy (and therefore a clear contrast with the current incumbent), someone who was decisive and would stand up for Russia both at home and abroad. His image of decisiveness was significantly enhanced by his launching of the second Chechen war (which unlike the first was initially widely popular) and his reaction to the wave of bombings in August and September 1999. This public exposure of Putin was part of the Kremlin's attempt to present him as the preferable candidate and thereby structure the electoral contest.

[39] Although in late December 1999 a long statement by him appeared on the government website and was published in *Nezavisimaia gazeta*, and in February he issued an open letter to electors. Respectively, Vladimir Putin, "Rossiia na rubezhe tysiacheletii," *Nezavisimaia gazeta*, December 30, 1999 (the website is www.gov.ru/ministry/isp-vlast47.html) and Vladimir Putin, "Otkrytoe pis'mo Vladimira Putina k Rossiiskiim izbirateliam," *Izvestiia*, February 25, 2000.

[40] Monitoring by EIM showed that across all channels Putin received 29.4 percent of the coverage with Yavlinsky next with 11.3 percent; in terms of news coverage, Putin's share was 43.3 percent with the next 10.6 percent for Yavlinsky and Zhirinovsky. Portrayal of Putin was overwhelmingly positive compared with that of his challengers, which was generally negative. EIM, "Monitoring the Media Coverage of the March 2000 Presidential Elections in Russia. Final Report," August 2000, pp. 44–6. Also see Ostrow, Satarov, and Khakamada (*The Consolidation*), p. 98.

[41] Yevgeniia Borisova, "And the Winner Is?," *Moscow Times*, September 9, 2000. Also Mikhail Myagkov and Peter C. Ordeshook, "The Trail of Votes in Russia's 1999 Duma and 2000 Presidential Elections," *Communist and Post-Communist Studies* 34 (3), 2001, pp. 353–70.

1991). The strategy used in 1999–2000 was a blueprint for success in 2003–4 and 2007–8.

Putin clearly learned from the Yeltsin experience and set about creating a system that would neuter potential opposition coming from the Duma and overwhelm any electoral challenge. He introduced a series of significant changes to the political structure in the early 2000s that had a direct effect on regional government and representation in the Federation Council. These will be discussed in Chapter 4. He also introduced a series of measures that had the effect of tilting the electoral arena even further in favor of the party of power. On July 11, 2001, a new law on political parties was introduced that regulated the party system while providing the authorities with an array of legal grounds on which they could liquidate parties.[42] The law also doubled the minimum membership to 10,000 and specified that a party had to be truly national (meaning that regional and governors' parties were effectively ruled out); they had to have a minimum of a hundred members in at least forty-five regions and fifty members in each of the other forty-four. Parties could not appeal to sectional interests. Provision was also made for state support for parties that received at least 3 percent of the PR vote, won 12 SMD seats, or 3 percent in the presidential election. Parties that failed to get 2 percent of the vote would have to return the state funds they had received. The law also limited the creation of electoral blocs, which could now comprise only three members, one of which had to be a party. This was a significant limit on the involvement of small groups. More stringent rules relating to registration were also introduced. A party had to hold a founding congress attended by at least 150 delegates from at least 45 regions, at which its leading bodies would be elected and its program adopted. The party could then be registered nationally in the Ministry of Justice, after which its regional organizations were registered at the regional level, with the central ministry finally validating its registration. Following registration, the party's observance of the rules would be monitored, and any breaches could result in deregistration. Parties were also made the only type of organization able to contest elections. This more stringent registration system seems to have resulted in the disappearance of many smaller parties, although by mid 2003, fifty-one parties had been registered.[43] A new law on elections that was signed into law in December 2002 replaced the 5 percent threshold by one of 7 percent to

[42] For the grounds on which parties could be refused registration, have their registration revoked, or be liquidated, see Sean P. Roberts, *Putin's United Russia Party* (London: Routledge, 2012), p. 110.

[43] Sakwa (*Putin*, 2004, 1st edn.), p. 116.

take effect from the 2007 election, and mandated that regardless of the number of votes they received, at least four parties (up from three in the 2003 election) should enter parliament via the PR list system.[44] From the 2003 election, those parties that gained representation in the parliament via the PR list system would be able to nominate a presidential candidate, and both the party and candidate would gain resources for extra media exposure compared with those not nominated by a party. The ability of the authorities to withdraw registration from a candidate was restricted.

The measures introduced in the early 2000s not only gave a more regularized basis for party development, but destroyed alternative forms of political organization that had been prominent at the regional level and that had given regional actors a degree of autonomy from the center. There were two principal sorts of such organization, business corporations and administrative structures headed by the governors. The basis of power of the former was primarily economic and the latter administrative, and in the second half of the 1990s, these machines dominated political life in many of the regions. Throughout much of the country, these machines had crowded out political parties, with potential candidates for election seeing them as more likely to generate success than political parties; in the 1999 election, candidates supported by these machines did better than those with party support.[45] The regional roots of such machines posed a challenge to central control, and Putin's reforms, in particular the requirement that only parties could contest elections, along with the changes in mode of selection of the governors, destroyed the control such machines had been able to exercise. Following this the governors came under increased pressure to join UR, which most ultimately did, although they often bore this membership lightly (see Chapter 4).

As the 2003–4 electoral cycle approached, Putin and his advisers rejigged their political tools. In December 2001, Unity merged with OVR to create United Russia, a party that was no less slavish in its adherence to Putin's political platform than Unity had been. However, what was now important was that the Kremlin's party of power included many of the governors, thereby locking into Putin's electoral machine a group that formerly had been outside it and that had been in a position to control the conduct of elections at the regional level. The Kremlin also spun off another party, Rodina, designed to attract votes from the KPRF. This combination of moves, reinforced by a pliant pro-Putin media and

---

[44] In 2009 this was changed to allow a couple of representatives from parties that received between 5 percent and 7 percent of the vote to enter the Duma. Sakwa, (*Crisis*), p. 345.
[45] Hale (*Why Not Parties*), p. 179. In the SMD seats, business corporations often ran their own candidates. On LUKoil, see Hale (*Why Not Parties*), pp. 164–5.

UR's ability to make use of state resources,[46] brought success in the 2003 parliamentary election, which eighteen parties and five blocs contested. United Russia took 37.6 percent of the vote and almost half the SMD seats, the KPRF 12.6 percent and Rodina 9 percent,[47] with liberal parties almost completely excluded from the Duma: Yabloko won only four seats and SPS three, despite last minute attempts by the Kremlin to help them in order to gain at least a semblance of liberal opposition in the parliament. When the Duma met, many deputies elected as either independents or under the banner of other parties switched sides to United Russia, which finished up with 300 deputies. This was a sufficient majority to pass not only normal legislation, but constitutional amendments too. It represented the overwhelming dominance of the electoral/parliamentary machinery by the Putin machine and removed the parliament as a potential site of significant opposition challenge. The election was characterized by the administrative manipulation of vote counting and significant media bias. The OSCE declared the parliamentary election to be free but not fair and failed to meet international legal standards, with the parties unable to compete on an equal basis. It also pointed to the inclusion of senior state officials on party lists who did not for the most part intend to take up their seats as a "direct and blatant deception of voters."[48]

This result was sealed with the presidential election of 2004 in which Putin won 71.3 percent of the vote in the first round. It had been clear from the outset that Putin would win, and many leading politicians who might have been expected to run (including Ziuganov), refused to do so; indeed the communist candidate Nikolai Kharitonov had sought to withdraw from the race, but the Central Election Commission refused to allow him to do so in order to retain the appearance of competition.[49] The call for a voter boycott of the election by the liberals was ineffective,

---

[46] For example, see the comments in OSCE Office for Democratic Institutions and Human Rights, "Russian Federation Elections to the State Duma 7 December 2003," January 27, 2004, pp. 12–14, www.osce.org. Accessed January 7, 2009. On the media failing to provide "impartial or fair coverage," see p. 16. Subsequent pages discuss the obstructions faced by some candidates and deficiencies in the balloting (e.g., open and group voting) process.

[47] White (*Understanding*), p. 32.

[48] OSCE Office for Democratic Institutions and Human Rights, "Russian Federation State Duma Elections 7 December 2003: Statement of Preliminary Findings and Conclusions," www.osce.org. Accessed January 7, 2009. This appeared to have been toned down by the final report where it was referred to as "misleading to the voter." OSCE Office for Democratic Institutions and Human Rights, "Russian Federation Presidential Election 14 March 2004. Election Observation Mission Report," June 2, 2004, p. 11, www.osce.org. Accessed January 7, 2009.

[49] Kharitonov, who received 13.7 percent of the vote, gained significant media coverage in return for not pulling out of the race. Sakwa (*Putin*, 2nd edn.), p. 116.

countered in part by administrative manipulation, which ensured a high turnout, and by their basic lack of resonance with the electorate. Again Putin refused to actively campaign, thereby marginalizing his opposition. The election was characterized by media bias,[50] fraud, and the substantial use of state resources by the Putin team.[51] According to one study, the 2004 election appears to have witnessed the most extensive fraud of any election to that time, with unprecedented levels of augmentation of turnout and allocation of those extra votes to Putin.[52] The Kremlin's dominance was confirmed with the 2007–8 electoral cycle.

The law on parties was modified in October 2004 to take effect from January 1, 2006, to make registration of parties more difficult. What was now required was a minimum membership of 50,000[53] with branches having at least 500 members in half of Russia's regions with a population of 500,000 and branches with at least 250 people in all of the other regions. Financial and reporting responsibilities were made more onerous, and parties had to remain active (i.e., to participate in federal, regional, and local elections at least once every five years) to retain registration. All parties had to undergo reregistration before the law came into effect, a process that resulted in thirty-five registered parties by October 2006, with twenty organizations having been unable to satisfy the criteria (including Putin critic Mikhail Kasyanov's National Democratic Union and the Russian Communist Workers' Party of Viktor Tiulkin).[54] The law also banned the creation of electoral blocs, forcing small parties to merge if they wanted to remain viable actors in electoral competition. A new election law adopted in 2005 (and amended on twenty-six occasions between its adoption and spring 2012) eliminated the SMD mode of election, mandating that all 450 members of the State Duma had to be elected by the PR party list system, a change that reduced the power of regional officials and placed the process more directly under the control of central authorities and eliminated the possibility of independent candidates.[55] Parties represented in the Duma were able to nominate candidates for

[50] According to the report of OSCE observers, the "State-controlled media displayed clear bias in favour of the incumbent in news presentation and coverage of the campaign." OSCE, 2004, pp. 1, 15–17. The privately owned media were less pro-Putin in their treatment.

[51] OSCE, 2004, pp. 10–12. This included obstruction of some opponents. Levitsky and Way (*Competitive Authoritarianism*), pp. 198–9.

[52] Myagkov et al. (*Forensics*), pp. 119–25. For some figures on this, see OSCE, 2004, pp. 31–5.

[53] As of January 1, 2010, this was reduced to 45,000, with a further reduction to 40,000 foreshadowed.

[54] Sakwa (*Putin*, 2nd edn.), p. 105.

[55] Although this followed and was officially justified in terms of the Beslan siege, it had been presented in draft form on August 31, 2004, before the siege. Sakwa (*Putin*, 2nd edn.), p. 118.

the next election without going through the usual formalities.[56] Others had to collect the signatures of 200,000 electors or pay a deposit of 60 million roubles (about US$2.5 million). If more than 5 percent of the signatures were deemed to be invalid or if the number of signatures fell below the minimum after invalid signatures were removed, the party would be refused registration for the election; this made de-registration easier given the earlier figure had been 25 percent of invalid signatures. Amendments in 2006 and 2007, respectively, abolished the provision that enabled voters to vote "against all," and the minimum turnout requirement. Also in 2006, the 2002 law against political extremism was amended to ban parties from contesting elections if one or more of their members were convicted of extremism, and restrictions were placed on canvassing and on the direct criticism of a rival candidate on television or in agitational materials (this did not apply to radio or printed publications).[57] In 2006 parties were forbidden to include representatives of other parties on their candidacy lists, and once elected, MPs were forbidden from switching parties. These changes, on top of those from 2001–2, tilted the electoral playing field heavily in favor of any political forces that were well organized in the center and which, like the Kremlin team, could exercise significant influence through administrative means over the conduct of the elections. They also made it more difficult to get elected. This was borne out by the 2007–8 election cycle.

Eleven parties contested the parliamentary election in December 2007, three others having been disqualified on the grounds of invalid signatures (Greens, People's Union, and Peace and Unity Party); some parties were also refused registration in particular regions, for example, SPS in Vologda, Pskov, Tiumen, and Dagestan.[58] UR remained the party of power representing Putin, but in October 2006 the Kremlin engineered a new party, Just Russia, from the merger of Rodina, the Party of Life, and the Party of Pensioners.[59] This took up a position on the center left, was designed to leach votes away from the communists and publicly declared its support for Putin.[60] The campaign was fought in the shadow of the forthcoming presidential election and the question of Vladimir

---

[56] They also had a privileged position in nominating representatives to the electoral commissions.
[57] Sakwa (*Putin*, 2nd edn.), p. 122.    [58] Sakwa (*Crisis*), p. 66.
[59] On the early development of Rodina and the Pensioners' Party and the way the regime destroyed them as independent entities because they had become too oppositionist, see Horvath (*Putin's Preventive Counter-Revolution*, 2013), pp. 57–63, 148–57. In February 2007, the People's Party also joined.
[60] On the founding and performance of Just Russia, see Luke March, "Just Russia – From 'Second Leg' to 'Footnote'?," *Russian Analytical Digest* 102, September 26, 2011, pp. 7–10. On the so-called "spoiler parties," see Sakwa (*Crisis*), p. 249.

Putin's future. The constitutional limit of two consecutive terms meant that Putin could not stand for the presidency in 2008. Nevertheless, there was significant pressure for him to engineer a change in the Constitution to enable this, something which United Russia's dominance of the Duma seemed to make a possibility.[61] However, despite such pressures and the very high opinion poll support Putin enjoyed, he refused to take this course, instead agreeing to head UR's list of candidates (even though he was not a party member) and saying that if UR won the election and an acceptable person was chosen as president, he might consider becoming prime minister.[62] Within this context, UR's campaign was again centered on the party's close association with Putin.[63] Indeed, it tried to cast the election as a referendum in support of Putin, while his refusal to participate in debate not only sidelined the opposition but also reinforced this impression of a referendum rather than an election. In various speeches during the campaign, Putin called on the people to vote for stability and a continuation of what they had had for the past eight years. When the results were announced, UR had won 64.3 percent of the votes and 315 of the 450 seats; the KPRF was a distant second with 11.6 percent of the vote and 57 seats;[64] Just Russia, which was caught in an impasse in that it could only hope to eat into the communist vote by criticizing Putin and UR, but if it did this it threatened to erode UR's position and thereby undercut its original raison d'etre (and this is what it did, causing the Kremlin to attempt to undermine it during the campaign), gained only 7.7 percent of the vote, just less than the LDPR which gained 8.14 percent.

Again the election was free but hardly fair.[65] The electoral terrain was heavily weighted in favor of UR by the changes in electoral regulations, and the media was highly biased in favor of what was seen as Putin's team.[66] They had been able to use the resources of the state freely (even if only to ensure a high turnout, which was seen as essential to legitimize the election in both Russian and international eyes and a means of adding

---

[61] This had already been done in Belarus, Kazakhstan, Kyrgyzstan, Tajikistan, Turkmenistan and Uzbekistan. On the popular "For Putin" movement, see Sakwa (*Crisis*), pp. 242–3.

[62] *Rossiiskaia gazeta*, October 2, 2007.

[63] The UR election manifesto was entitled "Putin's Plan: A Worthy Future for a Great Country." On the decision to support UR rather than Just Russia or Civic Force, see Sakwa (*Crisis*), pp. 230–31.

[64] For the results, see White (*Understanding*), p. 40.

[65] For discussions see Myagkov et al. (*Forensics*), pp. 125–6 and Sakwa (*Crisis*), pp. 252–8.

[66] For figures on the relative exposure of the different parties on various television channels, see Stephen White, "Elections Russian Style," *Europe-Asia Studies* 63 (4), 2011, p. 536. On the state-owned channels, UR received more coverage than all of its opponents combined.

votes to UR's total), and there were a large number of violations of various kinds in the conduct of the election.[67] There had also been some harassment of opposition candidates and movements, including the breakup of meetings by police and the arrest of opposition figures.[68] In many places of work, employees were instructed to vote for UR and threatened with reprisals if they did not.[69] The integrity of the electoral process was also called into question by the way Putin headed UR's list but had no intention of stepping down from the presidency to take up a Duma seat. While prominent politicians had done this in the past, the fact that it was the president doing this was particularly telling. Also given the prohibition in the electoral regulations on "negative campaigning" and UR's refusal to take part in debate, the party was effectively put beyond criticism. Further placing a pall on the process was the absence of credible foreign observers owing chiefly to a dispute between the OSCE and the Central Election Commission about the conditions under which such observers could operate.

When it came to the presidential election, there were four candidates. The Kremlin candidate was Dmitry Medvedev. He had been chosen by Putin[70] and publicly recommended by him, and Medvedev had undertaken publicly that, if elected, he would appoint Putin as prime minister. He was clearly seen as Putin's man, and benefited from Putin's popularity. Medvedev barely campaigned at all, playing the part of the statesman and relying on Putin's aura to get him across the line. But there was also manipulation of the regulations against the opposition. Potential opposition candidates from parties unrepresented in the Duma or in one-third of regional legislatures had to collect 2,000,000 signatures within a three-week period that overlapped with the Russian holiday season, while one candidate who claimed to have collected the required number of signatures (former prime minister Mikhail Kasyanov) was then eliminated on the grounds that some of these were forged.[71] When the votes were counted, Medvedev gained 70.3 percent of the vote, far ahead of his nearest rival, the communist Gennady Ziuganov, who received

---

[67] *Moscow Times*, December 5, 2007, reporting a report by the Golos Foundation. See the full report on www.golos.org. White (*Understanding*), pp. 40–41. On ballot box stuffing, see Sakwa (*Crisis*), p. 245.

[68] OSCE Parliamentary Assembly, "Russian Duma Elections 'Not Held on Level Playing Field' Say Parliamentary Observers," December 3, 2007, www.oscepa.org. White (*Understanding*), p. 40, Sakwa (*Crisis*), pp. 240–42, 248.

[69] White (*Understanding*), p. 41. There had been few international observers at this election due largely to obstruction from the Russian side. Sakwa (*Crisis*), pp. 215–17.

[70] On the choice, see Sakwa (*Crisis*), Chapter 8.

[71] On potential candidates prevented from running, see Sakwa (*Crisis*), pp. 277–80.

17.7 percent. Again while the vote may have been free,[72] the weight-ing of the whole process against the opposition was clear for all to see. Medvedev enjoyed the advantages of incumbency (as deputy prime min-ister and via Putin), the support of Putin and UR, and the support of the media,[73] and against these three forces, no opponent could hope to be successful. Also Medvedev's refusal to campaign, marginalized the opposition. And as in 2004, local and regional leaders were pressed to get out the vote. There was also fraud in the election,[74] and the whole process was therefore weighted heavily against the opposition.

The Russian electoral authoritarian system seemed established as a well-oiled machine following the 2007–8 elections, but this appearance was thrown into question by the December 2011 parliamentary election. There had already been some dissatisfaction with UR's performance leading in to the 2007 election, with the creation of Just Russia in part a response to this,[75] and in the period leading in to the December 2011 election there were further indications of problems. In the local and regional elections held on March 13, 2011, the vote for UR was down by about 20 percent compared to the last Duma elections in the same regions, and whereas during the elections held in the preceding autumn the party got more than 50 percent of the vote in five out of six regions, in 2011 it failed to gain 50 percent in seven of the twelve regions where elections were held.[76] Furthermore, the trend in the party's long-term support had been, with fluctuations, generally down. In April 2009, the Levada poll of voting intentions had support for UR at about 63 percent. Over the succeeding two and a half years, the level generally trended down, and by mid November 2011, some two weeks before the poll, its support level had dropped to 53.7 percent.[77] While short-term fluctua-tions in the polls may have been sufficient for the people around Putin to have hoped that UR could get close to its performance in 2007, those very fluctuations reflected how uncertain UR's political base was. There was no suggestion that it was not going to be the most popular party, but its ability to maintain its former level of dominance was under question.

This can only have been strengthened by the wave of criticism of UR that washed through Russian society. Dissident blogger Aleksei Navalny's

[72] There was only limited international scrutiny of the voting.
[73] Medvedev received 17.4 times more airtime than his three opponents on NTV and on Channel One 4.2 times. Sakwa (*Crisis*), p. 297.
[74] Myagkov et al. (*Forensics*), pp. 6–9.
[75] See Luke March, "Managing Opposition in a Hybrid Regime: Just Russia and Parastatal Opposition," *Slavic Review* 68 (3), 2009, p. 514.
[76] *Novaia gazeta*, March 16, 2011.
[77] For the Levada figures, see www.levada.ru/25–11–2011/noyabrskie-reitingi-odobreniya-i-doveriya-reitingi-partii. Accessed December 12, 2011.

reference to "the party of crooks and thieves" gained resonance in Russian society; in late November 2011 while 33 percent of people claimed never to have heard the phrase, in answer to a separate question 46 percent believed it referred to UR.[78] This fed into the general perception about high levels of corruption in the administrative structures of the country at both regional and central levels, and with many officials party members, this perception clearly leached into the party. Criticism of its connection with corruption by two of its founding fathers, Yury Luzhkov and Mintimer Shaimiev, albeit after they had been pushed from office, can only have reinforced this.[79] In addition, there was a feeling that having been the dominant party for eight years, it had run out of steam and this was responsible for the economic difficulties of the immediate past. Although such a judgment may have been harsh given the international financial crisis, it is one that Putin himself obliquely acknowledged in the aftermath of the election.[80] Over the year this combination of an image of a tired party filled with people who used their official positions for personal gain gathered strength among sections of the Russian people, and, fueled by the attacks of opposition forces, eroded the party's support base.

Putin seems to have been aware that this was happening and took two measures designed to bolster the party's flagging fortunes. First, at the May 6, 2011, UR party conference, he proposed the establishment of

---

[78] www.levada.ru/06-12-2-11/vybory-v-gosdumu-chast-2-o-edinoi-rossii-narodnom-fronte.slovosochetanii-partiya-zhulikov. Accessed December 12, 2011. In answer to the question about to which party this phrase referred, the second ranked party was the Liberal Democratic Party which received 3 percent; 44 percent said it was hard to answer. According to another poll, in answer to the question as to whether they agreed with the view that UR was the party of hooligans and thieves, respondents answered (in %):

|                  | April 2011 | June 2011 | November 2011 | January 2012 |
| ---------------- | ---------- | --------- | ------------- | ------------ |
| Yes              | 32         | 33        | 37            | 41           |
| No               | 46         | 47        | 44            | 43           |
| Difficult to say | 23         | 20        | 19            | 16           |

Gudkov et al. (*Rossiiskie*), p. 9.

[79] *Novaia gazeta*, March 21, 2011. For a survey that showed 40 percent of people believed that UR represented the interests of the oligarchs, 34 percent bureaucrats, 32 percent major businessmen, and 32 percent siloviki, see Gudkov et al. (*Rossiiskie*), p. 16. A third believed that it represented their interests. Gudkov et al. (*Rossiiskie*), p. 13.

[80] See his comments to the heads of the public reception offices of UR on Tuesday, December 6, Interfax, December 6, 2011.

an All-Russian People's Front (ARPF).[81] This was to be an organization anyone could join (including members of other parties) and they could then gain a place on UR's election list. The proposal soon attracted significant interest as organizations from many walks of life and many individuals sought to join the new body. It was clearly designed as a mobilizing mechanism, a means of attracting new voters to UR and thereby reviving the party. Second, was an attempt at giving party members an appearance of real power in the selection of candidates through the introduction of primaries.[82] So-called "people's primaries" were held by UR and the ARPF between July 21 and August 25, 2011, leading to the nomination of a large number of candidates for inclusion on the party's electoral list; according to the head of UR's Supreme Council, Boris Gryzlov, 4,700 candidates were nominated for the party's 600 list positions.[83] But the choice of the final list still lay with the party leadership, so that all that the primaries could do was to generate suggestions. In the event, neither development seems to have had much impact on UR's fortunes; on August 25 Putin abandoned primaries.[84] Although party leaders must have been aware that UR's position was eroding, six weeks before the election there was still a feeling among some at the top that UR could get up to 60 percent of the vote overall,[85] but this was not realized in the election.

The 2011 election, which was for a new five-year term (the presidential term was also increased, but to six years), was contested by only seven parties, with a number of others denied registration and therefore unable to participate.[86] UR was again the party of power bearing the Kremlin's banner, but since the last election Just Russia had abandoned its former support of UR and sought to stake out a position as an autonomous opposition force. The KPRF and LDPR appeared as the other major contenders, although for a time a new party called Right Cause, and headed (until September 2011) by the billionaire Mikhail Prokhorov but

---

81  *Vedomosti*, May 10, 2011. For information on the Front's early organizational structure, see the report in *Nezavisimaia gazeta*, May 30, 2011.
82  Primaries had actually been tried in UR in the run up to the 2007 Duma election. Darrell Slider, "How United is United Russia? Regional Sources of Intra-party Conflict," *The Journal of Communist Studies and Transition Politics* 26 (2), 2010, p. 270.
83  *Kommersant*, August 15, 2011.
84  Although this was not before, two days earlier, saying that primaries should be instituted for all parties to determine their candidates. *Vedomosti*, August 30, 2011.
85  *Vedomosti*, October 13, 2011.
86  For a discussion of the difficulties experienced by Yabloko, Right Cause, and the Patriots of Russia in gaining regional registration for concurrent elections in the regions, see *Kommersant*, October 31, 2011.

seen by many as another Kremlin front party, was thought by some to be likely to gain Duma representation. The campaign was bland, although for the first time there were televised debates that gave all parties some media exposure. As with earlier parliamentary elections, these were held under the shadow of the scheduled presidential poll in March 2012. This was particularly important in this case because of the September 24, 2011, announcement that Putin would run for the presidency with Medvedev likely to be his prime minister, followed on November 27 by UR's endorsement of Putin for the presidency. This form of political "castling," while not totally unexpected, was not greeted positively by some sections of the population (especially in the major cities), and this may have contributed to the outcome of the vote. In light of this, the public booing of Putin at a martial arts exhibition in November, action that perforated the image of Putin as popular beyond question, may have been the public signal which crystallized people to act. When the votes in the parliamentary poll were tallied, UR had retained a majority of seats in the Duma but had lost the constitutional majority it had gained in 2007, and it failed to achieve the majority of popular votes as it had in the last election; UR had 49.32 percent of votes and 238 seats, KPRF 19.19 percent of votes and 92 seats, Just Russia 13.24 percent of votes and 64 seats, and LDPR 11.67 percent of votes and 56 seats. Yabloko, Patriots of Russia, and Right Cause all received less than 3.5 percent of the vote and failed to gain representation in the Duma. Turnout was 60.2 percent. The vote for UR had dropped 15 percent while that for the other three parties in the Duma had increased substantially in proportional terms; that for KPRF and Just Russia almost doubled.

The conclusion of the international observers[87] was that the election was not fair. They pointed to "the convergence of the state and the governing party" that created the lack of a level playing field in favor of the ruling party, the denial of registration of some parties, the lack of independence of the election administration,[88] the partiality of most media outlets, and undue interference by state officials at different levels.[89]

---

[87] OSCE/ODIHR, "Russian Federation. Elections to the State Duma 4 December 2011. OSCE/ODIHR Election Observation Mission. Final Report" (Warsaw: OSCE/ODIHR, January 12, 2012), www.osce.org. Accessed February 2, 2012.

[88] For the CEC Chairman banning opposition party advertisements, see *Vedomosti* November 28, 2011.

[89] For some evidence of this from the campaign, see *Kommersant*, October 25, 2011; *Moskovskii komsomolets*, October 24, 2011; and Irina Berliand and Marina Stupakova (eds), *Razgnevannye nabliudateli. Fal'sifikatsii parlamentskikh vyborov glazami ochevidtsev* (Moscow: Novoe literaturnoe obozrenie, 2012). For a discussion of views about different levels of fraud, see Anatoly Karlin, "Measuring Churov's Beard. The Mathematics of Russian Election Fraud," www.darussophile.com. Originally accessed January 7, 2013.

Table 3.1. *2011 Election: public opinion polls, cf. voting*

|  | UR | KPRF | LDPR | Just Russia |
|---|---|---|---|---|
| VTsIOM November 19–20, 2011 | 53.7% | 16.7% | 11.6% | 10.0% |
| VTsIOM Exit poll | 48.5% | 19.8% | 11.42% | 12.8% |
| Vote | 49.32% | 19.19% | 11.67% | 13.24% |

Voters were reported to have been offered bribes, others faced with threats, and in some areas carousel voting occurred. The counting of votes was said to be characterized by "frequent procedural violations and instances of apparent manipulation, including several serious indications of ballot box stuffing." The reference to ballot box stuffing was supported by the wave of popular reports of electoral abuses transmitted by social media and then given a run in some of the mainstream media, and it was this perception of widespread electoral fraud that stimulated subsequent popular demonstrations (see Chapter 2).

But we do not really know how pervasive electoral fraud actually was. While we cannot get an accurate measure of this, a couple of factors counsel caution in assessing its dimensions. First, the vote for UR fell by a considerable amount. Had the regime sought to use major systematic fraud, one would have expected the decline to have been less severe and to at least have enabled UR to claim 50 percent of the vote. Second, the voting outcome is broadly consistent with polling data (Table 3.1).[90]

On the basis of the last poll before voting, UR is the only party to have done considerably worse in the actual vote, while in comparison with the exit poll data, UR and Just Russia gained more votes and the others lost votes, but in all cases the difference was less than 1 percent and therefore within the margin of error. This does not mean that there was no vote manipulation, because there are sufficient reports to suggest that it was present. However, it does suggest that that manipulation was not on a scale sufficient to affect the result. It is also consistent with the possibility that such manipulation was not all in favor of UR; after all UR representatives did not administer the count in all areas. But even if this

His tentative conclusion is that fraud probably amounted to 5–7 percent of the vote. For a critical report by the NGO Golos (The Association of Non-Profit Organizations "In Defence of Voters' Rights"), see "Statement of the GOLOS Association on the Results of the Elections of Deputies for the State Duma December 4, 2011," *Russian Analytical Digest* 106, December 21, 2011, pp. 9–10.

[90] www.levada.ru/28.11–2011/sotsiologi-otdayut-edinoi-rossii-nemnogim-bolshe-50-golosov and www.regnum.ru/news/1475239.html. Accessed January 7, 2012. Also see Gudkov et al. (*Rossiiskie*), p. 22.

sort of electoral fraud did not tip the balance, the significant advantages UR received through the conduct of the campaign and the resultant lack of a level playing field did shape the outcome.

In response to the popular protests, both Putin and Medvedev denied there had been widespread electoral abuse. They did, however, fore-shadow a number of changes designed to increase competition in the system, including restoration of the direct election of regional leaders while retaining a "filter" on who could stand, a simplified procedure for political party registration and reporting (there were still to be no regional parties), provision for a reduced number of signatures required for candidates to stand for election (this fell from 40,000 to 500), restoration of the system of single member districts in the 225 Duma electoral regions that would ensure that each region would have at least one representative in the Duma, and broader representation of political parties in the electoral commissions.[91] In addition, in November 2012 a new council was established to give parties that did not receive a seat in the Duma a voice on issues.[92] Putin also announced the establishment of webcams in all polling stations and use of transparent ballot boxes as means of countering fraud, with these to be in place by the presidential election.[93] These were in addition to the earlier announced reduction of the threshold for Duma representation from 7 percent to 5 percent to take effect from the 2016 election.[94] More immediately, a number of governors in regions where UR had performed poorly were removed.[95] However, none of these changes were aimed at the main cause of unfairness in Russian elections, the use of access to state resources to tip the grounds of the contest in favor of the party of power. Indeed, some worried (correctly) that the reduction in numbers required to register a party would lead to the further fragmentation of the opposition, and was therefore another attempt to give the party of power an advantage.

At one level, the changes introduced after the 2011 election may be seen as a sign of regime weakness: concessions delivered under pressure from below. But this would be to misread the essential dynamic of the situation. The weakness of the opposition vis-à-vis the regime meant that

[91] Dmitry Medvedev, "Poslanie Prezidenta Federal'nomu Sobraniiu," December 22, 2011, www.kremlin.ru. Accessed January 4, 2012.
[92] www.russiatoday.com, November 30, 2012. Accessed December 1, 2012.
[93] "Razgovor s Vladimirom Putinym. Prodolzhenie," December 15, 2011, http://premier .gov.ru/events/news/17409. Accessed January 7, 2012.
[94] *Novaia Gazeta*, October 12, 2011.
[95] Ilia Mikhalchuk in Arkhangelsk (31.9 percent of the vote), Anatoly Brovko in Volgograd (36.2 percent), Sergei Darkin in Primor'e (33.4 percent), Viktor Kress in Tomsk (37.5 percent), Boris Gryzlov in Moscow region (32.5 percent), Leonid Polezhaev in Omsk (39.6 percent), and Dmitry Dmitrenko in Murmansk (32 percent).

rather than being the thin edge of a wedge leading to more concessions from the regime, they were part of the reason why opposition mobilization declined. The changes were strategic moves designed to blunt opposition charges, not concessions to opposition demands, and what they reflect is not that the regime was weak, but that it was sufficiently flexible to be able to meet the challenges thrown up before it.[96]

The loss of support for UR led some to believe Vladimir Putin might suffer a similar rejection in the March 2012 presidential poll. Five candidates stood for election in an atmosphere where there was a heightened awareness of the issue of electoral falsification. Not only were larger numbers of international observers present, but large numbers of ordinary Russians were also mobilized to be on the lookout for any attempts to fiddle the vote. As in the past, Putin refused to campaign, including being the only candidate to refuse to participate in the televised debates that gave all candidates some free media exposure, but he did issue six programmatic articles in the popular press in which he addressed broad questions of Russian development and its future. While all candidates were able to campaign freely, the campaign was clearly tilted in Putin's favor by unequal treatment in the media and by his ability to use state resources.[97] In the final result, Putin received 63.60 percent of the votes, followed by Gennady Ziuganov 17.18 percent, Mikhail Prokhorov 7.98 percent, Vladimir Zhirinovsky 6.22 percent, and Sergei Mironov 3.85 percent. Fraudulent manipulation of the vote did occur in some localities,[98] but its dimensions do not appear to have been particularly large. Putin's vote exceeded that of two exit polls, but not by a significant margin: VTsIOM's exit poll awarded him 58.3 percent and FOM's 59.3 percent compared with his result of 63.6 percent; with a margin of error of about 3 percent, this means his vote exceeded the lowest exit poll by somewhere between 8 percent and less than 2 percent.[99] Putin's victory in the first round, and no one disputed that he had scored many more votes than his nearest competitor but some claimed that falsification had

[96] On the importance of institutional adaptability, see Martin K. Dimitrov, "Understanding Communist Collapse and Resilience," Martin K. Dimitrov (ed.), *Why Communism Did Not Collapse. Understanding Authoritarian Regime Resilience in Asia and Europe* (Cambridge: Cambridge University Press, 2013), pp. 3–39.

[97] See the press release OSCE, Office for Democratic Institutions and Human Rights, "Russia's Presidential Election Marked by Unequal Campaign Conditions, Active Citizens' Engagement, International Observers Say," March 6, 2012, www.osce.org/odihr/elections/88661. Accessed March 8, 2012.

[98] See the report by GOLOS, "Association GOLOS – Domestic Monitoring of Elections of the President of Russian Federation, 4 March 2012: Preliminary Report," *Russian Analytical Digest* 110, March 16, 2012, pp. 8–16.

[99] For these figures, see "Final Results of the Presidential Elections," *Russian Analytical Digest* 110, March 16, 2012, p. 20.

pushed him over the 50 percent mark thereby removing the need for a second round, seemed to suggest that the potential crisis to the electoral authoritarian regime that was believed to be reflected in UR's performance in December 2011 was not real. However, this is not the case. The performance of UR in the December election was not the sort of performance that one would expect from the sort of dominant party able to stabilize a party-oriented electoral authoritarian regime.

Presumably Putin and those around him will want to retain a competitive authoritarian electoral mode of legitimation, if only because this enables them to continue to tap into the international norm of democracy as a claimed basis of regime authority.[100] This would require the continued presence of UR, or a party to replace it. If previous experience is a guide, one option would be to replace UR with another party of power. The history of Russian political development has had as one of its continuing themes the replacement of one party of power by another when the former was deemed deficient in some way: Russia's Choice was followed by Our Home is Russia, which was succeeded by Unity which was then submerged into United Russia. The model of all of these was the same, with the party formed from above and based primarily upon state officials; only UR was able significantly to bolster this by attracting a rank-and-file membership. The essence of the party of power was the same, a party based overwhelmingly in official structures and drawing its strength in large part from its ability to leach resources from the state. But the replacement of UR by a clone would not be as easy as it had been earlier. Not only would the new party have to satisfy the requirements of registration, but the tying of party funding to electoral performance would create an initial problem of where the party's start-up funds were

---

[100] This desire to invest an election with legitimacy is reflected in the conduct of the election for the Moscow mayor's position on September 8, 2013. The existing mayor, Sergei Sobyanin, had been appointed to this post in 2010, but following the introduction of the measure to provide for the election of governors, stood down from this post to trigger an election which he was sure he would win. But Sobyanin and his supporters in the Kremlin realized that simply holding an election was insufficient; there also needed to be the perception that it was truly competitive, and this required a credible opponent. Accordingly when the 2011–12 protest leader Aleksei Navalny (who had flagged he would stand against Sobyanin) was found guilty and sentenced to five years in prison on fraud charges, that sentence and his appeal were immediately suspended, thereby clearing the way for him to take part in the election. During that process and during the campaign itself, the mayor's office actually provided him with various forms of assistance designed to boost his performance. Ultimately, he received a higher vote than many had expected – 27.2 percent to Sobyanin's 51.4 percent - and despite his claims about irregularities in the vote (especially in terms of boosting Sobyanin's vote above 50 percent so there would be no second round), it was generally seen as being fair. On the election, see the reports in *Russian Analytical Digest* 136, September 16, 2013, pp. 1–11.

to come from, and although this could be solved by cross-subsidy from the state, this would leave the party open to the same criticisms leveled against UR. Furthermore, UR is much more substantial in terms of party organization, Duma representation, and membership than any of its predecessors, and therefore liquidation of the party would be a messy process. Nevertheless, the heightened public profile of the All-Russian Popular Front and Putin's accession to its leadership in mid 2013 is consistent with the idea of promoting this as a potential replacement in 2017–18.[101]

But if the party is to be an effective means of electoral legitimation, it must both escape the negative image it has acquired and begin to perform the tasks expected of it (see Chapter 4) in a more effective fashion. If it could mobilize popular support and co-opt the opposition, unite the elite, control parliament and state, and be a mechanism for the distribution of patronage, it may be able to unite pro-regime forces, isolate and marginalize those opposition forces it could not co-opt, go some way toward restoring its image, and thereby stabilize political power. It would be a big job to improve party performance in this way, but given the example of parties like the People's Action Party in Singapore and the weakness of opposition forces in Russia, it might not be impossible. However, in order to achieve this, there needs to be a change in the relationship with the leader (see Chapter 4).

If the deficiencies of UR as a dominant party are part of the explanation for the poorer than expected performance of the party in the 2011 election, the question arises as to why the opposition did not do better. As Bunce and Wolchik[102] argue, the key factor in opposition success in elections has been the election campaign that they mounted rather than anything about the regime itself. Successful electoral strategy involved opposition unity (involving not just opposition parties but civil society groups and democracy promoters from abroad), improving the quality and transparency of the electoral process through such measures as election monitoring, exit polls, and parallel vote counting, and an ambitious campaign designed to increase voter registration and turnout, and projection of the conviction that real change was possible through the election. This sort of strategy, which Bunce and Wolchik argue was successful in Slovakia in 1998, Croatia and Serbia 2000, Georgia 2003, Ukraine 2004, and Kyrgyzstan 2005, was certainly not evident in Russia.

---

[101] Yulia Ponomareva, "Putin's Popular Front to Replace United Russia?," *Russia Beyond the Headlines* June 18, 2013, www.rbt.ru. Accessed June 19, 2013; Anna Arutunyan, "Putin's Front: The End of Politics?," *Moscow News*, June 17, 2013.

[102] Bunce and Wolchik (*Defeating Authoritarian Leaders*).

But an important factor in this has been that, despite the problems of UR, the regime has retained the capacity to blunt each element of this strategy. The generation of phantom opposition parties, harassment of opposition leaders, and the design of electoral laws have all helped to undermine opposition unity. Continuing control over the administration of the ballot, including limitations on independent observers, limited the possibility of independent monitoring of the vote, while continuing wide-scale media control both limited the capacity of the opposition to campaign effectively and to suggest that the possibility of change was real. Furthermore, since coming to power in 2000, Putin has emphasized a notion of Russian greatness that has involved the rejection of any sense of external "interference," thereby imposing a negative construction on the activity of external democracy promoters and their domestic partners. Positive action has been taken against such activities (see Chapter 2), including the election monitor Golos. The regime's ability to continue to wield such weapons shows that regime capacity remains a crucial factor shaping what the opposition can do and therefore, Bunce and Wolchik notwithstanding, electoral strategy alone is insufficient to overcome the regime's entrenched power. The capacity to structure the electoral process in Russia has thus far limited the effects of any deficiencies in the performance of UR.

The trajectory of development of the Russian electoral system since the emergence of independent Russia in 1992 has thus been in an authoritarian direction. Under Yeltsin, this course seems to have been motivated less by a clear vision of what sort of system he wished to see on Russian soil than by the desire to defeat his immediate foes and prevent the communists from making a comeback as the rulers of the country. To do this he utilized the resources of the state unashamedly, mobilized independent media outlets, and benefited from wide-scale electoral fraud. While some attempts were made to shape the system in a more permanent sense – the early banning of the communist party and the attempts to create a party of power first in Russia's Choice and then Our Home is Russia – these were failures, and Yeltsin was left basically to manipulate political and social forces as he found them. In part this was because Yeltsin lacked the tools to control autonomous political activity. Rather than being able to direct political forces, he was in a position where he had to seek alliances and agreements with them. The instability of such agreements, and the absence of mechanisms to ensure their enforcement, meant that although Yeltsin did drive the electoral system in an authoritarian direction, he was unable to stabilize it.

This was in direct contrast to the endeavors of Vladimir Putin. From the outset of his time in power, Putin emphasized the need for a strengthening of the state, which he saw as involving the reinforcement of the so-called "power vertical."[103] This was envisaged as the creation of a cohesive power machine centered on the presidency that drew into it all aspects of political life, which hitherto had played themselves out autonomously. His actions in terms of regional officials, the media, and civil society are discussed elsewhere in this book. With regard to the electoral system, parties, and the parliament, Putin implemented a series of measures designed decisively to tilt the system in favor of the party of power and its patron, the president. Not content with simply the advantages of incumbency and the exploitation of state resources to defeat opponents, he sought to restructure the system and the way it worked, significantly increasing the level of regulation of the electoral system (the 2005 election law was 325 pages long, cf. 29 pages for the 1994 version) and reducing its competitiveness. It was under Putin that the fraudulent manipulation of the ballot seems to have been most marked. The study by Myagkov et al. has shown how augmented turnout figures were associated with artificially heightened support for Putin in the 2004 election. Local and regional leaders had been aware in earlier elections of the potential they had to deliver votes to the Kremlin and the political and career implications of this. In 1996 many of those leaders had been somewhat ambivalent about Yeltsin while in 2000 they had been torn between Fatherland-All Russia and Putin. But in 2004 with Putin certain to win, plus the fact that he had already indicated he was calling them into line through the construction of the "power vertical," there was a strong incentive for local and regional leaders to produce high levels of support for Putin. The same logic applied in 2008 for Putin's candidate Medvedev. This does not mean that such fraud was not promoted from the center, but that it was at least as much in the interests of lower level leaders to engage in this as it was for the center who wanted an overwhelming display of popular support; they showed their loyalty by over-fulfilling the center's expectation about electoral support. The presidency seemed to become something virtually within the gift of the incumbent, and the parliament, through the dominance of the party of power, was co-opted into the presidential process of ruling. Opposition was allowed, as long as it had no prospect of success.

While electoral fraud (such as ballot box stuffing, the reallocation of votes, carousel voting, use of absentee certificates) played a part in all of the elections discussed here, more important was the way in which the whole field of the election was tilted in favor of the Kremlin and against opposition forces. This was achieved chiefly through the application of

---

[103] On strengthening the state, see Chapter 4.

what has been called "administrative resources," and these have been a direct result of the ability to exploit the resources of the state. This has been enjoyed by successive presidents and by the parties of power, with the latter being much more adept at this after 2000 than before. The mobilization of administrative resources heavily weighted the process against opposition forces, being more influential in this than the direct fraud on the ground. This was a structural feature of the electoral system, and one which undercut the competitive potential embedded in an electoral process.

The structuring of electoral competition by both Yeltsin and Putin had a clear and direct effect on the way in which the party system developed, including denial of political parties as effective vehicles of opposition activity. The increasingly high barriers and complex procedures for registration of a political party that were imposed over the years had the effect of reducing the number of parties that could become active in the political arena. Combined with the Putin-era prohibitions on sectoral and regional parties and the insistence on a broad base of membership across the Federation, this meant that only nationally oriented parties were likely to be able to satisfy the formal requirements for participation; by mid 2011 there were only seven political parties in existence, the four represented in the Duma (UR, KPRF, LDPR, and Just Russia) and three lacking such representation (Yabloko, Right Cause, and Patriots of Russia). Furthermore, the initial electoral arrangements for the State Duma, with 50 percent elected on a central list proportional representation basis and 50 percent in single member district constituencies, made it difficult for powerful parties to develop. In order to maximize their chances under this combined system, parties had to have both a powerful central office able to construct a list of reliable members for the PR section of the ballot, as well as a network of branches across the country to cater to the SMD side. In practice, no party was able to achieve this on a regular basis, with most concentrating their efforts on the central list PR section. In theory, a PR system is meant to encourage powerful parties with an effective machine at their heart, but this has not been the result in Russia. Even the shift to the election of all members by PR in 2007 has not clearly had this effect. And in any event, the shift to this system where all are elected on the basis of lists drawn up in Moscow, meant that party leaderships were concentrated in the capital where they were more vulnerable to control or at least supervision by the regime. With the restoration of the SMD basis of election for 2017, the party structures will again be pulled in two directions, between center and region.

But the weakness of the party system does not only stem from regime design. During the 1990s the Russian party system was a classic case of an unconsolidated party system, characterized by a high level of fragmentation, significant electoral volatility, and the crowding out of parties (especially at the regional level) by non-party political machines.[104] Explanations for this state of affairs have ranged from those focusing on the deficiencies of the parties themselves – lack of resources, ineffective organizational structure, absence of (agreement about) clear policies, personalized basis of the party's identity – to explanations based on the broader constituency – popular apathy and suspicion of all parties, the absence of clearly defined constituencies upon which parties could build sustained profiles. The presidential nature of the system and the fact that governments are neither embedded in the Duma nor responsible to it, with the consequent absence of an institutional imperative to gain a majority in the assembly to establish a government, denied legislative impetus to the development of a coherent party system. Similarly Yeltsin's decision, followed by his presidential successors, not to become a member of any party seemed to downgrade parties by suggesting that the leading political actor did not need to be a party member. All of these factors inhibited the development of parties and thereby hamstrung the capacity of potential oppositionist forces to act in an organized fashion.

The people around Yeltsin and Putin also sought to marginalize political parties through the creation of successive "parties of power." Through successively Russia's Choice, Our Home is Russia, Unity, and United Russia, the regime sought to capture the center ground electorally. Success was achieved in 2003 and 2007 and less so in 2011 in a process that culminated in the exclusion of liberal parties from the Duma. The dominance of the party of power effectively pushed to the margins many of the independently organized parties, both through the effect of the electoral juggernaut and through the attraction of the members of other parties (and of leading administrators) into its ranks. Part of the success of UR was a function of a significant change in the relationship between president and parties. Yeltsin had openly eschewed party membership, claiming he would govern for the whole country. In contrast, while Putin did not join UR while president, he openly associated himself with the party (in April 2008 he became party leader while still not being a formal member), so that it was widely recognized as "his" party. On declaring his intention to step down from the presidency in September 2011, Medvedev also openly associated himself with UR. This "official" nature of the party was reinforced by the fact that in early 2011, nearly two-thirds of its membership worked in the state bureaucracy.[105]

[104] See the discussion in Gel'man ("Feckless") pp. 545–6.
[105] Sakwa (*Crisis*), p. 23.

As well as creating the party of power, at various times those around the president have sought to create other parties not just to give the impression of electoral competition, but to take the ground away from potential oppositionists; this is Wilson's "virtual opposition."[106] The use of the state's administrative resources to underpin such party development was in some quarters seen as a guarantee of success, but in fact all of these attempts have failed. The center-left Rybkin Bloc failed to enter the Duma in 1995, and Rodina, which gained a total of thirty-seven seats in the 2003 Duma, were both designed to displace the KPRF as the principal party of the left (or at least to weaken it by stealing votes from it) by dominating the center-left of the political spectrum, but neither gained such predominance. Similarly Just Russia, formed in October 2006 from the coming together of Rodina, the Party of Life, the Pensioners' Party, and, in February 2007, the People's Party and designed to draw votes from the communists, gained thirty-eight seats in the 2007 Duma.[107] Just Russia maintained itself into the 2011 election, but was still not able to capture the center-left ground. In 2011 there was also an attempt to create a party with a clear pro-market orientation and designed to pick up the liberal-right constituency, Right Cause, but like its leftist counterparts, it was unable to establish itself as a solid representative of that constituency.

In addition to the generation of such parties aimed at establishing a semblance of competition in the system while excluding genuine competitors, the Kremlin also engaged in a process of buying off oppositionists. Through the doling out of positions such as committee chairmanships in the Duma and the provision of state largesse to Duma deputies and their constituents, the authorities sought to suborn opposition figures in the same way that occurs in all legislative systems. This has also applied at the party level, where from the party's inception the Liberal Democratic Party of Russia has been the beneficiary of Kremlin largesse. Although during elections, particularly presidential elections, the party leader Vladimir Zhirinovsky has generally been very critical of the president and his policies, under all three presidents in practice the LDPR has generally been a loyal supporter in the Duma. This is because the party has been the recipient of sometimes significant "administrative resources" directed to it by the authorities, especially during elections. This sort of situation of Kremlin funding of opposition parties, and thereby in part muting

---

[106] Wilson (*Virtual Politics*).

[107] For the argument that the fear that Just Russia could split support for the elite and thereby damage UR, leading to a decline in its support by the Putin elite just prior to the 2007 election, see Sakwa (*Crisis*), pp. 65–6.

their opposition, has been a feature throughout the entire post-Soviet period,[108] and is a clear case of the co-optation of the opposition by the regime.

But the opposition has also been ignored. Successive presidents have given very little attention to listening to the complaints of the main opposition party the KPRF, let alone the marginalized opposition. This reached its apogee in the 2000, 2004, 2008, and 2012 presidential elections when Putin and Medvedev effectively refused to campaign. They presented themselves as the statesman, above politics, who would not deign to argue with the opposition about their policies. By simply enunciating their position in such a way that everyone was expected to follow and which brooked of no possibility of opposition, their opponents were left with nowhere to go. By ignoring them, the president/future president rendered them irrelevant.

Thus, in its approach to the electoral and party system, the regime has adopted a sophisticated strategy involving four elements. Repression was used openly as a short-term measure in 1993 and more subtly throughout the whole period, while co-optation, marginalization, and ignoring of the opposition have also been prominent throughout the entire period. This reached its most developed form under Putin who, through the greater effectiveness of the party of power, was better able than Yeltsin to reduce the Duma to a generally tame supporter, and to blunt the electoral opposition. This has meant that the regime has been able to construct a competitive authoritarian electoral system that has enabled regime control of party-based opposition to match that of opposition in the streets.

---

[108] Wilson (*Virtual Politics*), pp. 113–29, 203–36. Even the communists have been the beneficiaries of such largesse.

*Part II*

# Structuring the regime

# 4    Structuring institutional power

Of the two dimensions of rule identified in Chapter 1, the structuring of both public political activity and the way the regime operates internally, the former is dependent upon the latter. If the regime can ensure that the machinery of administration works effectively and is at the command of central decision makers, the capacity for controlling public activity will be enhanced. So too will the stability of the regime because a smoothly functioning bureaucratic structure should ensure better policy outcomes and fewer occasions of domestic conflict. Following a discussion of strategies for building a responsive administrative structure, this chapter focuses on how successive presidential administrations have sought to build a centralized and responsive administrative machine in Russia.

The development of effective institutional machinery of government and administration is not an easy task, especially when a regime inherits that machinery from a former regime, as was the case in Russia. In attempting to establish control, to create a system that is responsive to central decision makers, two essential strategies were evident in post-Soviet Russia: a reliance upon building networks of personal loyalty, and a dependence on organizational means. In principle, these two strategies generate different sorts of imperatives that result in different sorts of regimes.

A reliance upon personal loyalty creates a personalist regime in which the dominant political actor is the individual leader. Of course no leader can rule without an institutional structure supporting him/her. Even when popular commitment is charismatic in nature (see below), the stability of rule requires an administrative machine. This may take the form of a party, but military rule can also be characterized by the dominant figure of an individual personality. In some cases of personalist rule, such a formal structure as a party or military is replaced by the leader's more informal personal clique, which assumes leading positions in the power structure. But although personalist rule requires some form of machinery to stand upon, its claims for authority are very different from those of such a machine. In a personalist regime, the basis of the leader's authority is that leader himself, including the message he represents, rather than organizational considerations like position or rank. His dominance stems not from any office he holds but from his very person and the promise that he embodies.

Personalist regimes are often seen in terms of charismatic leaders. Charisma[1] is a form of authority in which the followers invest all of their trust in the leader, following him blindly and accepting his definition of reality as their own. While this extreme form of domination whereby followers sink their capacity for independent thought into obedience to the leader may be rare in practice, enthusiasm for an individual leader and the message he projects is a common phenomenon. Where leaders are seen to embody the promise of a bright new future (Mao, Hitler, Peron), commitment on an ideational basis can be both widespread and intense. But as well as this, a material basis for commitment has also been identified for many dominant leaders. Through their control over patronage, and in particular their ability to dispense jobs (which can lead to increased access to material benefits) and material benefits, leaders can attract and retain followers for often considerable periods of time. Both ideational and material sources of commitment can thus operate to the benefit of individual leaders.

The pure personalist regime, although there is always a structure of some sort to sustain the leader, usually does not possess the machinery necessary to dominate the state the way a party can. Certainly the followers of a leader may be placed in major posts throughout the state structure, but this is usually in a less organized fashion than when a party does this. Pure personalist leadership resting on commitment to the leader lacks an institutional infrastructure that can function independent of the leader; bureaucratic norms and mores mean little if overwhelming authority lies with the individual leader. Accordingly the institutional structure sustaining such a leader is rarely sufficiently organizationally robust and developed to be able to carry its authority into the interstices of the state. As a result, the leader usually sits at the top of the state structure, but his capacity to control that structure is organizationally not well developed; he exercises what Michael Mann refers to as "despotic" power rather than "infrastructural" power.[2] In this sense, the essential political

---

[1] For the classic statement about charismatic rule, see Max Weber, *Economy and Society. An Outline of Interpretive Sociology* (eds Guenther Roth and Claus Wittich; Berkeley: University of California Press, 1978), pp. 241–54, 1111–56.

[2] Mann ("Autonomous Power"), pp. 109–36. Infrastructural power is power exercised through routine administrative methods, despotic power through the use of extraordinary means, for example, respectively, the collection of taxes through a regularized system of deductions from pay packets by employers, cf. armed police knocking at individual doors.

dynamic of the personalist regime is that that regime sits apart from the state in contrast to the situation in the party regime.

The most common organizational means for new leaders to establish control over an existing state machine is through the institution of the political party. The important thing about such authoritarian party regimes is that once in power, the party does not limit itself to filling public elected office. They also seek to control the state machine through the insertion of their members into its most important posts as well as, often, many of the less important more routine positions throughout the apparatus. The result is a lack of a clear distinction between party and state, often reflected in the absence of any separation between the finances of the government and those of the ruling party. Party regimes thus often see an effective merging of party and state structures, or at least significant overlap.

Two types of party can be identified in authoritarian polities: single and hegemonic. The single party regime is one where there is only one party allowed to function, and elections lack party choice, although in some cases limited choice may be allowed between different members of the same party. The ruling party is the only party in the system. The USSR was a case of this type of system. The hegemonic party regime is one where there is a ruling party that dominates a political system in which there are other, "opposition," parties present, but they are unable to mount a real challenge to the ruling party because of the advantages the system accords to the ruling party.[3] Mexico under the PRI until the mid-late 1990s was a case of a hegemonic party system. Both types, single and hegemonic, rely at base on the commitment of party members to maintain party dominance, and while in individual cases such commitment may rest on a range of factors, scholars have identified two basic sources of this. The first source of commitment[4] is belief in the values and positions for which the party stands. Such values are often formalized into an ideology, but this is not always the case; they may consist in Linz's "distinctive mentalities,"[5] in the message enunciated by a dominant leader, or in an ethos arising out of common shared experience (such as participating in a revolutionary struggle). But whatever form it takes, this type of commitment is ideational. The second source of commitment is based on the expectation of personal

[3] For a discussion of this type of party, see Giovanni Sartori, *Parties and Party Systems. A Framework for Analysis* (Cambridge: Cambridge University Press, 1976), pp. 230–38 and Chapter 3 above.

[4] In some instances, for example, ethnic parties, common identity could also be a source of commitment.

[5] Linz ("An Authoritarian Regime"), pp. 257–9.

advantage. By belonging to the party, its members hope to be able to gain significant advantages that they would not otherwise obtain. These can be in the form of jobs, pay, or access to material advantages not otherwise available. This is often seen in terms of patronage, and in contrast to ideational commitment, is commitment based on material gain. Both types of commitment can coexist in both single and hegemonic party systems.

Barbara Geddes argues that party regimes tend to be more long lasting than other types of regime, and she attributes this chiefly to their role in mitigating elite conflict.[6] However, this view is too restrictive. In practice, the role ruling parties play in regime maintenance is more extensive than this. There are seven ways in which a ruling political party can help stabilize an authoritarian regime:

1. control of the electoral process (see Chapter 3). In competitive authoritarian systems where elections are a means of filling substantive positions within the system and a means of systemic legitimation, the ruling elite must have some mechanism for accumulating sufficient votes
   to consolidate its position. The party does this by dominating the electoral process, as ruling parties crowd out opposition parties and deny
   them the space in which to organize and mobilize. Extensive party
   membership and the range of party organizations throughout society
   also facilitate any attempt by the party to steal elections through fraud.
2. mobilization of the population in support of the regime. Particularly in
   those systems where the scope of the ruling party is extensive, like the
   ruling communist parties, they can play important roles in mobilizing
   the populace into the activities of the regime, creating displays of unity
   and devotion that can help to create an aura of popular support and
   commitment. This may not only increase the sense of isolation among
   would-be opponents, but can also generate a sense of commitment
   and ownership among the populace to the regime and its goals. In
   this sense, mobilization can be both a positive regime-building force

---

[6] Geddes ("What Do We Know"), p. 131. Also see Brownlee (*Authoritarianism*), p. 30, where he argues that the particular institutions of authoritarian rule were more important in determining regime survival or fall than the presence or absence of elections. This underpins his point that elections are a symptom of regime change, not a cause. Benjamin Smith qualifies this by arguing that party leaders who had to face serious fiscal and political crises in the early stages of the party's life built parties that were organizationally robust and could provide both strong administrative leadership and contain elite conflict, while those leaders who did not face such challenges produced parties that were less powerful and came to rely on "continuing access to patronage rents." Smith ("Life of the Party"), pp. 421–51. Smith also suggests that the longevity of the Soviet and Mexican cases may so distort the analysis of the length of party regimes that Geddes' general finding may be questionable.

and a more negative, controlling force. One aspect of mobilization is recruitment of people into political life. By its nature, a party will usually seek to attract members, and given the access such a party can provide to political power and material resources, party membership is seen by many as an attractive proposition. But this can create a structural problem for the party: if there is too little rotation and promotion of cadres, ambitious cadres can become frustrated, but if there is too much movement, office holders can feel threatened.

3. control of the parliament. By gaining a dominant position within the parliament, the ruling party can prevent this body from being captured by opposition forces and from becoming a site of opposition activity.

4. maintenance of the unity and stability of a ruling elite. Through its access to state resources and its role in career advancement, the party is able to reward conformity and punish dissidence, thereby limiting the effect of individual ambition and conflict.[7] Even if individuals and groups do not get their way on particular issues, continued membership of the party can not only guarantee them continued involvement in the political game (and therefore the possibility that their view may prevail in the future), but ensures that they retain access to the benefits of power. While party membership continues to promise such benefits, it helps to curb the effects of elite dispute. Furthermore, the party can provide a means for the working out of such disputes that does not challenge regime stability. Through its own internal processes and procedures, the party can help to work out disputes in a way that does not call into question the formal structures of the regime by both separating the conflict from those regime structures and by providing gains for dissident factions/individuals even when they lose in the particular dispute at hand. It enables political bargains to be reached and individual ambitions accommodated.

5. management of elite succession. The party's ability to provide the mechanism for resolving elite problems, with its internal structure and processes providing a means for sorting out particular leadership disputes, means it is well placed to resolve questions of leadership succession. For example, who should stand in a presidential election can be resolved behind closed party doors, thereby obviating a messy public spat, and given its dominating position, the ruling party can usually ensure that its candidate wins in any election. Furthermore,

---

[7] Brownlee (*Authoritarianism*), p. 33. The whole book contains an argument about the role played by parties in resolving conflict and the consequences when this is not done. He cites the successful cases of Egypt and Malaysia, which had such a party, and the unsuccessful ones of Iran and the Philippines, which did not.

when incumbents of the top state posts are about to move on, they want to ensure that they are replaced by someone who will be loyal to them and what they believe (and will protect them in the future). Common party membership may be seen as an indicator of this. Furthermore, the control the ruling party exercises can act as a disincentive to elite splits by showing all sides in the party that they would be better off remaining united than they would if they split. Frustrated ambition may be best assuaged by remaining in the party if that is the most effective route to high office; the guarantee of regular potential access to high office can be a powerful incentive to unity.[8]

6. control of the state. The appointment of party members to leading positions at various levels of the state apparatus, added to high cohesion (or discipline) within the party, is a means for the party to exercise control over the state. There are a number of aspects of this. First, by becoming embedded in the state machine at a variety of levels, the party is better able to control the policy levers than if it exercised broad supervision only. Better control of the policy levers should mean greater ability to implement the policy it desires and, therefore, presumably better enable it to meet the expectations made of it. Greater control could therefore facilitate greater success. Second, greater control also implies increased capacity to use the coercive arms of the state to act against opposition, both potential and actual. Control of the state apparatus makes repression a much more realistic strategy on the part of the party for handling challengers. Third, control of the state gives control over resources that would not otherwise be available for the party. This enables it to carry out its patronage functions more effectively and to reward its supporters.

7. dispensing of patronage. It can do this through its control over economic resources (both through the state and independently) and over jobs. Once it has control over the state, the party's access to both resources and jobs is immense, and therefore it can act as a major dispenser of patronage within the system. Such patronage may be important for ensuring the running of the system, and has at times been seen as a potential substitute (at least in part) for coercive control.

These two strategies for controlling the state, reliance upon personal loyalty and organizational structures, reflect an essential tension in all

[8] Mexico is a good example of this. There the rule from 1933 about no reelection to the presidency (i.e., only one term) and the resultant (from 1963) six yearly turnover of that office meant the PRI had a regular opportunity to reward leading figures with the fruits of office. A similar opportunity existed at lower levels, where there was to be no reelection of governors and no immediate reelection for seats in federal and state legislatures.

political systems contained in the relationship between formal institutions and their incumbents. A system is highly institutionalized when the institutions of which it is constituted possess a high level of normative authority. The normative authority of an institution is high when the incumbents in that particular institution possess only limited room for action outside the rules and patterns of the institution. When people have to abide by the rules of the institution, and they do for most of the time, that institution has a high level of normative authority; people abide by the rules of the institution because it is the right thing to do, although fear of the consequences of acting otherwise may also be relevant. When incumbents of offices are little restrained by the rules of those offices, the institution has limited normative authority. Low levels of institutional normative authority go with higher levels of personalized power, and vice versa. Although we need to be wary of generalization, democratic regimes are usually more highly institutionalized, that is, their institutions possess higher levels of normative authority, than non-democratic regimes. A simple illustration of this is the binding nature of constitutions in democracies, cf. their more instrumental nature in authoritarian regimes. Because of the adoption of these two strategies in Russia, personalist and organizational, this tension has been strongly evident in the post-Soviet attempt to build an effective administrative structure.

## Regime development in Russia

While the collapse of the Soviet Union meant the demise of the ruling communist party and the removal from office of many of its chief officials, this did not mean the disappearance of most of the institutional structures of which the Soviet system consisted. Some of the main institutional structures – government ministries, legal hierarchy, security apparatus, military, and the regions – remained intact, even if given the breakup of the federation the jurisdiction of many of these bodies was greatly changed. Furthermore, given that there was no process of lustration undertaken in Russia, and therefore leading officials throughout these structures were not banned from continuing in office, in the administrative hierarchy there was significant continuity of personnel from the Soviet to the post-Soviet period. This meant that, despite the change in political circumstances, much of the organizational culture of the Soviet bureaucracy was carried forward into the post-Soviet era, a situation consistent with the political culture argument surveyed in Chapter 1. This organizational culture, meaning the patterns of action and the assumptions underlying them that characterized the Soviet bureaucracy, continued to structure administrative life after 1991. Although some of these patterns and assumptions may have taken on different forms in the post-Soviet period, their essential continuity with pre-1991 is clearly evident. A number of these have been important.

The first element of the Soviet organizational culture was the high level of centralization. The ethos of the party, and the whole Soviet system, was a centralizing one. Expressed in the formula "democratic centralism," this assumed that each level of the structure was strictly subordinate to those above it, and that the most important questions were resolved at the higher levels. The focus of this was the dominating role played throughout most of Soviet history by the Politburo. This small group of men (only three women were members of this body, E.A. Furtseva as a candidate in 1956–7 and then a full member between 1957 and 1961, A.P. Biriukova as a candidate in 1988–90, and G.V. Semenova 1990–91; E.A. Stasova served as a temporary member for three months in 1919[9]) dominated Soviet politics, and this was the institution where all of the most important decisions were taken. The main exception to this was during the Stalin period from the early 1930s, and especially during the war, when it was often bypassed by the leader and his immediate associates.[10] Nevertheless, this was the key decision-making body from its formation in 1919 until the late 1980s.

Within the Politburo the General Secretary[11] was the leading figure, generally being acknowledged as the leader of the party. While Stalin was clearly the dominant figure in the regime from the early 1930s, other general secretaries have enjoyed differing degrees of power and autonomy, but even the weakest (Konstantin Chernenko) was accepted as the leader. This combination of individual (General Secretary) and collective (Politburo) leadership generated strains within the Soviet political structure, but it nevertheless survived for some sixty years. A similar situation applied at regional levels where party first secretaries (sometimes called in the West "prefects"[12]) usually enjoyed the same sort of primacy in relation to their immediate colleagues as the General Secretary at the center.

---

[9]  John Lowenhardt, James R. Ozinga, and Erik van Ree, *The Rise and Fall of the Soviet Politburo* (New York: St. Martin's Press, 1992), pp. 128–9.

[10]  On this, see Lowenhardt, Ozinga and van Ree (*Rise*), p. 35. At other times important decisions also were taken outside the full Politburo but by Politburo members (e.g., the decision to invade Afghanistan in 1979; Roderic Braithwaite, *Afgantsy. The Russians in Afghanistan 1979–89* (London: Profile Books, 2011), Chapter 3.); but in general terms, this was the repository of supreme power.

[11]  Between 1953 and 1966 this position was called First Secretary.

[12]  Jerry F. Hough, *The Soviet Prefects. The Local Party Organs in Industrial Decision-Making* (Cambridge, [Mass.]: Harvard University Press, 1964).

The centralizing ethos was countered to some degree by another structural tension, between the principles of bureaucratic rationalism and those of patrimonialism (a manifestation of the organizational/personalist tension noted above). These are two alternative ways of managing a hierarchical structure. The former, bureaucratic rationalism, involves a structure operating on the basis of the formal rules designed to structure bureaucratic procedure. These involve predictability, following set procedures, and appointment and promotion on the basis of technical skills and competence, and reflect a high level of institutionalization or institutional normative authority. The latter, patrimonialism,[13] involves the structure being run on personalist lines, according to the instructions of the leader. At the extreme, the leader treats the structure as his own property and dispenses it to his supporters. The basis of appointment and promotion is loyalty and support of the leader. These are two ideal types, with structures in practice often combining elements of both bureaucratic rationalism and patrimonialism in their modus operandi.

The Soviet system was one in which bureaucratic rationalist principles appeared very strong. There were formal rules that purported to govern the functioning of the society's main structures, including the party, and a whole panoply of legislation designed to structure popular activity. However, the functioning of these principles was in practice undercut by the operation of patrimonial principles. Since the origins of the regime, the currency of power within the central institution (the party) was personal support. Leaders possessed chains of followers, tied to the leader by the prospect of material reward. Policy agreement could play a role here, but for many it was the prospect of promotion and material advancement that was central. Personal following could be aggregated at each level of the party, with the leader at each of those levels associated with leaders at higher levels, thereby creating chains of support stretching the length of the party. Popularly labeled "family groups" at lower levels and "factions" at higher levels (despite the formal prohibition on factions stemming from 1921), these personal support groups constituted

---

[13] The classic statement of both of these is Weber (*Economy and Society*). On patrimonialism, see Weber (*Economy and Society*), vol. II, Chapters 12 and 13. For some literature on patrimonialism, see Guenther Roth, "Personal Rulership, Patrimonialism, and Empire-Building in the New States," *World Politics* xx (2), 1968, pp. 194–206; Robin Theobald, "Patrimonialism," *World Politics* 34 (4), 1982, pp. 548–59; Linda Kirschke, "Semipresidentialism and the Perils of Power-Sharing in Neopatrimonial States," *Comparative Political Studies* 40 (11), 2007, pp. 1372–94; Anne Pitcher, Mary H. Moran, and Michael Johnston, "Rethinking Patrimonialism and Neopatrimonialism in Africa," *African Studies Review* 52 (1), 2009, pp. 125–56; and Karsten Bechle, "Neopatrimonialism in Latin America: Prospects and Promises of a Neglected Concept," GIGA Working Paper No. 153, November 2010.

pyramids of power based upon personal association.[14] Maintenance of these associations was of primary importance for figures at all levels of the party, and therefore they were often willing to subvert bureaucratic rational principles for the purpose of alliance maintenance. However, this did not mean that they could completely disregard the formal rules. When political conflict broke out, those who could be charged with breaching the rules were vulnerable. Accordingly leaders at all levels had to balance adherence to the formal rules with what was necessary to maintain the informal alliances and, in the case of lower level officials, the local autonomy from the center that was a feature of "family group" rule. This was one source of the spread throughout the Soviet system of what came to be called "informal practices."

Informal practices, sometimes also called an "economy of favors,"[15] thrived in all spheres of Soviet life and constituted major means for people to get on with their lives despite the formal rules. Often tasks could be achieved only by circumventing the rules and using informal channels; an oft-cited example is the way that, in order to meet their annual plan targets, factory managers often had to source supplies outside the plan through "fixers," who acquired what was needed illegally. Of course, informal procedures exist everywhere as a means of oiling the wheels of official structures, but in many areas of life in the USSR, such procedures were central to the actual functioning of the system as a whole. Officials at all levels were able to act with considerable autonomy as long as they produced the goods in the eyes of their superiors. The result was that although the party and other structures were in theory highly centralized and disciplined, in practice they could be quite articulated with the different levels exercising a lot of autonomy from higher level control.[16] It was this centrality of informal processes that led many to see the Soviet regime as thoroughly corrupt.

Corruption was clearly a problem in the USSR, and not solely in terms of practices that did not accord with the established rules. The use of office for personal gain occurred throughout the Soviet period, but it seems to have reached new heights during the Brezhnev years (1964–82),[17] a period during which many post-Soviet officials gained

[14] On the early stages of this, see Graeme Gill, *The Origins of the Stalinist Political System* (Cambridge: Cambridge University Press, 1990). There is a large literature on this phenomenon in Soviet politics.

[15] Alena V. Ledeneva, *Russia's Economy of Favours: Blat, Networking, and Informal Exchange* (Cambridge: Cambridge University Press, 1998).

[16] On this, see Gill (*Origins*) and Graeme Gill and Roderic Pitty, *Power in the Party. The Organization of Power and Central–Republican Relations in the CPSU* (Basingstoke: Macmillan, 1997).

[17] Gill and Pitty (*Power in the Party*), Chapter 3.

their start in bureaucratic life. Many officials were able to build up their personal wealth, with the leadership generally turning a blind eye.[18] By the end of the Soviet era, the perception that officials were corrupt and that official position was the road to wealth was widespread. This perception was strengthened by the way that the experience of many ordinary Soviet citizens was that, in their dealings with officials (and police were particularly notorious in this regard), their cause was aided immeasurably by payment of a bribe.

This combination of elements – the tension between centralism and local autonomy, between bureaucratic rationalism and patrimonialism, and the ubiquity of informal practices (including corruption) – were all prominent parts of the Soviet organizational culture. And they have all found echoes in the post-Soviet organizational culture and thereby in structuring the way political institutions work. But what was also crucial about the Soviet organizational culture was the central role of the party. As the primary integrating mechanism for the system as a whole, the party was crucial to the way these phenomena played out. Its absence after 1991 was no less central to the shaping of institutional development. As indicated in Chapter 3, Yeltsin generally eschewed the use of a party of power. Although some attempts were made to create such a party – initially in the form of Russia's Choice and then Our Home is Russia – Yeltsin had little to do with these, and they soon foundered. Rather than relying upon a dominant party as a mechanism to integrate the political structure, Yeltsin sought to rely upon a combination of personal charisma (see Chapter 5) and the development of certain state institutions as the means to project his authority and pull all parts of the structure together. But in relying upon the enhancement of the existing bureaucratic structure, Yeltsin was dependent upon structures emanating from the Soviet legacy that he publicly sought to reject.

As noted above, the formal institutions of state – executive, legislative, administrative, and judicial – were all inherited from the Soviet era, and until some of them were substantially renovated under the terms of the new 1993 Constitution, continued to function after the fall of the USSR. However, Yeltsin's intention from the outset was to mold a new system different from that of the Soviet to rule in Russia. In doing so, despite the democratic rhetoric and the inconsistency of many of his actions, he

[18] Although Andropov did launch an anti-corruption campaign in 1979–80. See Konstantin Simis, "Andropov's Anticorruption Campaign," *The Washington Quarterly* 6 (3), 1983, pp. 111–21. Also Luc Duhamel, *The KGB Campaign against Corruption in Moscow, 1982–1987* (Pittsburgh: University of Pittsburgh Press, 2010).

laid the foundations for the later elaboration of the authoritarian system under Putin.

Yeltsin's attention was split among many issues relating to the structure of the new state in the early 1990s, but none was as all-consuming or as politically dangerous as his desire to strengthen the institution of the presidency.[19] A new post grafted on to the parliamentary constitution of the RSFSR in 1991, the presidency was not initially the dominant institution in the system that its incumbent wished it to be. Accordingly in 1992–3, Yeltsin sought to expand the power of this institution. Two aspects were relevant, the administrative and the legislative. Politically, the development of the administrative side of the presidency was relatively unproblematic. This took the form of the creation, development, and strengthening of the Presidential Administration. This body, which was the personal organizational machine of the president and responsible only to him, was developed on the basis of the apparatus of the defunct Communist Party of the Soviet Union. It performed the basic housekeeping functions for the president, but it also developed a broad supervisory and watching brief over everything that happened in Russia. Its departments effectively shadowed the government, providing a separate pseudo-governmental apparatus in the hands of the president alone. It was the eyes and ears of the president, as well as a major source of advice; it was the source of much of the drafting of presidential decrees and decisions, and acted as the central channel of access to the president himself. This body was staffed by people appointed by and loyal to the president – indeed one, Valentin Yumashev, who headed the body from March 1997 until December 1998, married one of Yeltsin's daughters shortly after leaving office – and became one of the most powerful entities in Russian politics.[20] The size of this body continued to expand in the

---

[19] The desire to strengthen the presidency may have been one factor in Yeltsin's refusal to call for new elections in the aftermath of the August 1991 putsch. New parliamentary elections then would have strengthened the parliament by giving it a renewed mandate, and it may have strengthened the democrats (who would have been expected to do well following the putsch) and increased his reliance on them. For the argument that Yeltsin did not seek an early transformation of inherited Soviet institutions (which they argue could have been achieved through a new constitution ratified at the same time as an election) because he saw no need for such a change, had no clear plan of what to do, was temperamentally averse to such radical change, and gave a higher priority to economic than political reform, see Ostrow, Satarov, and Khakamada (*The Consolidation*), Chapter 2. For a discussion of what he calls "super-presidentialism" in post-communist states, see Fish (*Democracy Derailed*), Chapter 7. For a more general treatment of what he calls "semi-presidentialism, see Robert Elgie, *Semi-Presidentialism. Sub-types and Democratic Performance* (Oxford: Oxford University Press, 2011).

[20] On early aspects of the Presidential Administration, see Eugene Huskey, *Presidential Power* (Armonk: M.E. Sharpe, 1999) and Eugene Huskey, "The State-Legal Administration and the Politics of Redundancy," *Post-Soviet Affairs* 11 (2), 1995, pp. 115–43.

early 1990s, and by 1994 the permanent professional staff amounted to 2,180 with thousands of other auxiliary staff and its budgetary allocation exceeded that given to the parliament.[21] It also came to be an important stepping stone to the top job, with both Putin and Medvedev spending time within the Presidential Administration, Medvedev as its head (October 2003–November 2005). The head of the Presidential Administration was effectively the president's chief of staff.

Expansion of the power of the legislative side of the presidency was politically much more contentious because this brought Yeltsin into direct conflict with the parliament (the Congress of People's Deputies and the Supreme Soviet). It may be that by the beginning of 1992, this conflict (although not the way it was ended) was inevitable. By this time the pure lines of the parliamentary system had become blurred. The creation of the Russian presidency and the conception of it as an activist post (principally seen in terms of leading the struggle against the Gorbachev-led Soviet center) blurred the parliamentary principles inherited from the Soviet experience (although these had already been blurred by the creation of the Soviet presidency in 1990). This was strengthened by the granting to the president of (temporary) emergency powers to drive through reform in November 1991, and by the establishment that same month of a non-party "reform government" responsible primarily to the president. This process was given constitutional standing by the way in which, over time, amendments to the Constitution (which was the 1978 RSFSR Constitution) made both the president and the parliament the sovereign state power. In this sense there was a fundamental constitutional issue that needed to be resolved, yet neither side seemed willing to adopt the flexible sort of approach required. The parliament under its speaker Ruslan Khasbulatov from early 1992 adopted an adversarial approach to Yeltsin's exercise of presidential power and the policies with which he was associated, while Yeltsin made no attempt to build up a power base through consolidation of the support he had earlier enjoyed within the parliament. Fueled by a combination of policy differences (especially over economic policy), institutional ambitions, and personal aspirations (Yeltsin vs. Khasbulatov), the conflict between president and parliament dominated 1992–3 until September when Yeltsin closed the parliament (and suspended the Constitutional Court), used military force to disperse those deputies who had remained in the parliament building, and called parliamentary elections and a referendum on a new constitution for December.[22] However, as shown in Chapter 3,

---

[21] Huskey ("State-Legal Administration"), p. 116 fn. 5.
[22] On the course of this conflict, see Gill and Markwick (*Russia's*), pp. 140–66.

the results of the election and referendum were more ambiguous than Yeltsin had hoped they would be.

On the plus side for Yeltsin's drive to create a powerful presidency, the draft Constitution that had been drawn up in his office and that he had laid before the people, was formally ratified in the referendum, even if there were later suggestions that some of the results had actually been falsified to ensure its adoption.[23] Although the new Constitution imposed some limitations on the powers of the president (the parliament could impeach the president although this was a difficult process, his nominee as prime minister had to be ratified by the parliament, legislation including the budget required parliamentary assent, and his veto of laws could be overturned by a two-thirds majority in both houses of the parliament), it also made the presidency the most powerful institution in the Russian system. The president defined the "basic directions of the domestic and foreign policy of the state," could initiate legislation and issue decrees, edicts, and directives, which had the force of law,[24] appointed the prime minister ("with the consent of the State Duma") and government ministers (on the proposal of the prime minister), meaning the government was responsible to the president. He nominated candidates to head the Central Bank and to the Constitutional Court, the Supreme Court, the Supreme Arbitration Court, and the Procuracy, formed the Security Council, appointed his representatives in the Russian regions, diplomatic representatives, and the head of the armed forces. The president could introduce a state of emergency and suspend civil freedoms and veto legislation adopted by the State Duma. All of the so-called "power ministries" (those principally concerned with foreign affairs, defense, security, emergencies, and justice, reflecting his constitutional responsibility for security, defense, home, and foreign affairs) were directly subordinate to the president while others were subordinate to the government. He could also, under certain circumstances, dissolve the Duma while being relatively immune from impeachment because of the complexity of that process. However, the president did rely on the parliament for the passing of all legislation, including the budget, and this is where the outcome of the election was less successful in Yeltsin's eyes.

---

[23] To be adopted, the constitutional draft required the participation of at least 50 percent of registered voters and the approval of a majority of those who voted. Official figures declared a turnout of 54.8 percent and a positive vote of 58.4 percent, but it was later suggested that in fact only 46.1 percent of the electorate had actually participated. *Izvestiia*, May 4, 1994. Also *Nezavisimaia gazeta*, June 28 and July 19, 1994.

[24] Although they could be specifically rescinded by the parliament or annulled by the Constitutional Court.

As indicated in Chapter 3, the 1993 election returned a pro-Yeltsin minority to the State Duma while the opposition scored 43.3 percent of the vote. The strong opposition showing in the Duma election was repeated in 1995, so that for the length of Yeltsin's presidency he had to face a Duma within which those opposed to him constituted a considerable force. This lack of control over the parliament led Yeltsin to rely heavily upon his decree powers to get measures he supported introduced, and meant that on a number of occasions he narrowly escaped impeachment votes in the house. Thus, although the parliament was less powerful than the president, a hostile Duma could act as both a brake upon and an irritant to the president, as well as encouraging him to seek even greater centralization of power in the presidential apparatus.

Yeltsin's desire for a parliament that would not cause him any trouble seemed more successful with regard to the upper house, the Federation Council. Initially Yeltsin had wanted to turn the appointed Federation Council established in August 1993 into the upper house of the new federal parliament, but he could not gain support for this.[25] Instead it was decided that it should be popularly elected at the same time as the State Duma.[26] It was to consist of two representatives from each of the eighty-nine subjects of the federation, and in December 1993 was elected in open competition. Although the result was that there were a lot of independents in the new house, many members were leading local politicians, governors of the regions, and presidents of the republics. Although the Council did not take an anti-Yeltsin stance, and in fact assisted the president in a number of areas,[27] because of the local responsibilities of many of its members, it was difficult to get any real routine in the way the Council functioned. Following considerable debate, during which Yeltsin unsuccessfully sought to have regional leaders (most of whom he had appointed personally, see below) automatically become members of the Council, it was decided that the head of the regional legislature and the head of administration (governor) from each of the subjects of the federation would be members of the Council. Once this principle was established (although the means of its realization would be changed), it gave local elites a firm foothold in the central state apparatus, but while their tenure depended upon local electorates, their willingness to act as

---

[25] Sakwa (*Russian Politics*, 3rd edn.), p. 133.
[26] This was not contained in the Constitution, which declared only that the Federation Council would "be composed" of two representatives of each of the then eighty-nine regions of the Russian Federation.
[27] Sakwa (*Russian Politics*, 3rd edn.), p. 133. The Council did reject some of his nominees to the Constitutional Court in 1994.

agents of the center remained under question. The old tensions between central and local imperatives reasserted themselves. But there seemed to be little Yeltsin could do about this at this stage.

The uncertainty that seemed to surround the Federation Council was a reflection of that which characterized the whole federal relationship. Russia inherited from the USSR an ethno-federal system in which the leaders of the subjects of the union had been encouraged by Yeltsin in 1990–91 to adopt an expansive view of the powers and autonomy each of those subjects should enjoy. While this may have been an effective strategy when Yeltsin was trying to undermine Mikhail Gorbachev and the Soviet Union, it was counterproductive to any desire to create a centralized, or even workable, state. There was some formal regularization of relationships through the Federal Treaty signed in March 1992 (although Tatarstan and Chechnya refused to sign) and then the Constitution ratified in December 1993, but in practice many of the regions gave scant regard to Moscow's wishes and Yeltsin tended to deal with them generally on a bilateral basis. This was given an institutional form by the conclusion between February 1994 and June 1998 of forty-two power-sharing treaties between the leaders of forty-six regions and the center, but because the terms of each of these were different, they brought no consistency or coherence to federal relations, and they did not substantially increase central control. The absence of clear and agreed rules on federal relations meant that these were subject to continual negotiation and re-negotiation, and they were vulnerable to political exigencies; federal fiscal relations were at times subject to this.[28]

The inability of the center to project its control effectively over the regions,[29] and even to keep abreast of what was going on in those regions,[30] was despite Yeltsin's wide use of appointment to fill lower level executive positions. During 1991 Yeltsin appointed heads of administration, soon called governors, in all of the country's provinces (but not in the republics) as an interim measure until such posts could be filled by

[28] Daniel Treisman, "The Politics of Intergovernmental Transfers in Post-Soviet Russia," *British Journal of Political Science* 26 (3), 1996, pp. 299–335; Daniel Treisman, "Deciphering Russia's Federal Finance: Fiscal Appeasement in 1995 and 1996," *Europe-Asia Studies* 50 (5), 1998, pp. 893–906; Daniel Treisman, *After the Deluge: Regional Crises and Political Consolidation in Russia* (Ann Arbor: University of Michigan Press, 1999). For a contrary view, see Alastair McAuley, "The Determinants of Russian Federal–Regional Fiscal Relations: Equity or Political Influence," *Europe-Asia Studies* 49 (3), 1997, pp. 431–44. In the words of one observer, the governors bartered political loyalty for economic concessions. Mendras (*Russian Politics*), p. 127.

[29] This is reflected in the center's reliance on the FSB for keeping the governors under control. Brian D. Taylor, *State Building in Putin's Russia. Policing and Coercion after Communism* (Cambridge: Cambridge University Press, 2011), p. 126.

[30] Mendras (*Russian Politics*), p. 129.

election. However, Yeltsin also banned gubernatorial elections (except in republics) from October 1991 until 1993, when he allowed elections to take place, but when pro-Yeltsin candidates lost seven of the first eight elections, he restored the ban, until it was finally lifted in autumn 1996.[31] Such elections were not held in most regions until December 1996, although most of the republics had been allowed to elect their governors. In most cases, former oblast communist party leaders were appointed to these positions.[32] Reflecting concerns about the effectiveness of central control and monitoring, Yeltsin also instituted a new position in 1991, the presidential representative who was appointed to the regions to monitor the work of the regional administrations. The representative was charged with ensuring that local legislation was compatible with national laws and had the capacity to recommend the removal of local officials who were not acting satisfactorily. The representatives were meant to constitute a direct line of presidential power into the regions, but in practice they proved largely ineffective. They lacked any power base or independence from local authorities (without funding of their own they were reliant upon the local administrations whose work they were to supervise) with the result that many of them seemed to act more as the agents of the regions to the center than of the center in the regions. They were not an effective means for the projection of presidential power. Throughout the Yeltsin period, therefore, central control over the regions remained weak. With no replacement for the former CPSU that had been such an important integrative mechanism during Soviet times, the center was unable to establish close continuing control over officials in the regions. The high level of formal centralization beside the weak actual centralization evident in the Soviet organizational culture was thus also characteristic of the Yeltsin era.

In the immediate aftermath of the 1993 elections, Yeltsin also turned his attention to the coercive apparatus of the state, bringing these more directly under presidential control. Initially in late 1991, Yeltsin had sought to incorporate the newly formed Russian KGB, called the Inter-republican Security Service, into a new super ministry of Security and Internal Affairs, an attempt to incorporate all of the former Soviet and RSFSR police and security agencies into one body, but this was rebuffed in the Constitutional Court[33] leading to the recreation of separate ministries of Security and of Internal Affairs. Following the abolition of the

---

[31] He actually allowed elections in thirteen provinces in 1995, of which his candidates won ten. Hale (*Why Not Parties*), pp. 34–5.
[32] Sakwa (*Russian Politics*, 3rd edn.), p. 225.
[33] See the report in *Izvestiia*, January 15, 1992.

Ministry of Security (which was the lineal descendant of the KGB in internal matters) in December 1993 and its reorganization into the Federal Counter-Intelligence Service (FSK), it plus the Foreign Intelligence Service (SVR, a lineal descendant of the KGB), the Federal Border Service (FPS), and the Federal Agency for Government Communications and Information (FAPSI, which was to exercise oversight of the media) all came under direct presidential oversight.[34] In April 1995 the FSK was reorganized and became the Federal Security Service (FSB), in which form it was to become much more prominent. As well as these security agencies, and apart from the military that was under the direct command of people appointed by the president, there were two other military-style formations. The Ministry of Internal Affairs had a powerful military apparatus in its own right; indeed, it was this force that spearheaded the military actions in Chechnya beginning in December 1994. And there were forces specially tasked with guarding the political leadership, the chief of which in the mid 1990s was the Presidential Security Service (formally this had been part of the Federal Security Service FSO) headed by Yeltsin crony Aleksandr Korzhakov. Despite the apparent diversification of security agencies, the primacy of the president in their oversight, formally exercised through the Security Council,[35] gave the incumbent of that office potentially a powerful weapon. However, this could be wielded only by a strong president, and in the closing years of Yeltsin's rule the security apparatus seems to have operated with considerable autonomy from effective presidential oversight.

Yeltsin's attempt to build an integrated central political machine thus fell far short of the actual construction of such a structure. A number of factors contributed to this. One is that there was a basic ambivalence in Yeltsin himself. While at one level he clearly favored the concentration of power in his own hands and in those of his supporters, because this was seen as the best guarantee against a slippage back toward the Soviet past, he also believed that the hyper-centralization of the USSR had been an important factor in its collapse. This was fundamental to his support for "democracy," although this became less strong as the decade wore on and he came to believe that it was the weakening of "order" that

---

[34] The SVR as a result of a law of July 1992 and confirmed in another law of December 1995. Sakwa (*Russian Politics*, 1996, 2nd edn.), p. 72. Although this was formally shared with the parliament and the Prosecutor-General until the December 1995 law subordinated it only to the president.

[35] The Security Council had no autonomy from the president. From its reorganization in 1994, the membership comprised the heads of the security, law enforcement, and judicial agencies, while its administrative functions were performed by members of the Presidential Administration. For a succinct discussion of this, see Sakwa (*Russian Politics*, 2nd edn.), pp. 145–6 and Gill and Markwick (*Russia's*), pp. 133–5.

was in part responsible for the social and economic (not to mention political) difficulties of the late 1990s. This sort of ambivalence meant that he was never forcefully committed to the construction of a powerful, centralized apparatus. But also important was the effect of his health, which deteriorated sharply in the middle of the decade and remained problematic throughout. This meant that even if he had been firmly committed to the building of a powerful authoritarian structure, he would have been physically limited in his capacity to carry this out. Yeltsin's physical frailties were also important in preventing him from developing and projecting any real sense of effective personal authority (see Chapter 5).

But as well as these personal factors in Yeltsin's failure to develop an effective political machine was his unwillingness to use a party of power. As argued in Chapter 3, he made no attempt to use the successive potential parties of power to consolidate his position or project his authority. Instead of creating a party to carry out those tasks a ruling party should fulfill, outlined at the beginning of this chapter, Yeltsin chose to attempt to combine a reliance upon charismatic authority (which was soon found to be inadequate) with some institutional construction. But because he eschewed a party structure, he lacked the institutional means to integrate the diverse parts of the emergent Russian polity. The potential power inherent in the presidential office could not be realized, the parliament remained essentially subject to opposition control, the center possessed little real capacity for the projection of effective power over the regions, and despite the organizational division of the power ministries/security apparatus, these remained in effect largely autonomous. Despite personnel changes over the decade, the state machine continued to be characterized by the Soviet organizational culture dominated by central–local strains, tension between bureaucratic rational and patrimonial principles, and informalism. But it was like the Soviet organizational culture of the late 1980s rather than earlier in that there were significant limits to the operation of centralism compared with the other elements. Yeltsin had been unable both to exert and project his authority in such a way as to integrate principal actors throughout the system into a political machine focused on the presidency. The fear that many had during the 1990s that Russia might break up was vividly reflected in the continuing strength within the state machine of patrimonial principles and informal patterns of action. Like many aspects of the period of his rule, at the time Yeltsin stood down there was much that was unfinished; the machinery of the state structure remained loosely articulated and his personal authority was insufficient to compensate for this.

## The reengineering of the state

His successor, Vladimir Putin, most markedly through his construction of the so-called "power vertical," moved with alacrity to create a more centralized political machine that, by the end of his second presidential term in 2008, constituted a potent weapon for a Russian president to use to both consolidate and wield his power.

If by 1999 the presidency had seemed debilitated because of the relative infirmity of its incumbent, Putin's elevation to the post injected a new sense of energy and dynamism into it, and with this an impression of increasingly centralized power. The activist style Putin adopted (see next chapter), his willingness to act in response to perceived challenges, and his continuing high levels of public popularity portrayed the president as a powerful actor and someone who it was dangerous to oppose. Instead of someone who let things drift, Putin gave the impression of a man who wanted to lead and to be seen to be leading. Accordingly the presidency was propelled even more into the central institution of the system, and other actors were discouraged from opposing him. The appearance of a reinvigorated presidency was reinforced by the 2008 decision to increase the term of the president from four to six years, thereby further attenuating the mechanism of popular control rooted in the electoral process. This image of a reinvigorated presidency was buttressed by the reorganization of the Presidential Apparatus, including through the populating of it by people with personal associations with Putin (see next chapter).

The position of the president seemed to be changed in 2008 with the election to that post of Putin protégé Dmitry Medvedev and the subsequent appointment of Putin as prime minister. While constitutionally presidential powers were not affected by this arrangement, in practice the situation was unprecedented: the less powerful prime ministership was held by a person whose popularity and personal authority generally exceeded that of the president. The dynamics of this relationship will be discussed further in the following chapter, but in institutional terms the so-called "tandem" did not affect the fundamental strength of the presidency. The two incumbents were in general agreement on issues, and although there may at times have been differences of emphasis in what they said and did,[36] there were no major public disagreements; both were following the same broad policy program. Medvedev may have shadowed Putin in terms of public profile, but this was marginal, and the reemergence of Putin as president (and Medvedev as his prime minister) in 2012 confirms the continuing primacy of the presidency. However, it also

[36] See Gill (*Symbolism*), Chapter 3.

confirms the importance of the individual incumbent for the capacity of the post to realize its potential.

But presidential power has also been shown to be subject to limitation as a result of the structure of presidential and prime ministerial executive government, and this is reflected in the increasing isolation of the president. This seemed particularly evident during the early stages of Putin's return to the presidency in 2012, when he seemed both more withdrawn and more frustrated than he had been during his earlier terms. One key to this phenomenon is the relationship between the president and his ministers. Although he has the decisive role in appointing the prime minister and the ministers, and despite the often publicized meetings between the president and his ministers, most are not really responsible to him and do not work on a day-to-day basis with him. Ministers' interactions are mainly with the prime minister, who acts as an intermediary between ministers and president. If the president seeks to play an activist role, this structural relationship can act as a real constraint on presidential power. And given that the president has generally sought to have a weak prime minister (President Medvedev was the exception, but he had little effective say in this) in order to avoid potential political challenge from this person, the prime minister is then often unable to play this intermediary role in a satisfactory fashion. The better the relationship with his ministers that the prime minister has, the more likely he is to be a powerful figure. Therefore for the president, there is a real dilemma: a powerful prime minister is likely to be most effective in his relationship with the ministers and therefore potentially more of a challenge to presidential dominance, while a weak prime minister who might not appear as a potential threat to the president would be likely to be less effective in mediating between the president and ministers. What this means in practice is that the president is somewhat cut off from the policy sphere; witness how often the president makes an announcement and the substance of it remains unimplemented, and the president publicly criticizes this lack of fulfillment.

This problem of isolation also affects the elite as a whole. In any society where there is not freedom of the press and a vigorous civil society, there is a problem of information flow to the apex of the regime. Officials at all levels will tend to cover up mistakes, put a positive gloss on developments, and generally try to protect themselves by painting a positive picture of what is going on in their particular sphere. This means that there is not only an information flow problem, but also a problem of implementation; how can the ruling elite get officials at lower levels of the bureaucratic structure to do what they want them to do? The usual regime response to this dilemma is to generate another, parallel, institutional structure to watch over and act as an alternative disciplinary mechanism for use against lower level officials. In most authoritarian systems, this has been the political party, but in some, like Stalin's USSR, the security apparatus has performed this function. In contemporary Russia, the so-called ruling party United Russia does not perform this function (see below), and neither does the security apparatus. The elite therefore must try other means. The so-called Putin cult (see next chapter) may have been one attempt to create a figure who would command the sort of authority that is missing institutionally, but as the Soviet experience shows, even in a much more closed environment than contemporary Russia, the leader cult could not bring about this sort of official obedience in a sustained fashion.

The major alternative form in which regimes seek to establish such systematic lower level obedience, and thereby create one of the necessary conditions for effective institutional functioning, is through the bureaucratic structure itself. Central here is the application of the rules of the hierarchical structure to the incumbents of office, or the strengthening of the normative authority of the institutions. The problem in Russia is the aforenoted tension within the organizational culture between two sets of operating principles that are largely incompatible: the bureaucratic (or organizational or institutionalist) and the personalist. Bureaucratic principles assume that officials carry out their functions on the basis of the bureaucratic rules associated with their positions in particular and with the bureaucracy as a whole. Personalist principles assume that the bureaucratic rules are less important than the personal loyalties of officials to particular superiors. In the former case officials do things because the rules say that they should, in the latter because the boss says that they should. These contrasting principles are at work in all bureaucratic structures to some degree; even the highly rationalized bureaucracies of advanced liberal democracies can have their personalist elements. The problem is when the structure is not overwhelmingly dominated by one or the other principle. When both principles are strongly entrenched within the hierarchical structure and guide major parts of the activity of that hierarchy, these competing modus vivendi make it difficult for the exercise of effective leadership. The attempt to apply bureaucratic principles can be blunted by personalist-based protection of lower level officials by higher, while the appeal to personalist loyalty and reliance on personal authority may run into the barrier of adherence to bureaucratic rules. This is the situation that applies in Russia. The continuing strength of both personalist principles and bureaucratic rules means that it is difficult for the elite to combat the tendency of higher level instructions to simply get lost in the lower levels of the apparatus. This is a particular problem for a president who wants to exercise expansive powers and poses a significant dilemma for the development of the system. Any strengthening of bureaucratic principles at the expense of personalist ones would erode much of the basis upon which President Putin has sought to rule and would threaten to constrain his personal authority. But any expansion of the personalist principle would threaten to turn the structure even more into a patrimonial hierarchy and thereby rob it of the incentive to pursue the sort of development that the country needs. The more the structure rests on personal loyalty, the greater its reliance on individual reward, and therefore the higher the likelihood of substantial rent-seeking by officials. In the short term, therefore, the tension between these two operating principles acts as a significant constraint on the effective exercise of central power in Russia.

Putin seems to have been aware of this, so as well as reinvigorating the presidency, he moved to project central control throughout the federal state structure and to eliminate what was seen as excessive local autonomy on the part of regional leaders.[37] In May 2000 he created seven federal administrative districts (in January 2010 Medvedev increased this to eight), each headed by a presidential envoy. The districts shadowed the existing military districts, and of the initial seven envoys, five came from security or military backgrounds. The principal aim was to strengthen central, presidential, oversight of politics in the regions, especially the activities of the governors.[38] Initially perceived as being powerful instruments of central control, the importance of these figures declined with the measure following the September 2004 Beslan hostage crisis to change the way governors obtained office. Governors had been popularly elected, although there was some modification to this principle when in July 2000 the President was given the power to remove governors who had breached federal laws and (through the State Duma) dissolve regional assemblies. A change in the law on regional elections that came into effect in July 2003 mandated that 50 percent of each regional parliament had to be elected on the basis of PR, a change that weakened the governors' capacity to control those parliaments.[39] In December 2004 the Duma adopted

---

[37] For an argument that Putin brought about the strengthening of the so-called "para-constitutional" institutions (i.e., norms that did not formally violate the letter of the Constitution but undermined the spirit of constitutionalism), see Sakwa (*Crisis*), pp. 49–51. The institutions Sakwa identified were the federal districts established in 2000, Presidential Council for the Implementation of National Projects (2005), and the Public Chamber (2005). It is not clear that any of these have had any real political effect.

[38] For a summary of their powers and responsibilities, see Cameron Ross, "Federalism, and Defederalisation in Russia," Graeme Gill and James Young (eds), *Routledge Handbook on Russian Society and Politics* (London: Routledge, 2012), p. 145.

[39] Sakwa (*Putin*, 2nd edn.), p. 104.

legislation giving the president the power to nominate governors.[40] This nomination had to be approved by the regional assembly, but if the assembly twice blocked the presidential nomination, the president could dissolve the assembly and insert an acting head into the region. There was thus considerable incentive for the assembly to approve whomever the president nominated. In effect, this integrated the regional governors into the presidential "power vertical."[41] This was modified in 2009 whereby the majority party in the regional legislature proposed three candidates for the governorship, one of whom the president was to approve, or he could ask for three further nominations, with the presidential selection being approved by the regional parliament. By the time this measure was introduced, UR dominated most regional parliaments, but in 2012 in apparent response to the postelection protests, popular election of the governors was restored; although the center retained the right to filter out undesirable candidates, governors retained some capacity to manipulate the process to limit challenge, and provision was made for the cancellation of such elections in "multiethnic" regions.[42] Greater control was also extended over the region's income, thereby restricting the ability of governors to use regional resources independently.[43]

The reduction of the independent power of the governors was also brought about through a restructuring of the federal upper house, the Federation Council. In 1993 the Council, had been elected via national elections while from 1996–2000 the heads of the regional executive and legislative branches were granted ex officio membership. In 2000 this was

[40] This has been seen by some as part of a "constitutional coup" enacted by Putin in the wake of the Beslan siege. Sakwa (*Putin*, 2nd edn.), p. 141. On September 13, ten days after the siege ended, Putin announced seven measures: presidential appointment of governors, replacement of SMD by PR in elections to the Duma, establishment of the Public Chamber, creation of voluntary controls to maintain public order, establishment of a "crisis management system" to wage the war on terror, reestablishment of the ministry for regional and ethnic policy, and establishment of a special federal commission on the North Caucasus. All can be seen as designed to strengthen the power vertical.

[41] Marie Mendras argues that the governors accepted this change because it freed them from the unpredictability of elections and the two-term limit. Mendras (*Russian Politics*), pp. 134–5. However, instead they were now subjected to the whim of the president, although they may have viewed this as an improvement if they assumed they knew better how to satisfy him than a potentially fickle electorate.

[42] In such regions, the regional legislature could cancel such elections, and would choose three candidates from among whom the president would select the new governor. On the operation of so-called "presidential" and "municipal" filters, see J. Paul Goode, "The Revival of Russia's Gubernatorial Elections: Liberalization or Potemkin Reform?," *Russian Analytical Digest* 139, November 18, 2013, p. 9.

[43] Taylor (*State Building*), p. 147 and Hale (*Why Not Parties*), p. 201. The most important element of this was the introduction in 2000 of a new tax code that centralized control over taxation revenues and shifted the income from some taxes from the regions to the center.

changed so that the two branches each sent a delegate to the Federation Council, and this became a full-time position.[44] The effect of this was not only to deny the governors an automatic seat in the upper house, thereby denying them both a regular forum in which to meet and a channel into national elite politics,[45] but to undercut the autonomy of the upper house since many of the delegates chosen to represent the regions had little connection with those regions; one result was a major increase in the number of members of the Council coming from Moscow.[46] The Federation Council became little more than a rubber stamp for the president's policies. As a partial sop to the governors, they were given representation in a new advisory body, the State Council, established in 2000, but this gave them an opportunity to be heard but little else. The system was changed yet again in 2012 with the legislative representative in the Federation Council to be elected from among the deputies to the regional legislature while the other was to be chosen by the governor.

As well as these measures to bring the regional authorities into the presidential power vertical, under both Putin and Medvedev major efforts were made to bring about greater coordination and consistency between on the one hand the regional charters, republican constitutions, and laws, and on the other the federal Constitution and laws. This actually began in June 1999 with the adoption of a law on the principles for dividing power between the federal government and the regions,[47] which paved the way for gaining greater coherence and consistency, while by mid 2005 all the treaties between Moscow and the regions had lapsed. This "harmonization" of the laws effectively reduced the formal room for autonomous action on the part of regional leaders. There was also a shifting of responsibilities and powers from the regions to the center, with increased central control over policing and the legal infrastructure (prosecutors, ministries, and courts)[48] and a centralization of finances through the central budget.[49] By reducing the difference between the legal infrastructure of the regions and the center and by tightening fiscal controls, the autonomy of the regions was thereby reduced. This shift in power is reflected in the fact that during the 1990s the number of

[44] On the mode of selecting these delegates, see Ross (*Federalism and Defederalisation*), p. 146. From 2011, delegates were meant to be chosen from among people elected to regional representative bodies, so that at least they had some sort of popular mandate.

[45] It also denied them the legal immunity they enjoyed as governor if they chose to take up the seat in the Federation Council themselves and thereby give up their governorship.

[46] Rostislav Turovsky, "The Mechanism of Representation of Regional Interests at the Federal Level in Russia: Problems and Solutions," *Perspectives on European Politics and Society* 8 (1), 2007, p. 77.

[47] Sakwa (*Putin*, 2nd edn.), p. 190.       [48] Taylor (*State Building*), pp. 138–44.

[49] Ross (*Federalism and Defederalisation*), p. 148.

local/regional civil servants rose while those at the center fell, but in the 2000s this pattern was reversed.[50]

Presidential oversight of the security apparatus, which was subject to neither party nor parliamentary supervision, was also strengthened under Putin. A major reorganization of the security apparatus in 2003 resulted in the substantial strengthening of the FSB (headed by Putin friend Nikolai Patrushev), which now absorbed the Border Guard Troops and some of the assets and functions of FAPSI, which was abolished,[51] and a new National Counter-terrorism Committee headed by the chief of the FSB was established to coordinate all efforts in the counterterrorism field. The partial reconsolidation of the power ministries/security apparatus and the upgrading of the FSB's status and power occurred against the background of the entry of siloviki into leading positions throughout the structure noted in Chapter 5. The director of the FSB is directly responsible to the president. At the same time the power ministries were reformed and rationalized,[52] ostensibly to eliminate competition and overlap, and they remained directly under presidential oversight, with both government and parliament having little role to play in the exercise of civilian control. A step in civilian control over the military occurred with the appointment of the first civilian defense minister (long-time Putin friend Sergei Ivanov, although his background was in the security apparatus; the first civilian without such a background was Anatoly Serdiukov 2007–12) in 2001; the removal of professional military men from this post can be seen as a strengthening of presidential control over the armed services. In addition, the Security Council, which had lost some of its importance during Yeltsin's second term, was reenergized and its tasks widened as Putin used it as an instrument for consolidation of his rule. This consolidation of the security services and their concentration under the president, plus Putin's almost sixteen years in the security service in the 1970s to 1980s,[53] were widely seen to herald a strengthening of praetorian elements at the apex of the political structure (see next chapter).[54]

In the measures discussed above, Putin was largely building on foundations laid by Yeltsin to create a much more effective central hierarchy of power. He sought to further this through something Yeltsin made no

---

[50]  Mendras (*Russian Politics*), p. 136.

[51]  Bettina Renz, "The Russian Power Ministries and Security Services," Graeme Gill and James Young (eds), *Routledge Handbook on Russian Society and Politics* (London: Routledge, 2012), pp. 212–13. Also see Taylor (*State Building*), p. 38.

[52]  For a list of those subordinate to the president and to the government in 2010, see White (*Understanding*), p. 80.

[53]  He was also briefly head of the FSB from July 1998 until August 1999.

[54]  On the importance of the security services in preventing popular protest, see D'Anieri ("Explaining"), pp. 331–50.

meaningful attempt to achieve, the creation of a party of power, successively Unity and United Russia. The electoral success of these parties in 1999, 2003, 2007, and (less so) 2011 has been noted in Chapter 3, as has the very significant weaknesses in the performance of UR. But regardless of the deficiencies of UR as a ruling party (see below), it did have one very important institutional impact: it was the means for integrating the Duma into Putin's power vertical. By gaining substantive control of the chamber (including committee chairs[55]), UR converted the Duma from a critic of the president into his handmaiden. This was also facilitated by the smashing of the power of the oligarch Mikhail Khodorkovsky and the associated takeover of Yukos, because before this Yukos had been actively sponsoring deputies in the Duma to protect its interests.[56] The denial of the Duma's autonomy has meant that it has not been able to exercise any discernible limits on the president and his actions, nor has it been an effective vehicle for the measured consideration of issues. The key to this has been the gaining of electoral majorities in the Duma and the discipline of party members, a discipline promoted by the opportunities for material advantage party membership involved and by the operation of a measure beginning in 2008 that deprived deputies of their seats if they voted against or left the party under whose banner they had stood in the election.[57] The development of the Public Chamber (see Chapter 2) has further impinged on the power of the parliament.

Another aspect of the development of this system has been the role of law. Those arguing for the development of a democratic system usually support the notion of the rule of law with the state and government being subordinate to the law and the judicial structure being independent. The concept that became dominant in Russia beginning during perestroika and extending into the post-Soviet period – pravovoe gosudarstvo – is usually translated as "law-based state." However, this conception is not without its uncertainty: does it mean the rule of law or rule by the law? And Putin's comments on this matter have not cleared this up. The former implies the rulers' subordination to the law, the latter the rulers' use of the law to rule. The former rests on the assumption that there is a basis of law over and above and separate from the state (natural law) while the latter sees the state as the basic source of law and therefore to some degree autonomous from it. The Russian tradition, especially as exemplified in the Soviet period, took this latter position. The

---

[55] Chaisty ("Federal Assembly"), pp. 93–4.
[56] On Putin's economic policies being actively hindered by such opposition in the Duma, see Tompson ("Putin and the Oligarchs"), pp. 188–91.
[57] Chaisty ("Federal Assembly"), pp. 94–5.

performance of post-Soviet actors has been ambiguous. From the end of 1993 presidents have complied with all of the rulings of the Constitutional Court, yet throughout this period significant pressure has been placed on successive prosecutors,[58] and there have been frequent reports of so-called "telephone justice" whereby authorities give directions to judges about desirable verdicts.[59] The financial dependence of the courts on local authorities has also increased their vulnerability. There have also been cases of the authorities using the legal system to attack those they considered to be potential or real threats, with the attack on the oligarchs in the early 2000s (including most spectacularly the proceedings against Mikhail Khodorkovsky), the arrest and trial of 2011–12 protest leader Aleksei Navalny, and the imprisonment of the Pussy Riot participants in 2012[60] the most prominent cases of this. Reports of the use of tax police and health inspectors and of traffic authorities harassing firms and people are legion. Judicial autonomy was also called into question by the fact that members of the Court were nominated by the president and approved by the Federation Council. In addition, Medvedev introduced a change whereby the head of the Court would be no longer elected by his peers but nominated by the president and confirmed by the Federation Council. All of this suggests that, despite some signs of independence on the part of the legal system, it remains the case that there is little barrier to the authorities using that system for instrumental ends.

The position of the law has also been weakened by the continued strength of the Soviet legacy of reliance upon informal practices and patterns of action to lubricate the formal process and enable people to function effectively to achieve what they wanted.[61] The ubiquity of this reliance creates a whole pattern of activity that takes place alongside but also intertwining with the formal rules and institutions. Relying substantially on personal contacts, this enables people to get around legal blocks and provides a degree of flexibility in the system that a focus purely on formal rules and institutions obscures. But while reliance on informal

---

[58] Sakwa (*Russian Politics*, 3rd edn.), p. 74.

[59] On judicial corruption, see Sakwa (*Crisis*), pp. 328–32 and Taylor (*State Building*), pp. 161–75. On "telephone justice" see Alena Ledeneva, "Informality and Informal Politics," Graeme Gill and James Young (eds), *Routledge Handbook on Russian Politics and Society*, pp. 379–81.

[60] A punk rock band that attempted to give an anti-Putin performance in Moscow's Christ the Saviour Cathedral in January 2012. Two members of the group were sentenced to prison for two years.

[61] See the works by Alena V. Ledeneva, *How Russia Really Works. The Informal Practices That Shaped Post-Soviet Politics and Business* (Ithaca: Cornell University Press, 2006); *Can Russia Modernise? Sistema, Power Networks and Informal Governance* (Cambridge: Cambridge University Press, 2013); and on Soviet practice, Ledeneva (*Russia's*).

practices can assist in ensuring that rigid rules, regulations, and structures do not stand in the way of people doing what they want to do, and therefore assist the system to function and thereby survive, it also undermines those rules. If the rules are, in practice, of little relevance to people's day-to-day behavior because of the role of informal relations, their normative authority will erode and they will have little importance for the structuring of behavior.

The combination of presidential appointive powers plus the organizational and mobilizational capacities of United Russia seemed to vest in the president (or in Medvedev's case the president and the prime minister who headed United Russia) a powerful instrument for dominating both national and subnational politics. And with the subordination of the security services to the president, a powerful centralized state machine seemed to be in formation, and one that bore some resemblance to its Soviet predecessor. The strengthening of the center's institutional power under Putin marked a significant contrast with the situation as it had developed under Yeltsin, but it did not in itself create a disciplined and efficient hierarchy subject to the president's will. The power vertical remained an impressive structure on paper, but in reality it was far from a smoothly oiled machine. In part this was because of the underdeveloped nature of the institutional structure and processes of which this vertical consisted. It was relatively simple, for example, for Putin to establish the federal districts with their presidential envoys, but it was much more difficult to create a mechanism whereby they were able to articulate effectively and consistently with existing regional machines. Similarly the weaknesses of UR discussed below show that the impressive party structure was not matched by performance. With institutional linkages underdeveloped, substantial power remained in the officials and their personal relations. This was clear in the relations between center and regions.

In the regions (i.e., at the administrative levels below the national), clear echoes of Soviet patterns of rule have remained. Regional politics throughout Russia has remained dominated by the informal political machines of local leaders. Sometimes, and certainly initially, these were the same people who had been prominent during Soviet times, especially during the 1990s, but often (and increasingly as time passed) these were people who had not held such office prior to 1991. Regardless of their provenance, conditions encouraged such leaders to develop and rely upon their own personal political machines. The early 1990s collapse of parts of the mechanism of economic distribution and the potentially threatening political environment resulting from the continuing tension between Yeltsin and his opponents encouraged local leaders to turn to those they could trust in seeking to administer their regions.

This involved associations that were horizontal, with fellow clique members at that level, and vertical between patrons and clients. This type of behavior had the potentially very real advantages politically of providing protection, and administratively of getting things done, but this was at the expense of the development, operation, and normative authority of the official institutions. Long time leaders like Yury Luzhkov in Moscow, Mintimer Shaimiev in Tatarstan, and Murtaza Rakhimov in Bashkortostan successfully combined local political, administrative, business, and social elites into an effective political machine that was able to run their respective regions for over a decade, in the process utilizing the official institutions in a largely instrumental fashion. However, all three were ultimately removed by the president using his formal powers, reflecting the tension that existed between the official rules and the personalist, informal practices.

The reality of personalist control within a structure of formal institutions and rules meant that changes to those institutions alone were unlikely to have much effect on the autonomy of regional leaders. Certainly the center could use formal institutional powers to remove leaders, but the strength of personalist ties frustrated the acquisition of real normative authority and power by those institutions. Accordingly if the center wanted to tighten its control, it had to come to grips with the personalist networks. One possible response was to attempt to destroy them, but this would have been impossible and in any case would have been counter to the principles that prevailed at the center (see next chapter). The other response was to co-opt them, and this is what Yeltsin, and much more successfully Putin, sought to do.[62] All presidents have sought to fill regional posts with people who had historical, usually career, ties with them personally, or who came from outside the particular region and therefore were not only not part of the local political machine but also owed advancement to the president.[63] This sort of patrimonial reliance on personal loyalty in effect constituted a bargain: obedience and loyalty by the client in exchange for security and the prospect of advancement, material reward, and potentially greater capacity to carry out their official responsibilities (because of better support from above). But there was always an element of uncertainty in this bargain: would the client remain loyal or would s/he be vulnerable to potential gains associated with an alternative patron? Will the patron remain loyal, or will he seek

---

[62] For one argument along these lines, see Henry E. Hale, "Eurasian Polities as Hybrid Regimes: The Case of Putin's Russia," *Journal of Eurasian Studies* 1, 2010, pp. 34–5.
[63] On replacements in the regional security apparatus, see Taylor (*State Building*), pp. 134–8.

to create vacancies to promote other clients? Can the patron continue to satisfy the expectations of the client? This third problem was a real issue given the potentially competing expectations of different clients and the limits resulting from economic downturn on the capacity of the center to provide resources. Furthermore, as the president approached the end of his constitutional term, the lame duck effect could also come into play.[64] This means that the institutional tightening of control under Putin remains only as strong as the patrimonial ties that underpin it.

This reliance upon patrimonialism is reflected, in part, in the failure of UR to develop as an effective ruling party. Unlike Yeltsin, Putin had sought, through the creation first of Unity and then its submersion into United Russia, to create a party of power. However, it has not been able to establish itself as a ruling party in the Russian system because it has not performed the seven tasks outlined at the beginning of this chapter that a dominant party should fulfill if it is to contribute to the stabilization of authoritarian rule.

First, in terms of the mobilization of votes and control over the electoral process, UR has generally been much more successful than its predecessor parties of power: in 1993 Russia's Choice won 15.5 percent of the party list vote, in 1995 Our Home is Russia won 10.1 percent, and in 1999 Unity won 23.3 percent. In 2003, UR won 37.6 percent, in 2007 64.3 percent and in 2011 49.3 percent. The greater ability of UR than its predecessors to win votes in the legislative elections reflects in part the way in which the party's principal sponsor, President Vladimir Putin, took over some of the policy ground which under Yeltsin had been occupied by Communist and nationalist forces.[65] The effect of this in 2007 may have been boosted by the successful launch of Just Russia as a tame opposition party designed to take votes from the Communists,[66] a role it ceased to play in 2011, which contributed to UR's poorer performance, while the personal levels of support for Putin himself also helped to sustain UR, especially in 2007.[67]

[64] Hale ("Eurasian Polities"), p. 39. This did not apply to Putin in 2008, argues Hale, because Putin's level of popular support ensured that one of his clients would win, and he retained the power to punish defectors through his roles as prime minister and head of UR. Also see Henry E. Hale, "Democracy or Autocracy on the March? The Colored Revolutions as Normal Dynamics of Patronal Presidentialism," *Communist and Post-Communist Studies* 39 (3), 2006, pp. 305–29.

[65] In discussing Unity, Regina Smyth describes this as the party moving to the center on key issues and the lessening of the polarization within the party system. The same arguments apply to UR. Smyth ("Building State Capacity"), pp. 555–78.

[66] See the discussion in Luke March ("Managing"), pp. 511–17.

[67] For a discussion of the basis of support for Putin, see Timothy J. Colton and Henry E. Hale, "The Putin Vote: Presidential Electorates in a Hybrid Regime," *Slavic Review* 68 (3), 2009, pp. 473–503.

The party's greater ability to mobilize the votes was also a reflection of the more substantial nature of the party itself. It possessed a much larger membership than any of its predecessors and competitors, and its organizational structure was more widely distributed throughout the country, although as will be shown below, that structure had real deficiencies. The greater organizational and membership resources provided UR with much greater canvassing capacity spread over a wider area, and even between 2007 and 2011 when the single member districts had been abolished and therefore greater power transferred to central party leaders, the ability to get out the vote still relied upon the exercise of organizational and personal resources at the local level. Furthermore, the presence of UR representatives in all of the electoral districts gave greater scope for the party to benefit from the sorts of electoral fraud that could be, and were, committed at this level.

But crucial too in UR's ability to garner voter support was its access to the substantial resources of the state. With state officials prominent in its membership at all levels, the mobilization of state resources in the interests of the party was a relatively simple matter. Access to state funds both for financing election campaigns and holding out the promise of benefits in exchange for electoral support were important advantages enjoyed by UR, something dramatically increased in the early 2000s by the vast flow of funds into state coffers as a result of rising energy prices. But access to the state was also significant in other ways[68]: selective enforcement of the law to favor UR and hinder its rivals, favorable coverage in the state media and legal harassment of the independent media, harassment of opposition politicians, use of the law to close or hinder the activities of opposition bodies, disqualification of candidates and parties on legal grounds, and the sabotage of opposition campaigning were all activities that tilted the electoral arena to the advantage of UR and involved use of the state and its resources.[69]

Clearly vote-getting was a primary function of UR, and it achieved this through a combination of genuine support (for party and Putin) and electoral manipulation. While it was able to achieve massive electoral support, it could act as a form of democratic legitimator of the system. But it was precisely its limitations and perceived failures in this regard that were laid bare in December 2011 (see Chapter 3).

---

[68] For one discussion of this leading in to the 2007 election, see White ("Elections"), pp. 533–5, 541–6.

[69] For one attempt to evaluate the extent of this, see Myagkov et al. (*Forensics*). But see the comments in Karlin ("Measuring").

The second area of dominant party activity is mobilization of the populace, and UR has been little involved in this. Certainly it has developed a mass membership,[70] but there is little evidence of vigorous and continuing intra-party life involving that membership. Members are not closely involved in the life of the party and there is no sense of it as an organization in which its members have either a large stake or a significant commitment of time and effort, perhaps reflecting the party's absence of an ideology and therefore a values-based foundation upon which commitment could rest. Those attempts that have been made at mobilization of people in support of Putin have been carried out by auxiliary organizations mainly designed to attract the youth into political activities. The most important of these has been Nashi, which has concentrated on the organization of public demonstrations in support of Putin and the development of a youth movement committed to Putin. Another youth organization, Molodaia Gvardiia, is formally affiliated with UR, and most of its attention has been devoted to attracting young people to the party, but overall, UR has paid little attention to popular mobilization.

The third area of activity is parliamentary dominance. In a presidential system like that of Russia, some mechanism is needed to mediate the relationship between president and parliament. This role is usually played by a political party. Under Yeltsin, with a polarized politics in which the policies pursued by the president were vigorously opposed by a significant section of politically active society and where the party of power fell far short of a majority in the lower chamber, tension and conflict between president and parliament were a constant of political life. Although this did not again reach the 1993 levels when Yeltsin unleashed the military upon the parliament, tense and unstable relations existed between the two throughout the decade. In contrast, in the 2000s the relationship was much more cooperative, with the two arms of the state frequently acting in concert. While this has in part been a function of the disappearance of policy polarization, it has also reflected the stronger position gained by the party of power in the parliament. Before 2003 Unity lacked a majority on the floor of the chamber, but through agreement reached with the communists (although this was later overturned) on the division of committee chairmanships, Unity was able to establish a leadership position within the parliament.[71] In 2003, UR was able to gain a majority in the chamber despite polling less than 50 percent of the vote by attracting 77 independent deputies or deputies from other

[70]  In February 2011, UR was said to have 2,597 regional and 53,740 local branches, and 2,073,772 members. Roberts (*Putin's*), p. 71.
[71]  On this see Smyth ("Building State Capacity"), pp. 570–71.

parties to its ranks, thereby giving it a total of 300 seats. In 2007 and 2011 the party gained a majority without attracting deputies from elsewhere. This has meant that under Putin and Medvedev, the party of power has been much more effective in ushering presidential legislation through the Duma than had earlier been the case.[72] Coordination between the Kremlin and the UR parliamentary leadership[73] effectively meant that the State Duma was incorporated into the presidential power vertical without the need for constitutional change.

While this incorporation rested in part upon the policy-mediating role of UR, it also reflects the party's role in the Duma as a machine for rent extraction and patronage. With the State Duma a major arena within which economic interests sought advantage,[74] this has been a rich field for rent-seeking behavior; the move against Khodorkovsky in 2003 was in part a response to the fact that Khodorkovsky had the support of sufficient Duma deputies to block some of Putin's program.[75] Both individual deputies and parties, but especially the party enjoying a majority position, could use their power to support or block measures in exchange for side payments. The prospect of increased monetary benefits could act as a powerful incentive for deputies to join UR and to toe the party line.[76] This was reinforced by the access UR had to state resources, which enabled the party to deliver benefits to particular constituencies as well as individual deputies; this was a significant tool that UR could use to attract deputies from single member districts when that system of election existed, although it could clearly apply to deputies elected on party lists as well.

Fourth, turning to elite unity, according to one study,[77] UR "consigns elite conflict to intra-party disputes, supplies strong incentives for elite coordination, and generates mechanisms for sanctioning defectors." However, this statement needs qualification. It may be that the party can play this role with regard to keeping lower level members of the administrative structure in line and providing a structured environment

---

[72] On UR performing this role, see Thomas Remington, "Patronage and the Party of Power: President–Parliament Relations under Vladimir Putin," *Europe-Asia Studies* 60 (6), 2008, pp. 959–87.

[73] On this, see White (*Understanding*), p. 68.

[74] On this, see Paul Chaisty, *Legislative Politics and Economic Power in Russia* (Basingstoke: Palgrave Macmillan, 2006).

[75] Angus Roxburgh, *The Strongman. Vladimir Putin and the Struggle for Russia* (London: I.B. Tauris, 2012), p. 76.

[76] See Remington ("Patronage"), pp. 959–87.

[77] Regina Smyth, Anna Lowry, and Brandon Wilkening, "Engineering Victory: Institutional Reform, Informal Institutions, and the Formation of a Hegemonic Party Regime in the Russian Federation," *Post-Soviet Affairs* 23 (2), 2007, p. 123.

within which political bargains can be reached and ambitions accommodated, but its success at the highest level is more problematic. Certainly under Putin there has been little evident conflict within the ruling elite. Although there have been some instances of leading figures falling out with the president – for example, former prime minister Mikhail Kasyanov, former finance minister Alexei Kudrin, and former defense minister Anatoly Serdiukov – the party has not been involved in such intra-elite issues. In part this may reflect the fact that many of the members of the central elite have not been members of the party. Only three of the sixteen cabinet ministers who took office in 2008 were members of the party, while a fourth was said to be close to it.[78] More importantly, neither Putin nor Medvedev were members (a 2004 law had declared that the president could not be a member of a party), even though Putin agreed to be its leader in 2008, although he did so without actually becoming a party member.[79] What this means is that the central part of the political elite has not belonged to UR, and therefore the party's capacity to maintain elite unity is limited. This is linked to the next point.

Fifth, while some have argued that UR can be a means for resolving succession questions,[80] in fact no party of power has been instrumental in determining who would become the next president. These decisions in each case – Yeltsin–Putin, Putin–Medvedev, and Medvedev–Putin – were made within the presidential (although in the last case, prime ministerial as well) circle, not the party. The party's role was restricted to acclaiming the choice and seeking to organize electoral support for the candidate. Even in the election, the candidate has not presented himself as the representative of the party or sought to run under the party's banner. UR has clearly not been a ruling party in that it has not controlled access to the leading position at the top of the political hierarchy.

The sixth arena of dominant party activity is control over the state. One of the most commonly noted characteristics of the membership of UR is the large number of state officials. Officials at all levels of the political structure joined UR, although it is striking that when Medvedev announced his "cadre reserve" in 2009, membership of UR does not seem to have been a consideration.[81] One of the most important groups

---

[78] Eugene Huskey, "Elite Recruitment and State–Society Relations in Technocratic-Authoritarian Regimes: The Russian Case," *Communist and Post-Communist Studies* 43 (4), 2010, p. 367. For only three members of Fradkov's cabinet (March 2004–September 2007) joining UR, see Gel'man ("Feckless"), p. 551.

[79] Party statutes had to be changed to make it possible for the party leader not to be a member. Roberts (*Putin's*), p. 120.

[80] Smyth, Lowry, and Wilkening ("Engineering"), 131.

[81] Only two of the initial one hundred were high profile UR members. On this and the general point, see Roberts (*Putin's*), p. 173.

of officials is the regional governors. Because of the political control and the control over state resources exercised by the governors at the regional level, they were significant political actors in their own right. Not only were they central to the successful implementation of policy, but through the political machines that they headed, they exercised major influence over elections in their regions.[82] During the Yeltsin period, many of these regional authorities acted independently and rejected central authority. As indicated above, Putin introduced a number of measures to rein them in, including the creation of presidential envoys to oversee their activity, reform of the upper house to remove their automatic membership, and most importantly presidential appointment to fill these posts. These measures, particularly the last, created a significant incentive for governors to toe the line, but this was something of a blunt tool. Attraction of them into a party of power would open up more opportunities for the center to influence the governors without creating the major political issue that removal could become. Involvement in such a party could create a positive incentive for gubernatorial cooperation, in the form of access to the resources that the party had at its disposal,[83] and balance the negative incentive posed by the threat of removal. The provision from 2009 that the dominant party in the regional legislature had the right to nominate candidates for governor from among whom the president would choose constituted another incentive for governors to join UR. The party's leadership actively encouraged gubernatorial membership; in November 2004 thirty-five governors were members, but by November 2008 only six of Russia's eighty-three governors were not members of UR.[84] Newly appointed governors increasingly came from within UR ranks: 38 percent in 2005, 75 percent in 2006, 85 percent in 2007, 86 percent in 2009, and 89 percent in 2010.[85] UR also won a dominant place in the regional (and many of the local) legislatures; between 2008 and 2011, UR consistently won over 80 percent of single

[82] For a discussion of these political machines and the role they played, see Hale (*Why Not Parties*). For reference to "parties of administration," see Kimitaka Matsuzato, "Elites and the Party System of Zakarpattya *Oblast'*: Relations among Levels of Party Systems in Ukraine," *Europe-Asia Studies* 54 (8), 2002, pp. 1267–99.
[83] For an argument suggesting that such access to resources was a significant factor in the timing of decisions by governors to join UR, see O.J. Reuter, "The Politics of Dominant Party Formation: United Russia and Russia's Governors," *Europe-Asia Studies* 62 (2), 2010, pp. 293–327; and Ora John Reuter and Thomas F. Remington, "Dominant Party Regimes and the Commitment Problem. The Case of United Russia," *Comparative Political Studies* 42 (4), 2009, pp. 501–26.
[84] Reuter ("The Politics"), p. 300.
[85] Some of these figures are rounded up. Ora John Reuter, "United Russia and the 2011 Elections," *Russian Analytical Digest* 102, September 26, 2011, p. 6.

member races in the regions,[86] and in 2010 the party held a majority of seats in all subjects of the federation except St. Petersburg (where it held twenty-three of fifty seats); in sixty-two of those subjects, it held a super majority.[87]

However, it is not clear what the party membership of state officials actually means. Most officials, initially including most of the governors, joined UR after they had obtained their substantive bureaucratic positions, and in the construction of the party in the regions, the party's reliance on the governors cast them as the more important regional actors and the party as secondary.[88] Joining the party was seen as something one ought to do, presumably for career reasons, and although this may have involved an assumption that party membership would aid future promotion, acquisition of their current offices was generally independent of any party effect. This may, of course, simply reflect the early stages of the party's existence, when official incumbents gained their positions prior to the party being an important factor, and therefore in the future the party could be a more significant influence in appointments. The figures above suggest that this may have been happening, but the effect of it upon party control over the administrative structure may be ameliorated by the effects of gubernatorial turnover. The replacement of governors with roots in their regions by people parachuted in by presidential appointment often meant that the newcomers found themselves in a position where they lacked control over the local political machine. This reduced capacity for control may be reflected in the party's performance in the 2011 election noted above and the inability of regional officials to deliver their regions electorally in the way they had in the past, and in the dispatch of government ministers into some regions to head the party's electoral list.[89] Furthermore, although local officials may formally have been party members, there is little evidence that they were actively involved in party life or made much of their party membership in the course of their official activities.[90]

---

[86] Reuter ("United Russia"), p. 3.

[87] Darrell Slider, "Regional Governance," Graeme Gill and James Young (eds), *Routledge Handbook of Russian Politics and Society*, pp. 157–9.

[88] For an argument that the unity of regional elites in UR is quite superficial, see Slider ("How United"), pp. 257–75. Furthermore, in the 2003 election, many UR members did not use the party label when campaigning. Hale (*Why Not Parties*), p. 136.

[89] Sergei Shoigu to Krasnoyarsk, Igor Shuvalev to Primor'e, Aleksandr Zhukov to Kaliningrad, Viktor Zubkov to Volgograd, Dmitry Kozak to St. Petersburg, Igor Trutnev to Perm, and Igor Sechin to Stavropol. Reuter ("United Russia"), p. 4.

[90] For the case of Khabarovsk krai where the governor actually undermined the official (and UR) policy of monetizing welfare benefits despite his party membership, see Aburamoto Mari, "Who Takes Care of the Residents? United Russia and the Regions Facing the Monetization of L'goty," *Acta Slavica Japonica* 28, 2010, pp. 101–15.

The final sphere of dominant party activity is that of patronage, and here there is more evidence of a party role. One type of patronage has been for the party to provide a path to electoral office. Since the 2007 election when the only path into the State Duma was through a party list and given that UR has possessed a majority of seats in the Duma, the principal route into the assembly has been through UR. Given the dominance UR has had in regional legislatures, this also applied in the regions. The ability of UR to both create legislative majorities and to maintain them may reflect in part the commitment of deputies to the policies propounded by Putin/the party,[91] but it also stems from the party's role in the Duma as a machine for rent extraction and patronage. Of commitment based on ideational or patronage concerns, the latter seems to have been more salient for UR members. But the party has been less successful as a patronage dispenser outside the legislative chamber, where patronage has generally flowed through state rather than party channels, and where there has been greater reliance on personal networks than party office. If the center has sought to direct funds or resources to particular parts of the country, this has been done more through the presidential apparatus, through things like budgetary allocations, and through the chains linking governors to the center than through the party.

In sum, UR has not performed all the tasks that dominant parties perform when they contribute to the stabilization of electoral authoritarian regimes. This reflects the nature of the system within which it operates. The type of political system in Putin's Russia has been a matter of some debate. Scholars focusing on society more broadly have been inclined to opt for a notion like "managed pluralism,"[92] a concept that seemed to find echoes within Russian officialdom in the notion of "sovereign democracy."[93] Others who have sought to focus on the party system have referred to it as a "dominant party system"[94] or UR as a "ruling party."[95] In her discussion of regime types, Barbara Geddes talks about a single party regime,[96] but her description of the role the party plays also applies to regimes in which one party is dominant although other parties

---

[91] For a general argument about the importance of ideology for a party, see Stephen E. Hanson, *Post-Imperial Democracies. Ideology and Party Formation in Third Republic France, Weimar Germany, and Post-Soviet Russia* (Cambridge: Cambridge University Press, 2010).

[92] Harley Balzer, "Managed Pluralism: Vladimir Putin's Emerging Regime," *Post-Soviet Affairs* 19 (3), 2003, pp. 189–227.

[93] For example, see *Suverennaia demokratiia: ot idei – k doctrine* (Moscow: Evropa, 2006).

[94] Gel'man ("Feckless").

[95] Levitsky and Way (*Competitive Authoritarianism*), p. 197.

[96] Geddes (*Paradigms*), p. 52.

may also be present.[97] She argues that in real as opposed to nominal single party regimes, "a party organization exercises some power over the leader at least part of the time, controls the selection of officials, organizes the distribution of benefits to supporters, and mobilizes citizens to vote and show support for party leaders in other ways." Although this is a more limited view of the tasks of a dominant party than sketched above, the two are consistent, and it is clear that under both UR has not acted as a dominant party. The chief deficiency in UR's performance relates to the first two tasks Geddes identifies, and crucially these are the two most important in defining the nature of the party.

From the outset, UR has been what one scholar has called an "appendage to power,"[98] an institution subordinate to another and, while at times it may be able to act autonomously, remains largely instrumental to the supreme power wielder. In Russia since 2000, that power wielder has been Vladimir Putin. There have been no instances when UR has been able to exert any decisive influence over president/prime minister Putin. In no election campaign in which Putin has competed has UR been a dominant element in the message he has projected; he has sought to project an intensely personal appeal, relying upon his image of integrity, strength, and personal commitment to appeal to the voters. It was his competence in the job rather than membership of any party that was the central plank of his election platforms, with the result that there was no room in this for UR. Indeed, Putin never became a member of UR, even though in 2008 he formally took over its leadership. While Putin did attend UR congresses, this was to deliver keynote addresses rather than to either listen to debate or seek guidance from party members. UR has not intervened decisively in policy discussions, nor has it been a significant actor in determining the identity of office holders.

While United Russia seemed organizationally to dominate the Russian political scene, it was a party that lacked both a strong internal structure and a clear ideological orientation. It was, both accurately and widely, seen as the establishment party, or the "party of bureaucrats" (chinovniki). It was the party that ambitious office holders joined as a means of promoting their careers; and while it may be that as time passes this order will reverse, it is striking that so many members attained high office before joining the party, so that rather than being the means to power, it was almost an additional quality of possessing that office. Moreover, the party that these local and bureaucratic elites joined did not have a highly developed internal structure. There were no powerful

---

[97]   This is reflected in the fact that she uses the PRI in Mexico as an example.
[98]   Roberts (*Putin's*), p. 33.

central organs, although the congresses the party held were reminiscent of those of its Soviet predecessor: long reports of impressive achievements greeted by enthusiastic and overwhelming support, and in 2007 and 2011 the reception and effective anointing of Putin in the same way that Soviet general secretaries had been treated. Nor was there a developed network of local organs linked together by a powerful machine. Even in the Duma the party could rely on the law to keep its deputies loyal and therefore did not need a strong party organization in the chamber,[99] although in practice it did develop an effective parliamentary organization. It remained largely a network of local and bureaucratic elites tied together in a loose structure headed by Putin, who seems to have devoted little of his time to the party. In this sense, rather than it being a ruling party, it was the party of rulers. Furthermore, this party of elites was tied together by the commonality of office-holding and the access to state resources that the party enjoyed rather than a shared commitment to a vigorous ideology. The party had no clearly defined program or set of policies, except for supporting the current president and his policies.[100] There was no clear organizational mechanism for working out party positions and no vehicle (such as a party newspaper or radio or television outlet) for propagating any policies developed. The party did not present itself in independent programmatic terms, and because it seemed not to stand for anything, it appeared as the placeholders' party par excellence.

This is consistent with Smith's argument about the relationship between the presence or absence of early struggle and a powerful party structure.[101] From the outset the party of power was created to fulfill limited tactical purposes: to marginalize the opposition electorally and to dominate in the parliamentary chamber. It was always seen instrumentally and never had to face the sort of existential threat identified by Smith. Furthermore, there was little subsequent attempt to develop the party institutionally or to give it a coherent organizational presence and structure. As a result, Russia has really had a hybrid personalist/party regime, a regime in which the primary dynamic has been the will of the leader rather than any institutional imperative. This does not mean that Putin has been a dictator and able to get his way on all things. He has had to act in a system in which a diverse array of forces can exercise political influence. Other political parties are not merely instruments of

---

[99] Beginning with the Fifth Duma in 2008, deputies had to vote with the party that sponsored them in the election, or at least not leave the party, or lose their seat. The ostensible aim of this amendment was to prevent the wholesale swapping of affiliation of deputies once the election was over and they had taken up their seats.

[100] This was publicly confirmed in *Izvestiia*, November 8, 2013.

[101] Smith ("Life of the Party").

Putin and his circle even if they have generally restricted their oppositional activity, despite restrictions there are autonomous groups within
society that seek to shape the political debate even if this is within limited
(and ill-defined) bounds, the media are not all subject to government
control, major economic interests can find room for maneuver and for
autonomous activity, and the bureaucracy is not monolithic but divided
in a number of ways – factions, "clans," political allegiances, and institutional loyalties are some of the fault lines that have been identified. In
addition, constitutional provisions may have developed some normative
authority (witness the refusal to change the Constitution to allow for a
third successive term), even if means have been found to circumvent
such normative restriction,[102] while the federal system too has provided
a limitation on central power. But even given this differentiated political
environment and the limited pluralism that characterizes it, it is clear
that the dominant political force has been Putin. This has had direct
implications for UR.

Putin's personal dominance, and the fact that it has not been wielded
through UR, not only sidelined the party, but did so in a very public way. The circumstances of the announcement of his swapping jobs
with Medvedev to return to the presidency was a clear illustration of this.
Because Putin has relied on the party only for the management of legislative elections and of business in the Duma, those other tasks undertaken
by a dominant party have not been well developed. The party has thus
not only appeared to be a second-order body, but has been so in reality
as well. Its inability to project an image of itself as anything other than a
tool of the leader thus stems in part from the limited functions it has been
able to perform and has been instrumental in the decline in the party's
image. But this sort of relationship between dominant leader and party is
not inevitable. There have been cases where leaders whose authority was
essentially personal have worked with parties that, although under their
control, neither acted nor were always seen as pure appendages of the
leader; Lee Kuan Yew and the PAP in Singapore and Mahathir Mohamad
and UMNO in Malaysia are good instances of this. In these cases the
party performed most of the tasks outlined above, even if its involvement
in elite affairs may have at times been more limited. In Russia, this may
be able to be achieved with little diminution of Putin's personal authority,
should he allow the party to expand and consolidate its functions and
decide to work through its channels. However, by opening the door to the
expansion of the party's institutional authority, this could also lead to the

---

[102] For an extended discussion of this in terms of what he calls the "dual state," see Sakwa
(*Crisis*).

ultimate displacement of personalism as the prevailing principle of political rule. This may be seen as a danger for Putin (especially if he seeks another presidential term in 2018), but only by gaining a degree of institutional autonomy, and thereby the capacity to perform all the tasks of a dominant party, can UR become the focus of a stable, party-oriented electoral authoritarian system. This would be a more secure basis for long-term stability than a continued reliance upon the personal authority of the president. However, such a course would require the agreement, or at least acquiescence, of the president for it to take place. This means that, as with so much else in Russia, the institutional development of the country depends significantly upon the predilections of the president.

The continuing strength of the patrimonial element has meant that informal practices and corruption have remained endemic to the functioning of the system. The proliferation of personal networks, or mechanisms for circumventing formal rules and procedures, and the reliance on personal contacts rather than impersonal structures erode the institutional integrity of the state. As people at all levels, and particularly the top, rely on informal mechanisms for getting things done, the primacy of the personal over the formal institutional is strengthened, and the shift of the regime in a personalist direction becomes more pronounced. This is associated with a strengthening of the tendency for the state apparatus to see itself more as a servant of the rulers and designed to further their interests than it is to serve the needs of the populace. This is a direct result of the strength of patrimonialism in the state structure and reflects both the continuing strength of the Soviet legacy and the effect of the two strategies employed by Russian leaders to engage in state-building, the reliance on personal connections and on organizational forms.

But although this tension has continued to bedevil the Russian regime, the institutional machinery of the state became much more effective and integrated as a result of the Putin regime's state-building activities than it had been under Yeltsin. This was because of the organizational measures introduced since Putin's election to the presidency: a general tightening of controls in the state structure and the development of an integrative political party which, for all its weaknesses, has been more effective than anything developed under Yeltsin. But also important has been the greater capacity of Putin to project his personal authority throughout the state and country at large. And this is linked to developments within the sphere of elite relations.

# 5 Elite stabilization

Central to the consolidation of an authoritarian political system is the creation of mechanisms to ensure that the political elite is not disrupted by developments within that elite itself. Of course no amount of institutional engineering or the judicious selection of personnel can guarantee against the clash of personal ambition among individual members of the elite and the potential destabilizing effects that this can have. Personal relations within the cabinet, politburo, junta, or court are subject to the vagaries of personality and the opportunities created by the course of events, neither of which is wholly under the control of the leading figure or figures in the elite. Nevertheless, leaders have generally tried to minimize the possibility of intra-elite disruption and the focus of this chapter is how successive Russian presidents have gone about this. Following a discussion of the nature of factionalism, the chapter analyzes the changing dynamics of elite relations, including the place of economic elites, and the development of the profile of the leader himself and the way these have been shaped under successive presidents.

The main focus is the central political elite. At the top of the elite is the president, whose constitutional and actual powers make him the pivot around whom the rest of the political elite turns. Although exercising influence over him is not the only means whereby power is manifested – other members of the elite have some independent decision-making power and the capacity to block is widespread – this is one of the principal dimensions of power within the elite. Below the president are the leading officials in the main bureaucratic structures of the state: government, government ministries, leading bodies like the Security Council, upper levels of the armed forces and security apparatus, the Presidential Administration, and the advisers of leading political figures. Not all of these people are of equal standing, for example, leading officials in the Presidential Administration are more powerful than most ministers and there is a hierarchy among government ministers, and the position of individuals can change over time. Power within this group is structured along two essential axes: personal relations and institutional position.

These are, of course, not completely separate; the position one occupies may be a function of one's relationship with a powerful figure (most importantly but not exclusively the president), and it is for most members of the elite a combination of these that explains their influence. But it is an important characteristic of this elite that the institutional position it is in is a bureaucratic one. Of the members of this elite, only the president is popularly elected; the remainder are appointed to their positions. This means that the elite is overwhelmingly a bureaucratic elite. Public politicians, party leaders, leaders of the parliament, regionally based officials, and (with some exceptions) leading figures in the private economic sector are not members of this central political elite.

Political elites in all systems are subject to factionalization and internal groupings as people cohere around different common elements to form a group that seeks to some degree to realize its own interests. Such bodies have been conceptualized in a variety of ways; for example, they have been referred to in Russia in terms of "clans" and cliques,[1] factions,[2] networks,[3] and informal relations.[4] These terms have been used, indiscriminately, to refer to a range of different types of groupings of people seemingly united on the basis of one or more of:

- common policy positions, for example, heavy industrialists, energy sector;
- common institutional locations, for example, those working in the finance ministry or the defense ministry;
- shared career experience, for example, the siloviki[5];
- common geographical origins, for example, regional family groups, the Pitertsy[6];
- personal acquaintance, for example, the "family"[7];
- common support for a particular leader.

These bases of association[8] are not mutually exclusive, but operate in cross-cutting and complex ways; for example, support for a particular

---

[1] For example, Thomas Graham, "Novyi russkii rezhim," *Nezavisimaia gazeta*, November 23, 1995; Alexander Lukin, "Putin's Regime: Restoration or Revolution?," *Problems of Post-Communism* 48 (4), 2001, pp. 38–48; and Wedel (*Collision*).
[2] For example, Sakwa (*Crisis*). See pp. 103–13 for an extended discussion.
[3] For example, Andrew D. Buck, "Elite Networks and World Views during the Yel'tsin Years," *Europe-Asia Studies* 59 (4), 2007, pp. 643–61.
[4] For example, Ledeneva (*How Russia Really Works*).
[5] People who had career experience in the coercive apparatus of the state.
[6] People coming from St. Petersburg.
[7] A term used for those who were particularly close to Yeltsin in the second half of the decade.
[8] For a stimulating study that seeks to look at the culture of elite politics, see Ledeneva (*Can Russia Modernise*).

leader (such as Putin) could unite people across policy, institutional, and geographical positions, with the result that the actual basis of unity may be different for different members of the pro-Putin faction. To add to the uncertainty, such factions usually do not meet as corporate entities, issue collective statements, or even act in a coordinated fashion. Nevertheless, such factions exist and, sometimes just as importantly, are believed to exist by members of the broad elite. Observers of the Russian scene often use these sorts of conceptions loosely to construct explanations of Russian politics. However, there is little agreement about the names of the factions or their precise contours, usually little identification of the members of a faction, and no analysis of how these work or seek to exercise influence. "Explanations" often amount to little more than the assertion that particular policies are a function of the dominance of particular groups, with the logic here being that such a policy would be supported by such a group, for example, the more assertive foreign policy that followed Putin's election as president in 2000 reflects the dominance of the siloviki and their security concerns. Reflecting the way Soviet politics was often conceptualized in the West – a Kremlin-focused battle between different factions – Russian politics has been seen largely in terms of continuing factional conflict, but without a solid grounding in the empirical details of factional structures in the Kremlin. Of course, such details are very difficult to obtain, but this does not justify the excessively general nature of many explanations that have been offered. This chapter does not seek to identify precise factions but to explain the basic nature of the informal structuring of elite political life.

The context within which such factions exist at the summit of the political system comprises a combination of formal structures and rules and informal norms and practices. The former were embodied most importantly in the Constitution and the mass of legislation and of administrative regulations that governed the way leading political institutions were meant to function, the latter in the patterns of action and behavior that emanated from the conduct of politics at the highest level. The central focus of all of this was the presidency. As the leading institution in the political system, with the power to set the tone of politics as a whole, this was the key prize in any struggle for power. It was also the main point of influence, in the sense that if factions struggled to achieve policy ends, gaining influence with the president was the major way of seeking to advance this goal. It was not, of course, the only object of such attention; the government, parliament, and bureaucracy were also potential points of influence, but given their diffuse natures and differentiated memberships, they were intrinsically more difficult than the president from which to get a decisive response. Formally the key to factional success was attaining high level representation in the leading elite organs. If this could be achieved by any single factional group, not only could it dominate that particular organ, but it could also choke off the potential for rival factions to influence its deliberations. Where a faction had a member in leading decision-making or bureaucratic circles, their potential for influence was enhanced; where this was absent, that potential was reduced.[9]

Central to factional success has been the relationship with the president. This is related to the fact that the contours of elite politics are fundamentally shaped by the profile, power, and actions of a predominant leader, and these are, in turn, affected by those elite contours. The relationship between a predominant (and would-be predominant) leader and the various factions will be central to the shaping of elite dynamics. In principle, there are three basic patterns for the structuring of this sort of relationship:

1. the leader is a member of the predominant faction and uses his/her position to consolidate factional dominance.
2. the leader is a member of one faction, but that faction is not in a predominant position. The leader maintains his/her position either through cross-factional alliances or through a process of balancing the other factions. This latter option may amount to a strategy of divide and rule, but it could also take the form of general consensus-building.
3. the leader is a member of no faction. Although his/her position will require support from within the factions, he stands above them and seeks to limit factional differences and maybe balance their interests. This too could involve either divide and rule or consensus-building.

In principle, the first pattern, single factional dominance, should enhance regime functioning and stability, although in practice much depends upon the contours of the particular factional arrangements in play, for example, how united a faction is, the extent of personal dominance of the leader, the respective strengths of different factions. But whatever the precise contours of factional relations, a political leader must manage those factions and their differences. In the case of all three patterns, the leader will use a combination of weapons in an attempt to contain factional difference. In the Russian case, the presidents have followed different strategies in their attempts to deal with different patterns of elite relations.

---

[9] For some comparative comments along these lines, see Sakwa (*Crisis*), pp. 109–13.

### Elite unconsolidated

Yeltsin was a pattern 3 type leader: he was not a member of a major faction and sought to stand above the factions that existed during his tenure as president. In part this was a function of his personal history, in part his personal temperament. During the Soviet period, he had made his career by climbing the ladder of the party apparatus, chiefly in regional Sverdlov (which he left in 1985), and it was only here that he was in situ long enough to be able to create a substantial clientelistic following among officials. However, in the move that was the turning point in his career, in 1990 he rejected the party and, at least in public, all that it stood for. With few of those who might have been considered clients making this change with him, he entered post-Soviet political life without an established political machine or factional group to sustain him. Instead of relying on such a group, he adopted a two-pronged strategy: to generate a personal mass base through a charismatic appeal to the voters, and to ally himself with other groups, chiefly the so-called "democrats" around the political movement Democratic Russia. This proved to be a weak basis upon which to stand as the dynamics of politics unrolled during the 1990s. Perhaps recognizing this, from the outset he sought to bolster this through the appointment of supporters to leading positions, but in the early period of his presidency many such appointments reflected more a general policy agreement than personal/factional commitment. And given the nature of that policy agreement – on radical political and economic reform – it came under severe strain as the early effects of economic change pitched much of the populace into severe economic difficulty. This strain was particularly acute given the nature of the elite in the immediate post-Soviet years.

Just as many of the institutions of the former Soviet state were carried over into the post-Soviet period, so also large numbers of the officials staffing those institutions remained in situ. In the early years of the Yeltsin presidency especially, the Russian state continued to be administered overwhelmingly by officials who had held office prior to 1991. Generically referred to as the "nomenklatura," the name given to both the personnel mechanism whereby the USSR's main politico-administrative positions were filled and to those people actually filling those positions, these people were said to constitute 82.3 percent of senior administrative staff and legislators and 75 percent of the new political elite in 1993.[10]

---

[10] Kryshtanovskaia ("Transformatsiia"), p. 64. Also see Olga Kryshtanovskaia and Stephen White "From Soviet *Nomenklatura* to Russian Elite," *Europe-Asia Studies* 48 (5), 1996, pp. 711–33. On the prominence of former members of the nomenklatura in the early years – three-quarters of the Presidential Administration, almost three-quarters

There is no evidence that former members of the nomenklatura shared anything much except a history of service in Soviet officialdom. Some remained committed communists while others came to be supporters of the most radical privatization measures, and of course Yeltsin himself was a former member of the nomenklatura. While there was much talk at the time among both Russian and Western observers about how "the nomenklatura" could constitute a kind of fifth column within the Russian body politic opposing the proposed shift to democracy and the market, there is no evidence that they acted in this way systematically as a group. Certainly many of them did oppose the radical free market ideas espoused by various spokespeople for "reform," but many also supported such ideas.

Yeltsin's attitude to this group was somewhat ambiguous. While he was clearly opposed to "communism" and any hint of a reversion toward the communist past, he relied upon many people from the nomenklatura and appointed many of them to leading positions. This reflects his trust in those with whom he was either personally acquainted or who were recommended to him by those he trusted, and sits awkwardly alongside his opposition to perceived representatives of the communists who he publicly opposed. Here was the strength of personalist sentiments cutting through the rhetoric of regime change. The key principle for Yeltsin was loyalty. This quest for loyalty was reflected in the appointment of people who had earlier career experience working with the president.[11] Yeltsin's initial administration was dominated by former colleagues from Sverdlovsk (now Yekaterinburg), where Yeltsin had been obkom first secretary before being brought to Moscow in 1985. Among these were Yury Petrov, the first head of the Presidential Administration, Gennady Burbulis (State Secretary and First Deputy Prime Minister 1991–2), Viktor Iliushin (initially head of the president's secretariat and then chief personal assistant) and Oleg Lobov (chairman of the Expert Council). While none of these people remained close to Yeltsin throughout his two terms, a level of turnover that contrasts with that of his successors as president, and no one from Sverdlovsk was promoted into the elite after 1993, his reliance upon them initially shows this propensity to turn to long-time associates for support and sustenance.

Yeltsin's reliance upon protégés from Sverdlovsk was soon overshadowed by his reliance upon people who had come to his side after he

---

of the government and over 80 percent of the regional leadership – see Kryshtanovskaia and White ("From Soviet *Nomenklatura*"), pp. 727–8.

[11] For a distinction between "protégés" and "clients," see John P. Willerton, "Post-Soviet Clientelist Norms at the Russian Federal Level," Graeme Gill (ed.), *Elites and Leadership in Russian Politics* (Basingstoke: Macmillan, 1998), pp. 60–62.

became president in June 1991.[12] From the outset, his administration had strong representation from a group of people whose link with Yeltsin seems to have been essentially one of policy agreement. The chief representatives of this group were Yegor Gaidar and Anatoly Chubais, who were the driving forces behind economic reform. There were others who became linked with Yeltsin along the way, perhaps like Sergei Shakhrai, who had ushered the institution of the presidency through the Congress of People's Deputies in 1991, and Sergei Filatov, who had supported Yeltsin in the legislature and replaced Petrov as head of the presidential administration in January 1993 (he was replaced in January 1996 by Nikolai Yegorov). All of these incumbents of formal office owed their positions to the president. This does not mean that they always worked harmoniously; for example, conflict between Petrov and Shakhrai was a constant feature until Shakhrai's resignation in May 1992.[13] But it does mean that the president was able to shape the membership of the formal offices around him by ensuring that their incumbents had some loyalty to him. It was Gaidar and his close associates who were responsible for the introduction of radical economic reform in the early 1990s, culminating in the waves of privatization in the middle of the decade.

These criteria for appointment, personal loyalty and policy orientation, could potentially be in tension, which illustrates the complex nature of factional politics at the apex of political life. Standard accounts of the Yeltsin period see the initial primacy of a liberal faction reflected in the ushering in of the economic reforms, over a more statist group comprising officials and siloviki, with the latter emerging dominant around 1994,[14] which was then displaced in a "liberal counter-coup headed by Anatoly Chubais" in 1996, which was in turn replaced by business-rooted combines.[15] There clearly were these sorts of dynamics evident during the 1990s, but it is important not to exaggerate their effect. Membership of the different groups could be fluid and the domination of one did not necessarily mean the others were without influence. The rise and fall of influence was related overwhelmingly to presidential preference, although the nature of the groups themselves and the broader (especially

---

[12] According to one study, by 1994 there were five people in the executive branch whose association with Yeltsin predated June 1991 and fourteen who had achieved rapid career advancement by Yeltsin after that date. Willerton ("Post-Soviet"), p. 61.

[13] See Shakhrai's comments in *Rossiiskaia gazeta*, May 26, 1992.

[14] For the view that from this time power and influence oscillated between two groups, the "pragmatists" associated with Chernomyrdin, and the "conservative restorationists" associated at the time with Oleg Soskovets, see Thane Gustafson, *Wheel of Fortune. The Battle for Oil and Power in Russia* (Cambridge [Mass.]: The Belknap Press, 2012), pp. 89–90.

[15] Sakwa (*Crisis*), p. 90. For another, more structural, view, see Buck ("Elite Networks").

economic and security) context was also relevant, not least because individuals could embody different interests, for example, Chubais as a liberal economist, a St. Petersburger, and a representative of electricity interests, or Viktor Chernomyrdin as a representative of the gas interests, the energy sector more broadly, and a bureaucratic constituency in the form of the military–industrial complex. This sort of multiple identity made the policy environment central to the process of factional interaction, and given the weakness of the broad public debate of issues, factional interactions became the principal arena of policy debate.

But as policy became more problematic with the serious decline in economic conditions and the growth of political opposition to the basic policy direction, added to the fact that the defeat of the parliament in 1993 removed a major stimulus to unity among those around the president, Yeltsin's ability to sustain his position based on policy agreement was eroded. Accordingly he acted to bring into his entourage people who were less associated with radical economic change and more closely linked into the traditionally influential heavy industry/defense industry sectors of the economy. This does not mean that all members of the so-called "liberal" faction lost their influence – for example, Foreign Minister Andrei Kozyrev maintained his position until January 1996 while Chubais remained influential late into the decade – nor that there was a sharp reversal in policy, but it did mean that important people with whom Yeltsin now sought to create a coalition on the basis of policy possessed their own bureaucratic constituencies and power bases independent of the president; they were not solely reliant upon the president as the liberals had been. The nature of Yeltsin's relationship with key members of the elite therefore changed, with them possessing greater autonomy from the president than their predecessors had. This is well reflected in the development of the office of prime minister.

During his two terms of office, Yeltsin appointed six prime ministers after he acted in that role himself between November 1991 and June 1992: Yegor Gaidar June 15–December 9, 1992 (formally only "acting" because he was never confirmed by parliament), Viktor Chernomyrdin December 14, 1992–March 23, 1998, Sergei Kirienko March 23–August 23, 1998, Yevgeny Primakov September 10, 1998–May 12, 1999, Sergei Stepashin May 12–August 9, 1999, and Vladimir Putin August 9–May 7, 2000. The history of these successive prime ministers illustrates both the power of the presidency and the effect of personal idiosyncrasy. Three of these people, Chernomyrdin, Primakov, and Putin, were at times able to exercise significant power autonomous from the president, principally because of the political resources that they brought to the role, although Yeltsin's indifferent health was sometimes also important in this, especially for Chernomyrdin. Chernomyrdin was appointed when Yeltsin was under attack from the parliament, and he brought with him solid standing within the industrial complex (given his background as the last Soviet minister of the gas industry and his role as head of Gazprom, which he established) and therefore within sections of the parliament hostile to Yeltsin and within the state apparatus. He provided Yeltsin with a prime minister who could not be used against him by his enemies, and one that, although he was instrumental in the moderation of a number of Yeltsin's policies, generally gave solid policy and political support to the president. Ultimately he was sacked principally because Yeltsin and those around him believed that he had exceeded his authority when Yeltsin was ill and that he posed a threat to the president and his entourage. Primakov brought both a period as head of the foreign intelligence service (SVR 1991–6) and foreign minister as well as an extended career in official service prior to 1991, and widespread support within the parliament. However, his government did not enjoy significant support within the parliament despite Primakov's attempt to build a government that drew in parliamentary elements, and when he launched an anti-corruption campaign that threatened to approach Yeltsin himself and "the family," he was dismissed. Putin brought a career in the Soviet security service (the KGB), some time with the reformist mayor of St. Petersburg (Anatoly Sobchak) and then a series of posts under Yeltsin (in the Presidential Administration where he rose to be deputy head, then head of the security service, the FSB), before Yeltsin appointed him the fifth prime minister in two years.[16] Putin also brought to the post the promise of loyalty[17] and an apparent absence of threat to Yeltsin and those around him; this was realized by the decree granting Yeltsin and his family amnesty from prosecution (the decree was not specific to Yeltsin but applied to all presidents), adopted on December 31, 1999, as soon as Putin became acting president. In his shuffling of prime ministers in 1998–9, Yeltsin had clearly been trying to arrange the succession in such a way as to ensure the maintenance of the system he had created as well as the security of himself and those around him. Putin seems to have promised this in a way that none of his predecessors had done. Accordingly, not only was he appointed, but he also enjoyed more autonomy and authority in the brief period of his prime ministership than any of his predecessors. This was also connected to his personal qualities and the way he performed the responsibilities of his office.

[16] On his background, see Sakwa (*Putin*, 1st edn.), pp. 6–16.
[17] On his loyalty to his former patron, Anatoly Sobchak, see Sakwa (*Putin*, 1st edn.), p. 11.

Thus, it was clear that the role of prime minister was defined by what the president allowed (either by conscious decision or, in the case of Yeltsin's illness, by default) the incumbent of that post to do. If a prime minister became too independent or powerful, as Chernomyrdin and Primakov threatened to do, the president could dismiss them. Similarly if they did not perform up to the president's expectations, he could remove them. The prime minister had little effective autonomy except when Yeltsin was sick and thereby partly removed from the scene, a situation that greatly enhanced the capacity of Chernomyrdin to play a leading role. The prime minister had little in the way of an independent power base. Reliant on the president's continued support and favor, lacking any electoral basis, and without the bureaucratic structure below him that his ministers possessed (see below), his position was fundamentally weak.

This succession of prime ministers reflects two things relevant to the changing nature of elite politics and Yeltsin's role in it. First, the decline of policy orientation as the key factor in the formation of an alliance between Yeltsin and other key elements of the elite: the sharing of policy views was clearly central in the initial alliance between Yeltsin and the "liberals" represented by Gaidar, but by the time Primakov became prime minister, the chief factor at least for Yeltsin seems to have been to get someone who could blunt opposition attacks almost regardless of their policy views. Primakov's coolness towards major elements of Yeltsin's policies, especially with regard to economic reform, was clear. Similarly the key factor in the appointment of Putin seems to have been concern about elite politics and the opposition to Yeltsin within it rather than expressed policy preferences. In this way elite dynamics seem to have displaced policy as the key to Yeltsin's tactics. Second, the apparent growth in importance for key members of the elite to have a bureaucratic constituency upon which they could stand: the apparent free-floating nature of Yeltsin's initial allies, in the sense that their presence in the elite depended upon the accord between their policy views and those of the president, was replaced by people who worked in the politico-administrative structure and therefore possessed their own autonomous power bases. These were people promoted by Yeltsin only recently, but inevitably brought with them tails of officials who took up important offices within the bureaucracies which they came to head. In their alliance with Yeltsin, these people therefore had greater freedom of maneuver than that enjoyed by his initial allies in government because of the bureaucratic roots they possessed. This was especially true of government ministers.

Paradoxically, government ministers may have possessed greater autonomy within elite politics than the prime minister. Although they too were dependent upon the president's (and the prime minister's) continuing favor, they sat atop the government ministries, and therefore had access to significant resources in terms of expertise, implementation (and therefore blocking) capacity, and material goods. While formally their standing in elite political councils rested principally upon their claims to expertise, in practice their power lay rather more in their control over the levers of the state for the implementation of policy. And because their power rested upon the bureaucratic structures they headed, it remained a relative constant across time. They were clearly more influential in decision-making circles at some times and on some issues than on others, but their power over implementation remained relatively unchanged. These were thus an important group in the elite dynamic, not greatly involved in the various power plays that took place, but ever present and providing a stable bureaucratically based landscape upon which elite politics could be played out.

Elite political life was also significantly affected by the emergence of a new economic elite. Initially based largely on the former nomenklatura who were able to transform their politico-administrative positions into control over economic resources in the process of privatization,[18] and given particular prominence by the way in which they benefited from state largesse through the "loans for shares" scheme of 1995–6,[19] an elite group of very wealthy businessmen emerged. Prominent members of this group, who came to be called "the oligarchs,"[20] became associated with Yeltsin, initially through bankrolling his election campaign in 1996. Some, principally Boris Berezovsky and later Roman Abramovich, seem to have become quite close to Yeltsin, with the former at least being considered part of "the family" (see below). Structurally what is important about this is that it created an overlap and interlinkage between the political elite around Yeltsin and some of the major figures in the emergent economic elite. This gave those oligarchs both access to the very top of the political tree in Russia, as well as potential influence over policy issues. While it is impossible to quantify that influence, it was important in the shaping of an economic policy environment that was beneficial to

---

[18] There is a large literature on this. For example, see Gill (*Bourgeoisie*); Olga Kryshtanovskaia and Stephen White, "The Rise of the Russian Business Elite," *Communist and Post-Communist Studies* 38 (3), 2005, pp. 293–307; Olga Kryshtanovskaya and Stephen White, "From Power to Property: The *Nomenklatura* in Post-Communist Russia," Graeme Gill (ed.), *Elites and Leadership in Russian Politics* (Basingstoke: Macmillan, 1998), pp. 81–105.

[19] A scheme that resulted in many of the most significant industrial and mining concerns being taken over by businessmen with links into the political elite, including with Yeltsin.

[20] On the oligarchs and their emergence, see D.E. Hoffman, *The Oligarchs. Wealth and Power in the New Russia* (New York: Public Affairs, 2002).

their economic interests; for example, the decisions about the "loans for shares" scheme and the creation of so-called "domestic off-shore zones" (which were effectively tax havens) clearly emanated from business influence, and in particular from Vladimir Potanin. The role of business in government decision-making contributed to the sense of corruption that came to surround the regime, a view that became strengthened with the role of "the family" discussed below.

This role of business reflected the emergence of an economic elite based upon control over significant economic resources gained in large part through the acquisition of state resources by means that rarely were legal and open. The oligarchs rested on business empires that embraced, in the words of one observer, "their own financial and industrial potential, their own security services, protégés in various levels of organs of power, in the military and special services (including the Ministry of the Interior, the General Prosecutor Office [sic] and the courts), their own analytical centres, and their own allies in the ranks of the political opposition."[21] The development of such empires and their linkages into the upper levels of the political elite caused some to talk about the merger of power and property and even the "feudalization" of Russia.[22] But despite the fact that some members of this group managed to achieve high public office (Potanin and Berezovsky) and were able to exert some influence on policy, their position within the political elite and the corridors of power was never stable or consolidated. They continually faced resentment and opposition from some of the bureaucratically based elites – witness the 1994 raid by troops of the Presidential Security Service on the forces of oligarch Vladimir Gusinsky – and as the fate of this group under Putin was to show, their access was always dependent upon a favorably disposed president.

But this interlinkage was more extensive than personal relations with the president. Under Yeltsin a trend emerged, which accelerated under Putin, of the interlinkage of the political elite into the economy. One form this took was the appointment of political, or former political (including Yeltsin associates), figures into leading posts in the economy (for example, the 1998 appointment of Anatoly Chubais to head the electricity conglomerate UES). This was combined with the effective state corporatization of various economic sectors, with one effect being that major corporations began to act, in part, as effective arms of the state (including

---

[21] Oxana Gaman-Golutvina, "Changes in Elite Patterns," Richard Sakwa (ed.), *Power and Policy in Putin's Russia* (London: Routledge, 2009), p. 156.

[22] For example, Vladimir Shlapentokh, with Joshua Woods, *Contemporary Russia as a Feudal Society. A New Perspective on the Post-Soviet Era* (Basingstoke: Palgrave Macmillan, 2007).

in foreign relations); for example, Gazprom was often accused of acting as a foreign policy arm of the Russian state, and it was also instrumental in sustaining much of the economy when barter replaced the use of cash for many transactions in the early 1990s. These interconnections encouraged some to begin to talk of "state capitalism" in Russia, but more important than the label was the way in which there seemed to be a coming together of political and economic elites.[23] And in the eyes of many, it was the economic elite that was becoming dominant over the political.

An important aspect of this linkage between the central political elite and the emergent economic elite is not just that it gave political access to leading economic actors, but it also represented a means for the enrichment of members of the political elite. It constituted a potential channel for members of the political elite to gain continuing access to the growing private sector economy. With the development of the private sector, and particularly its corporatized sections, opportunities for the employment of officials leading to private enrichment were created. Officials could take up jobs in the economic sector while retaining contacts in the higher political echelons. It also facilitated the passage of material rewards from the business sector into state officialdom. Corruption, bribery of officials, payment for services, and greasing of official wheels were all facilitated by this elite linkage. In addition, this means that the links between political and economic elites and the economic rewards that could flow from these represented a means of bringing some stability to the political elite by providing an outlet for their material aspirations. This began under Yeltsin, and became more systematic under Putin.

As Yeltsin's power base within the elite shifted from policy allies to institutionally based figures, that basis became more diversified with the increasing influence of another person close to Yeltsin, Aleksandr Korzhakov. Korzhakov had become Yeltsin's personal security guard soon after Yeltsin shifted to Moscow in 1985[24] and when a Main Guard Directorate was established following the dismissal of the parliament in October 1993 to create a military force loyal to the president, Korzhakov was put in command. Over time he became personally very close to Yeltsin,[25] to such an extent that, prior to his sacking in the lead up to the 1996 presidential election, it was believed that he had displaced Yeltsin's official team as the main source of advice to the president. Indeed, during

---

[23] For more detail on the substance of this paragraph, see Gill (*Bourgeoisie*), Chapter 7.

[24] O. Prokhanov (ed.), *Kto est' kto v Rossii: Spravochnoe izdanie* (Moscow: Olimp, 1997), p. 328.

[25] For his account of it, see Aleksandr Korzhakov, *Boris Yeltsin: Ot rassveta do zakata* (Moscow: Interbuk, 1997).

the mid 1990s prior to his sacking, he is reputed to have exercised significant influence in some areas of policy widely separate from his security responsibilities. Following his dismissal, in the second half of the 1990s Korzhakov's informal role was taken by a wider group, euphemistically called "the family," which reportedly included Yeltsin's daughter Tatiana Diachenko, businessmen Berezovsky and Abramovich, Chubais, and successive heads of the presidential administration Valentin Yumashev and Aleksandr Voloshin. The part played by this informal clique was quite influential[26] and clearly had an impact on the exercise of presidential power, especially in those periods when Yeltsin was ill disposed because of sickness.[27] At the same time, increasing reliance was had on people who had had careers in the security apparatus and moved into the Presidential Administration, with Putin ultimately being the most important of these.

Thus, no single faction remained dominant during the Yeltsin years, with the president playing a highly personalized role in the process of government and in shaping the fate of the factions. Just as Yeltsin refused to set up a party to represent his interests in the Duma and among the electorate, he did not consolidate a factional base within the elite. His method of governing through the diverse parts of the political elite was to place his faith in people he believed to be loyal to him – among these favorites at various times were Soskovets, Gaidar, Chubais, Federov, and ultimately Putin – combined with the bringing together of people who were likely not to agree with each other. The former leg of this strategy, the appointment of favorites, saw a succession of people move into the close presidential orbit and then be expelled from it when they disappointed him.[28] No one was permanent, and all were expendable, as shown especially by the fate of Korzhakov. The second leg, a sort of divide-and-rule strategy, was most clearly reflected in successive governments, which meant that governments were almost inevitably fractious and unable to mount a united front before a willful president. This was a technique that may have been designed to increase Yeltsin's personal

---

[26] On the "boofish" atmosphere that often prevailed in this group, see Viacheslav Kostikov, *Roman c prezidentom. Zapiski press-sekretaria* (Moscow: Vagrius, 1997), Chapter 1; and Korzhakov (*Boris Yeltsin*), pp. 82, 252–3. For a view that "the family" was less important than often thought, see Colton (*Yeltsin*), pp. 422–5.

[27] Many commentators pointed to Yeltsin's mercurial personality and his mood swings, while Gaidar referred to his propensity to "fall into long periods of passivity and depression." Yegor Gaidar, *Days of Defeat and Victory* (trans. Jane Anne Miller; Seattle: University of Washington Press, 1999), p. 88.

[28] On Yeltsin's disappointment with Putin after he (Yeltsin) had retired, see Colton (*Yeltsin*), pp. 442–4.

room for maneuver by complicating the emergence of a dominant faction within the government, but what it also did was to make the tasks of elite management and of government more difficult than they should have been.

Yeltsin's strategy of building disagreement and discord into his governments ensured that conflict remained a continuing feature of elite life. This was a strange strategy to adopt, especially in the context of the increasingly unpopular economic program Yeltsin was pursuing. The widespread economic hardship generated by that program added to the inveterate opposition to Yeltsin embedded in the parliament and in other parts of public life ensured that political argument, disagreement, and conflict would remain a feature of elite politics even had Yeltsin's strategy not been in place. But what that strategy did was to ensure that while political debate raged in the public sphere, despite the central political elite's relative isolation from this sphere (see below), that elite could not present a united front to it. In this way, rather than preventing elite discontent, and therefore the ground from which potential challenges to his authority could emerge, Yeltsin's strategy actually encouraged this.

Unlike in Soviet times, when a leading official left office, it now no longer necessarily meant that he was driven from political life.[29] Many of those who left Yeltsin's direct service – like Gaidar and Chubais and later Kirienko, Primakov, and Stepashin – remained active within the upper echelons of Russian public political life although they ceased to be members of the central political elite. There was, after 1993, now a sphere of public political activity based in the parliament and in the life of the weak party system that could offer a place to those who had left the presidential circle. As noted in Chapter 3, a range of political parties had emerged, oriented around the parliament, and these provided vehicles that some such refugees could use to remain politically active. Divided by personality conflicts and policy differences, most of these parties remained small and ineffectual, and therefore did not constitute a very strong basis upon which individuals could hope to build a continuing political career. But simply through their existence, they represented a milieu within which presidential critics could take root. And given Yeltsin's failure to generate a party of power that could either absorb these

---

[29] The big exception to this during Soviet times was Yeltsin who, when removed as Politburo candidate and first secretary of the Moscow party organization, was not banished from Moscow but instead given a low-level job, which left him time to organize his later political rebirth.

parties and their spokespeople or drive them to the electoral margins, they remained continuing thorns in Yeltsin's side. Their constant criticism of him, allied to their relative success in the 1996 parliamentary election, meant that opposition to the president remained a continuing feature of political life.

Under Yeltsin, therefore, elite structures remained largely unconsolidated. Despite some interlinkage between key political and economic elites, there was little stability or system in the way in which different groups interacted. Bureaucratic elites located in the major structures of government continued to use the power their locations gave them to influence policy outcomes. Presidential advisers, including the Presidential Administration, sought to use their access to the president to achieve policy influence. Many of the oligarchs sought to parlay their economic wealth and power into political power in such a way as to enhance their personal economic positions (an aim that was clearly not restricted to this group). Legislators continually tried to inject themselves into the policy process, but were kept at arms length by the president and his supporters. And those public politicians who headed major parties or who had political standing because of their past service, danced around the edge trying to make their voices heard. There was little that was systematic about the way these different elites interacted, and there seem to have been few rules structuring their activity. Certainly the Constitution and formal legislation provided a framework within which this took place, but this sort of informal politics occurred within the penumbra of the formal political structure. It was not a replacement for the formal structure nor an alternative mode of functioning, although its mode of operation in many instances did displace or circumvent more formal processes, but was an add-on to that formal structure. It eased the wheels of the formal structure, and enabled political actors to play out roles without too much formal constraint. But constraint did exist. Formal rules were in place, and although their level of normative authority may have been uncertain, their mere existence could impose some restraint; for example, Yeltsin went ahead with elections when they were scheduled in 1996 despite the possibility of defeat, and after the end of 1993 he did not dissent from any decisions of the Constitutional Court, despite some of them going against him. But the very existence of these formal rules also meant that political actors could invoke them when it suited. In this way the formal institutions could be used instrumentally by political actors to achieve their ends, with those with most formal authority in the system being best placed to do this. Such instrumental use of the formal institutions and rules even further undermined the normative authority such bodies could generate.

This sort of situation was not unique to Russia. An informal politics alongside the formal institutions occurs in all political systems,[30] and their relationship is broadly similar to the Russian. The principal difference between various cases of this lies in the relative strength of the informal compared with the formal. Generally, the stronger the informal processes, the weaker the formal institutions, because the former can reduce the latter to a mere shell if everything depended upon personal relations unmediated by institutional constraints. But normally there is some approximate balance between these, although it may not be an equal balance. Under Yeltsin, the balance was weighted in favor of the informal. The newness of the constitutional rules and the greater propensity to rely upon personal contacts that resulted from the course of political conflict meant that the formal structure was slow to develop normative authority. The dominance of "the family," which was a classic manifestation of personalism over institutional authority, reinforced this. In this sense, then, levels of formal institutionalization were low and the capacity of informal politics extensive. This is a classic case of what has been called "neo-patrimonialism," where the political leadership and strategic elites strike a bargain that trades status, influence, protection, and material rewards for loyalty,[31] and manifested principally through patron–client networks.

Elite politics under Yeltsin was also characterized by its relative autonomy from social interests in the society at large. Certainly during this decade lobby groups developed to press their own particular interests on political decision-makers, but generally these were held at arms length and seem to have exercised little direct influence on decision-making. The State Duma was one crucial arena within which such interests sought to press their case,[32] but because this body was largely sidelined under Yeltsin, this gave them little access to the center of power. But generally during this period, social interests remained largely unformed, inchoate, and inarticulate, and possessed no clear channels into the elite. This does not mean that the elite was completely self-contained, lacking all contacts with elements outside that elite. Bureaucratic elites remained rooted in their bureaucratic hierarchies, and through them, had some continuing contacts with people outside the elite, even if these were

[30] Richard Sakwa initially discusses this in terms of a distinction between "system" and "regime," and then in terms of a "dual state," but seems to imply that it is not a common feature outside Russia. Sakwa (*Russian Politics*, 3rd edn.), p. 455; and Sakwa (*Crisis*).

[31] On "neo-patrimonialism," see Shmuel Eisenstadt, *Traditional Patrimonialism and Modern Neopatrimonialism* (Beverley Hills: Sage, 1973). Also see Vitali Silitski, "Tools of Autocracy," *Journal of Democracy* 20 (2), 2009, p. 44.

[32] On this see Chaisty (*Legislative Politics*).

generally restricted to other members of their bureaucratic structures. And members of the parliament and leaders of political parties moved within the society more regularly and, given their roles, should have maintained closer contacts with general society as a whole. But the central elite, focused on Yeltsin, did not possess these sorts of channels into society more broadly. Certainly, in the second half of the 1990s, they had links into the economy through their contacts with the oligarchs and sometimes their personal involvement in economic matters, but they were not strongly rooted in society as a whole. The elite was thus largely cut off from Russian society, relatively autonomous in its actions from the will of the mass populace. Yeltsin's initial strategy for generating personal authority could be seen in part as an attempt to overcome this isolation.

How a president seeks to play his role will not only shape the institutional contours of elite political organizations and help determine the personal composition of those bodies, but it can also have a significant impact upon the stability of elite politics. Rhetorically, Yeltsin espoused continued (although weaker as time passed) support for "democracy," and yet in practice he seems to have profoundly distrusted most of the solutions it threw up. He was able to work constructively with none of the parliaments he faced as president. In part this was because of the substantial level of opposition to him and/or his policies within each of those chambers – as reflected in the various attempts to impeach him – but it is also the case that he never seriously set out to work with them. Instead he spent much of the time, especially before the 1995 parliamentary election, working to get around or roll over parliamentary opinion. This is reflected in the large number of presidential decrees that Yeltsin used; these were used more sparingly in the second half of the decade, but this was also when the president was less activist in a policy sense himself.

Yeltsin relied on a mixture of charismatic authority, appeals to the good of Russia, and the authority of his office to project his power, all of which focused attention on himself as the main actor outside the institutional context of emergent Russian politics. He was the only actor who was important; those close to him were empowered by the reflected authority, but those institutions that were not part of this image of the presidency, like the parliament, had only a secondary part to play in the system. Yeltsin sought to project a sort of personalized authority that, had it been successful, would have created a charismatic relationship between himself and the Russian people. This is a relationship in which the followers of the leader invest all of their powers of independent judgment in that leader, accepting what he says as the truth and obeying him simply because he is who he is.[33] Charismatic authority transcends institutional structures, and is an intensely personal tie between leader and led. Initially Yeltsin sought to project this sort of authority. Resting upon his role in the collapse of the August 1991 coup attempt, in which he was widely acclaimed as the rock upon which the coup foundered, he presented himself as the father of the country and the one who knew best what it needed. He sought to maintain this through the 1993 clash with the parliament, but here his role seemed more ambiguous and therefore less able to be manipulated into the charismatic mold than had been the case in 1991. But in any event, his personalized authority was being eroded by this time by the effects of the economic reforms that had been introduced under his aegis. While charismatic authority is in principle oblivious to material rewards, the economic difficulties experienced by the Russian populace during much of the 1990s quickly eroded the popular image of him as the caring father of his people. The sense of charismatic authority was even further eroded by his illness and relative absence from the scene. An old, ailing man who was unable at times even to perform his official functions (and then when he did, he sometimes did so in a fashion that caused embarrassment to his people, often because of the effect of alcohol) could not project a charismatic image in a media environment like that in Russia. This means that Yeltsin's attempt to create a stable base in elite politics resting on the generation of popular support and commitment failed; the need to manipulate elections to manufacture popular support showed the limits of that support. And as with all leaders who seek charismatic authority, for those in the immediate close vicinity (Weber's "staff"), charisma rarely takes effect. His attempt to generate charismatic authority to use within the elite was a failure.

The combination of populism and aloofness that he seemed to cultivate after 1991 was maintained throughout his presidency, but it was unable to sustain a sense of personal authority. This was the case within the elite as well as more widely. For those most closely allied around him in the elite, Yeltsin was like a patriarch.[34] In Breslauer's words, "He treated his entourage as a family with himself as its head, rather than treating it as a corpus of professionals of which he was chief executive."[35] He seems to have perceived his relations with his close advisers and

[33] On charisma, see Weber (*Economy and Society*), vol. I, pp. 241–54, 1111–56.
[34] This follows George W. Breslauer, "Boris Yel'tsin as Patriarch," *Post-Soviet Affairs* 15 (2), 1999, pp. 186–200. This image is also reflected in Korzhakov (*Boris Yeltsin*) and Kostikov (*Roman*). For a discussion of Korzhakov's memoirs relevant here, see David Remnick, "How Russia Is Ruled," *The New York Review of Books* April 9, 1998, pp. 10–15.
[35] Breslauer ("Patriarch"), p. 190.

subordinates in personalized, familial terms, based on trust and personal commitment rather than official standing or rules. Disagreement could be seen as betrayal, although in many cases this was temporary, and obedience and servility only were expected. But this personalist vision also extended to the state and its resources. While there was significant debate about the extent to which Yeltsin and his family profited as a result of their positions at the apex of Russian politics,[36] it is clear that in his official capacity as president, he seems to have believed that it was within his power to give away the resources of the state. From his exercise of largesse in the quest for votes in 1996, to his acceptance of the acquisition of large sections of economic capacity by his businessmen allies, to his granting of extravagant concessions to Ukraine (including the acceptance of Crimea as part of Ukraine) and Belarus (the formal creation of a "union state" between the two countries), Yeltsin seems to have been prepared to treat the Russian state largely as part of his patrimony. While this was fundamentally important in shaping the trajectory of the state, it was also crucial for the conduct of elite relations. If things were seen as being within the gift of the president, this simply reinforced the personalist element of elite dynamics and undercut any process of institutionalization. It thereby added considerably to the unconsolidated nature of the elite under Yeltsin.

But the highly personalized style of Yeltsin contained a paradox. While it emphasized the personal power of the president, the reality in terms of his continuing involvement in elite politics was very different. Reference has already been made to his aloofness and to Gaidar's comment about his propensity to fall into periods of passivity. Whether this was due to temperament, alcohol, or illness, its effect was to leave much of the dynamic of elite life outside Yeltsin's direct involvement. Rather than being at the center of elite political life, Yeltsin sought to hover above it. This might not have mattered had he had effective subordinates who could keep elite dynamics under control. But he did not. The stripping away of most of his reliable political supporters and his increased reliance upon "the family" left him largely bereft of the capacity to guide elite affairs on a day-to-day basis. As a result it went on around Yeltsin with him unable to exercise any consistent or coherent shaping influence upon it. His involvement was episodic and isolated – although it could be dramatic and important, like the sacking of prime ministers – rather than continuing and consistent. And with conflict built into the elite as part of his strategy, this could lead to nothing other than the lack of consolidation

---

[36] For example, see Colton (*Yeltsin*), pp. 420–21 on the claims surrounding the Mabetex scandal.

of the elite. When Putin replaced Yeltsin as president at the beginning of 2000, he sought to remedy this by transforming the dynamic of elite politics.

## A consolidated elite?

The end of Yeltsin's tenure as president looked as though it was going to be marked by open conflict within the elite, essentially over who would follow him. The chief indication of this was the emergence of an alliance between Moscow mayor Yury Luzhkov, former prime minister Yevgeny Primakov, and Tatarstan leader Mintimer Shaimiev, who came together in a party called Fatherland-All Russia, which aimed to contest the forthcoming Duma election. It was clear that this was to be a dry run for the presidency, when probably Primakov would run. In the eyes of Yeltsin and those around him, this danger had to be fended off. The result was the creation of Unity discussed in Chapter 3, the promotion of Putin, and the resignation of Yeltsin, thereby pushing Putin into the leading position for the election. The potential split of the elite and the passing of real decision-making power into the hands of the electorate were thereby averted and the relative autonomy of the political elite confirmed. Such autonomy has remained evident throughout the post-2000 period, encompassing Putin's first two and later third term as president and the Medvedev interregnum. While the latter reflected a change in the identity of the holder of the preeminent office, it did not represent an interruption of many of the basic trends in elite relations established under Yeltsin and built on during Putin's first two terms.

When both Putin and Medvedev first became president, they relied overwhelmingly upon elite incumbents they inherited from their predecessor, but only Putin was able decisively to break away from this group and bring past associates into responsible positions within the elite.[37] Initially both new presidents were somewhat restrained by the fact that they were being ushered into power by their predecessor and they inherited a full team from him rather than having their own personal factions to sustain them. But given that both had worked in the Presidential Administration of their predecessor, they had presumably had some input into the appointment of at least some of the people they now inherited. Initially Putin was reliant upon Yeltsin's "family," chiefly head and deputy head of

---

[37] On the question of loyalty to Putin, cf. Medvedev in the Presidential Administration, see John P. Willerton, "Presidency," Graeme Gill and James Young (eds), *Routledge Handbook of Russian Politics and Society* (London: Routledge, 2012), pp. 83–4. And more generally in the elite, Willerton ("Presidency"), p. 89.

the Presidential Administration Voloshin and Vladislav Surkov, oligarchs Berezovsky and Abramovich, banker Aleksandr Mamut, former speech writer and chief of staff Yumashev, former head of the Kremlin "property department" Pavel Borodin, and Yeltsin's daughter Diachenko,[38] and he made little change in the personnel surrounding him in his first year in office. This may have been part of an agreement with Yeltsin,[39] but over time the profile of this group slipped as Putin was able to develop a much more systematic and centralized appointment process than that used by Yeltsin.[40] As a result, members of two other groups representing two aspects of Putin's earlier career were ushered into the circles of power, the security apparatus (siloviki), and the St. Petersburg group (Pitertsy), with these coinciding in the case of many officials.

In a development that has been much remarked on in the West,[41] Putin brought into the central apparatus significant numbers of people who had spent time in the security apparatus, the so-called siloviki. According to Kryshtanovskaia and White, the number of officials from a security, military, or other law enforcement background in leadership positions rose from 11 percent under Yeltsin to 25 percent by 2004; by early 2005 they constituted just under 25 percent of the top leadership, a little over 33 percent of the national government and slightly under 20 percent of each chamber of the Federal Assembly.[42] Although the cohesiveness and effectiveness of this group has been exaggerated,[43] their appointment

---

[38] Sakwa (*Putin*, 2nd edn.), p. 72. For the view that Voloshin was there to protect the interests of the family and prime minister Kasyanov the oligarchs, see Wilson (*Virtual Politics*), p. 102.

[39] See the discussion in Sakwa (*Putin*, 2nd edn.), p. 73.

[40] Eugene Huskey, "Putin as Patron: Cadres Policy in the Russian Transition," Alex Pravda (ed.), *Leading Russia. Putin in Perspective. Essays in Honour of Archie Brown* (Oxford: Oxford University Press, 2005), p. 162. The pace of this picked up in 2003–4.

[41] For example, Olga Kryshtanovskaia and Stephen White, "Putin's Militocracy," *Post-Soviet Affairs* 19 (4), 2003, pp. 289–306; Bettina Renz, "Putin's Militocracy? An Alternative Interpretation of the Role of Siloviki in Contemporary Russian Politics," *Europe-Asia Studies* 58 (6), 2006, pp. 903–24; Sharon Werning Rivera and David W. Rivera, "The Russian Elite under Putin: Militocratic or Bourgeois?," *Post-Soviet Affairs* 22 (2), 2006, pp. 125–44; and Taylor (*State Building*), esp. pp. 57–70 for ways of conceptualizing this group.

[42] Kryshtanovskaia and White ("Putin's Militocracy"), p. 294; and Ol'ga Kryshtanovskaia and Stephen White, "Inside the Putin Court: A Research Note," *Europe-Asia Studies* 57 (7), 2005, p. 1065. Also see some figures in Gaman-Golutvina ("Changes"), p. 160. On the group more generally, see Sakwa (*Crisis*), pp. 117–23, 137–42.

[43] On divisions within this group, see Taylor (*State Building*), pp. 65–9 where it is argued that most disputes were over material issues, personnel, and turf wars rather than ideology. For the suggestion that their frustration at missing out on the division of property and wealth in the 1990s added to the rising incomes evident in the oil sector in the early 2000s was instrumental in the move against Khodorkovsky and Yukos in 2003, see Gustafson (*Wheel*), pp. 275–6.

nevertheless reflects an attempt by the president to surround himself with people he believed he could rely on.[44] This silovik presence was slightly ameliorated when Medvedev assumed the presidency, and he sought to bring into office people he had been associated with, which meant more people from a civilian, and often legal, background.[45] But because Putin remained a powerful force at this time, and was therefore able to continue to influence the composition of the elite, Medvedev's presidency did not bring about a significant recasting of the elite away from the form it had taken under Putin.

The second group, the so-called Pitertsy meaning those who came from St. Petersburg, provided many of the economic liberals[46] who played a significant part in shaping Putin's economic policy during his first two terms in office.[47] But they were not restricted to economic matters, as shown by the career of the one who became most prominent, Dmitry Medvedev. Although Putin promoted both of these groups and was by background a member of both, he was never a captive of either. Not only did these groups lack the policy coherence (as opposed to the general overall statist world outlook) to constitute an effective political faction, but Putin was careful to maintain a balance in the influence they could wield. Indeed, his role has often been portrayed as one of balancing between various factions, and although he possessed ultimate authority in factional conflicts, he still sought to maintain a general equilibrium.[48] He was a classic pattern 3 leader (as was Medvedev).

As under Yeltsin, these factions were active through their embeddedness in the political process, but this was not in the "public" arm of that process, the parliament; the Russian elite under Putin has retained its bureaucratic origins and nature. Most figures at the apex of Russian politics came there through the bureaucratic structures of the state, with

---

[44] Although for the view that despite his service in the security apparatus, Putin remained an outsider in that apparatus, and these people were "not his fraternity," see Fiona Hill and Clifford G. Gaddy, *Mr. Putin. Operative in the Kremlin* (Washington, DC: Brookings Institution Press, 2013), pp. 114–18 (quotation p. 116).

[45] On the limited nature of the changes he made, and the argument that this was to avoid upsetting the factional balance, see Sakwa (*Crisis*), p. 317. However, this may also have been because Putin was able to block any appointments with which he did not agree. The reduction in silovik presence may also reflect Putin's need to overcome the opposition of some senior siloviki to Medvedev's accession to the presidency. Gustafson (*Wheel*), p. 360; and Sakwa (*Crisis*), Chapters 5 and 6.

[46] Defined as those who supported market economics and fiscal and monetary orthodoxy. Gustafson (*Wheel*), p. 265.

[47] On the Pitertsy, see Roxburgh (*Strongman*), pp. 65–6; and Gustafson (*Wheel*), pp. 232–4. On the early role of the liberals, especially with regard to tax reform, see Gustafson (*Wheel*), pp. 254–66.

[48] For example, see Sakwa (*Crisis*), esp. Chapter 6.

public competitive politics something they watched rather than engaged in directly. This meant that while the elite may have been factionalized, it was also quite homogenous: career background, ethnicity, and geography were not major points of division within the elite. Although neither Putin nor Medvedev was able to articulate a clear and programmatic view of Russia's future that could act as a mobilizing ideology for the elite,[49] there was a basic unity of outlook between siloviki and Pitertsy, centered principally upon notions of a powerful Russian state that contrasted starkly with much of the Yeltsin period. A broad policy consensus existed within the elite, and although there were differences over specific issues, the general coherence of outlook constituted a solid basis for elite unity. Within this, the fortunes of individual factions may have waxed and waned, but none ever really challenged the president, be he Putin or Medvedev, even if, as some suggest, Putin acted as a shield for Medvedev against factional pressure.[50] Each president also had a group of personal intimates who had direct access to him and with whom he mixed and would have discussed political affairs.[51]

Although the emergence of the siloviki and Pitertsy was much remarked upon, the most basic dynamic of elite relations remained rooted in the relations between those figures embedded in the bureaucratic structures, chiefly government ministries and the Presidential Administration. Political conflict in the new millennium remained present and, at times, extensive, but unlike under Yeltsin it concerned not grand questions of democracy, the market, and Russia's trajectory, but more mundane issues of immediate policy relevance. Government ministers frequently clashed among themselves over questions of budgetary allocation and policy direction,[52] ministers were also often the target of presidential criticism for failing to carry out what the president had ordered,[53] and

[49] Gill (*Symbolism*), Chapter 3. Also Chapter 2 above.

[50] For different views about the identity and nature of factions under Putin, see Sakwa (*Crisis*), pp. 117–30 and Ian Bremmer and Samuel Charap, "The *Siloviki* in Putin's Russia: Who They Are and What They Want," *The Washington Quarterly* 30 (1), 2006–7, pp. 83–92. Sakwa identifies what he calls siloviki, remnants of the "family," democratic statists, economic liberals and technocrats, big business, and regional "barons."

[51] Sakwa (*Crisis*), pp. 140–41; Kryshtanovskaia and White ("Inside"), pp. 1065–75; and Hill and Gaddy (*Mr. Putin*), pp. 244–9.

[52] For example, Philip Hanson, "The Russian Budget: Why So Much Fuss?," *Russian Analytical Digest* 121, December 21, 2012, pp. 2–5.

[53] For example, see Putin's comments on September 18, 2012, criticizing ministers for failing to make provision for spending promises he had made earlier, reported in *Kommersant*, September 19, 2012. Also note the campaign launched once Putin had been reelected in 2012 against officials holding bank accounts abroad, and the anti-corruption campaign in the same period that netted former Defense Minister Serdiukov and Agriculture Minister Yelena Skrynnik, among others.

reports of conflict and disputes within the political elite were standard fare in the Russian media. This was the normal sort of politics that goes on in any government, and while it may see reasonably stable alliances between ministers in cognate areas (e.g., defense and defense procurement) or possessing a shared outlook (e.g., economic liberals, technocrats), this politics was not one overwhelmingly shaped by factional difference. But also unlike the Yeltsin period, this was not a politics that threatened to shake the stability of the elite as a whole. Such differences were generally kept within the bounds of the elite, in the sense that although such differences may be reflected in public debate and discussion, there was no attempt to take the issue outside the bounds of the elite or to mobilize political forces from outside in an endeavor to achieve victory. Furthermore, under Putin, in the making of appointments to these leading positions within the state ministries, Putin placed a higher premium on personal loyalty than on technical expertise, reflected in fewer promotions from within ministries and the creation of a greater sense of cross-ministerial cohesion.[54] This was essentially a form of bureaucratic politics,[55] and it never threatened to destabilize the elite.

   One factor in this bureaucratic politics not destabilizing the elite is that this was taking place at a distinct second level in the elite hierarchy. While the already noted presidential inability to control the ministers was a frustration for the president and restricted the effective power he could wield, it also to some degree shielded him from the effects of such conflict. He was seen to stand above such conflict, seeking to exercise a guiding or even balancing role in this aspect of political life. As a consequence when things went wrong, blame could be deflected onto the relevant ministers (including the prime minister) and away from the president. This meant that the formal constitutional structure of relations between president and government was both a weakness of the system (at least in terms of maximizing presidential power) and a defense of the presidency. Here is one way in which the formal and the informal interacted in a complex and nuanced fashion.

   Central to this was the position of the prime minister, who could be the day-to-day mediator between president and ministers. During Putin's first two terms as president, three prime ministers held office: Mikhail Kasyanov May 7, 2000–February 24, 2004, Mikhail Fradkov March 1, 2004–September 12, 2007, and Viktor Zubkov September 12,

---

[54] Huskey ("Putin as Patron"), pp. 168–9.
[55] The "bureaucratic politics" nature of such differences was facilitated by the fact that Putin tended to avoid appointing people with overlapping spheres of responsibility. Hill and Gaddy (*Mr. Putin*), p. 231.

2007–May 7, 2008. All of these people were overshadowed by the popular president, whose authority was never called into question. However, a similar situation did not apply with regard to his successor. Medvedev had had a significant association with Putin, having worked in Sobchak's administration in St. Petersburg while Putin was there, managed Putin's election campaign in 2000, headed the Presidential Administration, and been deputy prime minister during part of Putin's presidency. Furthermore, just as Yeltsin had declared Putin to be his successor, so Putin promoted Medvedev to succeed him as president.[56] In response, Medvedev promised to appoint Putin as prime minister if elected, something he did as soon as he was inaugurated as president. Putin remained prime minister for all of Medvedev's term. This was a very different model to what had applied before. Although both Chernomyrdin and Kasyanov had remained prime minister for extended periods, neither had possessed the authority or standing that Putin had upon becoming prime minister. Furthermore, throughout Medvedev's presidency, it was not clear which of the two, president or prime minister, was actually the more powerful. While there seem to have been no serious conflicts between the two men,[57] there were discernible differences of nuance and emphasis between many of the positions they espoused. Reflective of the relationship between them is the fact that many who had been close to President Putin followed him into the government (and back to the presidency in 2012) while some of the leading people in Medvedev's presidential circle (including new head of the Presidential Administration Sergei Naryshin) had more established ties with Putin than with Medvedev.[58] Furthermore, Putin played a much more activist role as prime minister than any of his predecessors. He was projected through the press much more consistently than any of his predecessors, and was often shown as being more actively engaged in the resolution of practical issues and problems than the president (see below). The depiction of Putin as prime minister also suggested that the sort of demarcation that had seemed to apply in earlier years with the president alone being involved in foreign affairs while the prime minister concentrated on domestic (especially economic)

---

[56] For one discussion of the politics behind this, see Sakwa (*Crisis*), Chapter 5.
[57] Although Roxburgh (*Strongman*), pp. 296–316 argues that there were important differences of opinion.
[58] Mendras (*Russian Politics*), p. 229; and Roxburgh (*Strongman*), pp. 214–15. Putin also established a Government Presidium that included three ministers who were constitutionally responsible to the President. Membership included the seven deputy prime ministers and the ministers of Foreign Affairs, Defense, Interior (all responsible to the President), the Economy, Agriculture, Social Development and Health, and Regional Development. Mendras (*Russian Politics*), p. 230.

issues, may no longer have applied. Putin did become involved in foreign issues, especially the war with Georgia in 2008, in a way that none of his predecessors had done and that certainly seemed to imply an encroachment on presidential prerogatives. The higher profile of Putin during this period than earlier prime ministers had enjoyed, added to the fact that in 2012 Medvedev withdrew to allow Putin to return to the presidency, suggests that Putin remained the leading figure throughout. And when he returned to the presidency, he appointed Medvedev as his prime minister. While Putin was generally ascendant throughout the whole post-2000 period,[59] what is clear is that from 2008 Putin and Medvedev arrived at an arrangement which produced stability at the top, even if on another institutional basis to that which had gone before. This reflects the strength of personalist relations over institutional factors.

The restoration of Putin to the presidency also saw some change in elite contours at the second level. The new Medvedev government saw the introduction of a number of new ministers, most of whom were what has been described as "second-tier politicians";[60] five were former deputy heads of the ministries they came to head while the chief of President Medvedev's apparat (Surkov) became the chief of his prime ministerial apparat.[61] At the same time, many of the more important ministers under Prime Minister Putin moved into the Presidential Administration, although the influential former deputy prime minister Igor Sechin moved to headship of the state oil company Rosneft,[62] which he combined with secretaryship of the president's commission on the fuel and energy complex, a perfect example of the blurring of political and economic and state and non-state boundaries. This sort of elite movement from the government to the Presidential Administration as Putin became president shows that both personal relations with the president and institutional positions do matter. If either personal relations or institutional position alone was important, there would have been no need for "Putin's people" to change their institutional positions. President Putin's ability

---

[59]  This does not mean that there have not been some public differences over particular policies, but these have been neither serious nor continuing, and does not disturb the picture of the two men generally working together, but under Putin's guidance. For a discussion of such a difference and its meaning, see "Tax Fraud Bill Reveals Rift between Kremlin, Cabinet," *The Moscow Times*, November 13, 2013; and Stanislav Belkovsky in *Sobesednik*, November 18, 2013.

[60]  Hans-Henning Schröder, "Forward to the Past! The President's Message to the Federal Assembly," *Russia Analytical Digest* 124, March 18, 2013, p. 6.

[61]  The new deputy prime minister, Arkady Dvorkovich, had worked for Medvedev in the presidential staff while Medvedev was president.

[62]  Sechin became CEO and President of Rosneft in May 2012, having been made Chairman of the Board of Directors in April 2004.

to move his closest supporters into the institution most closely associated with the president, the Presidential Administration, contrasts with Medvedev's new government and the higher level of promotion within the bureaucratic structure of people whose claim to higher office rested more on technical/bureaucratic qualifications than personal relationship with the new prime minister.

Prominent in the contours of elite politics under Yeltsin had been the role of the oligarchs, and this relationship with big business was a key element in the early Putin years. As shown in Chapter 2, soon after coming to power Putin sought to craft a new relationship with the oligarchs. When leading businessmen were perceived to have breached the new rules Putin had laid down, he acted against them: Gusinsky and Berezovsky fled into exile, losing control over most of their assets in Russia, while Khodorkovsky was arrested and his company, Yukos, effectively nationalized.[63] This was the trigger for the reassertion of state control through state champions, principally Gazprom and Rosneft.[64] What Putin was doing was clearly asserting the primacy of the political elite over the economic elite. The perception that had been created in the eyes of many that the oligarchs ruled Russia while Yeltsin was president was destroyed as Putin showed that the basis of oligarch wealth and power was vulnerable to political pressure. But he also set about creating a second wave of oligarchs, leading businessmen who enjoyed Putin's support (often because of long personal association with him[65]) and were able to parlay access into economic power, and to mobilize that economic power into political currency.[66] During Putin's first two terms, the wealth of these oligarchs increased significantly,[67] but their capacity to wield independent political power within the elite was constrained. Furthermore, with a trend toward the corporatization of the economy during the pre-2008 period, with the state moving into a large number of major areas of economic life both through strategic investment and the insertion of state officials into leading posts in major corporations,[68] including people with established ties to Putin himself such as Aleksei Miller (Gazprom) and Igor Sechin (Rosneft),[69] the economic elite remained tied into the political elite,

---

[63] On the circumstances surrounding the arrest of Khodorkovsky and the breakup of Yukos, see Sakwa (*Quality*); Sakwa (*Putin and the Oligarch*); and Gustafson (*Wheel*), Chapter 7. Khodorkovsky was released in early 2014, and he immediately left Russia.

[64] Gustafson (*Wheel*), Chapter 8.

[65] Dawisha (*Putin's Kleptocracy*); and Applebaum ("How He and His Cronies"), pp. 26–30.

[66] On Gazprom and Putin in this regard, see Sakwa (*Crisis*), pp. 97–8.

[67] Gaman-Golutvina ("Changes"), p. 159.

[68] On the latter, see Huskey ("Putin as Patron"), pp. 175–6.

[69] See the discussion in Dawisha (*Putin's Kleptocracy*), pp. 281–2, 330–31, 336, 338–9.

but in a clearly subordinate position.[70] Although there appears to have been some attempt under Medvedev to moderate this trend, in structural terms little changed; politics retained its primacy in elite contours, with economics on a distinct second rung. The greater institutionalization of this relationship, principally through corporatization and the placement of political figures in leading economic posts, consolidated the political–economic elite nexus as a potential source of material reward for the former, and thereby further stabilized the political elite. Furthermore, under Putin, particularly during his third term, the presence of liberal economists and those who espoused a free market economy was much less evident than it had been under Yeltsin, a factor that also served to restrict the impact of Western views on the elite compared with the earlier period.

Important for the maintenance of any system of factional relations is the attitude of the most prominent figure in the elite, in this case the president. Note has already been made of the frequent changes in personnel under Yeltsin. There were also changes under Putin (and Medvedev), but they were much fewer in number, and generally when people were removed they were neither humiliated nor banished. In most cases when Putin removed someone from a post, he found that person another one.[71] By engineering such soft landings for people who were removed, Putin did much to ensure that an embittered opposition did not develop among former officials; most such people simply took on their new responsibilities and did not take up the political cudgels against their former boss, although ex-prime minister Mikhail Kasyanov was an exception to this.[72] Generally, when people were loyal to Putin, he returned that loyalty and protected them; dismissed officials were often moved to sinecures in/elsewhere in Moscow.[73] This is one reason why there was widespread surprise at the removal of Defense Minister Serdiukov in late 2012, who was seen as someone who had been very loyal to Putin. It is also a reason why there has been a high level of stability of the elite; if disaffected individuals are simply moved to another post in the general structure from which they can continue to enjoy the perks of office, they may be

---

[70] On businessmen being beholden to the Kremlin to conduct their businesses, see Dawisha (*Putin's Kleptocracy*), Chapters 6 and 7.

[71] For examples, see Sakwa (*Crisis*), pp. 115–16.

[72] On Kasyanov's activity in opposition, see Horvath (*Putin's Preventive Counter-Revolution*, 2013, pp. 63–5, 162–7. On Putin offering Kasyanov three jobs following his sacking, see Masha Gessen, *The Man without a Face. The Unlikely Rise of Vladimir Putin* (London: Granta, 2012), p. 250. Others who split from Putin include former Presidential Administration head Aleksandr Voloshin, economic adviser Andrei Illarionov, and PR specialist Gleb Pavlovsky.

[73] Huskey ("Putin as Patron"), pp. 164–5.

discouraged from taking up oppositionist activity. This is clearly designed as a measure to blunt potential challenges to the existing elite structure and to the president himself. Loyalty was important for Putin[74] because it brought obedience. The obedience he sought was not an obedience that turned everyone into yes men but one whereby a diversity of views could be expressed, but once a decision was made all fell in behind this. This could, of course, be a function of trust in the leader's abilities, but it could also result from a fear about the consequences of dissenting.[75] Whatever its source – belief in Putin, hope for benefits,[76] or fear of consequences – unity has been a powerful part of the elite ethos under Putin.

This notion of loyalty was an important underpinning of the dynamic of elite relations. The pattern of those relations that emerged under Putin was premised on the understanding that such relations did not involve a zero-sum game. Rather than a "winner take all" ethos, the spoils of both policy victory and material acquisition were shared to a degree among relevant groups, a process that helped to ensure loyalty to the general structure by giving all of the groups sufficient stake in it to dissuade them from seeking political advantage outside the existing elite structure. This also meant that defeat over some issue did not necessarily mean the destruction of the faction. This system, which recognized the legitimacy of a pluralism of interests within the elite, has since 2000 been presided over by Putin, one of whose major tasks has been to ensure that the system continues to function satisfactorily; he is an example of the "patronal president" identified by Hale.[77] But it is important to recognize that Putin has not only acted as a referee or balancer in this system; he has been a major actor in it, using its fluidity and dynamism to advance his own personal agenda. His success in managing factional differences is reflected in the fact that the government's policy agenda has generally been coherent and consistent over time and that the elite did not experience defections when it came under pressure at the time of the 2011–12 protests.

---

[74] On Putin, loyalty, and how this was a factor in Yeltsin's choosing of Putin in the first place, see Ostrow, Satarov, and Khakamada (*The Consolidation*), pp. 87–9.

[75] Hill and Gaddy's notion of "protection rackets" might be relevant here. Hill and Gaddy (*Mr. Putin*), pp. 239–40.

[76] The ubiquity of corruption, reflected both in the evaluations of international ratings agencies and in the speeches of Putin and Medvedev, may be important here because some of what is referred to as "corruption" will involve officials benefiting materially from their positions. The close links between politics and business at all levels means that those in politico-administrative positions are well placed to gain material wealth and benefits. Putin himself is said to enjoy a lifestyle far in excess of that possible on his salary alone. Roxburgh (*Strongman*), p. 291; and Gessen (*The Man*), pp. 254–7. For an extended argument that Putin created a system designed to benefit himself and his cronies, see Dawisha (*Putin's Kleptocracy*), Chapters 6 and 7.

[77] Hale ("Democracy"), pp. 305–29.

As argued above, the personality of the president is an important factor in shaping the dynamics of elite politics, and this was no less so in the post-Yeltsin years than it had been under Yeltsin. In contrast to Yeltsin, Vladimir Putin's three terms as president have been characterized by an image of Putin as an activist president, involved in both big picture issues and the nitty-gritty of detail. He appeared as someone who got things done, whose concern was doing the best for the country, and who expended his not inconsiderable energies in trying to deal with problems. Although unable to articulate a particularly clear vision of where the country was headed, he was able to project an image that it was headed in the right direction and that he was personally responsible for this. But unlike Yeltsin, he sought to convey this image not by generating a false picture of himself as standing up to his manifold foes, but by working with the parliament to solve the country's problems; he was shown as continually engaged in national affairs. He was clearly aided in this by the operation of first Unity and then United Russia (see Chapter 3), the two parties developed to promote Putin's policies and, through the winning of seats in the Duma, bring the parliament on side with the president.[78] In this sense Putin chose to work within the system, utilizing the powers vested in the presidency plus his ability to structure the political system in other ways to consolidate his personal position and avoid the continual elite tensions that had characterized much of the Yeltsin period. This was therefore a very different style of presidency, one in which large sections of the elite were encapsulated, in contrast to the Yeltsin presidency, where significant sections were excluded, but they were also subordinate.

But there was also a distinctly populist element to Putin's image. Resting upon continuing high popular approval ratings,[79] Putin appeared as an activist leader who could get things done. Benefiting from the economic turnaround that had followed the collapse of 1998, and adopting a more assertive attitude to the West, Putin appeared as a decisive leader whose policies were leading Russia back to the greatness that was its destiny. He appeared engaged and in control (despite an early hiccup with the Kursk affair in August 2000 where he appeared distant and uncaring), highlighted by his vigorous response to the various terrorist incidents during his presidency. But he also projected himself as a man of the people

---

[78] For one discussion of this, see Paul Chaisty, "Majority Control and Executive Dominance: Parliament–President Relations in Putin's Russia," Pravda (*Leading Russia*), pp. 119–37.

[79] Although over time these have generally trended down. By late 2013, 52 percent supported Putin's actions while 31 percent did not, the lowest approval and highest disapproval rating he had experienced to that time, www.levada.ru/03–12–2013/rossiyane-o-vladimire-putine and www.levada.ru/03–12–2013/vozmozhnye-rezultaty-prezidentskikh-vyborov. The downward trend was significantly reversed at the time of the takeover of Crimea and more general crisis with Ukraine in early 2014.

and in tune with their wishes. This was done not only through his major press conference each year and his open live question-and-answer sessions with the public, but through presentation of him involved in such things as judo, hunting, flying planes, riding motor bikes, scuba diving to locate ancient Greek vases and driving trucks. Pictures of his well-muscled body with his shirt off became cultural icons during his first two terms, although this macho image seems to have been less in evidence following his reelection in 2012. A cult of Putin emerged, reflected chiefly in the mass media and in the spate of books about him, although there was also a popularly based mocking, ironic side to this evident in many of the sorts of images and artifacts produced outside official channels.[80] Elements of a charismatic appeal have been present, but these have probably been overshadowed by the projection of the image of him as simply an activist, decisive, and competent leader.

The Medvedev presidency was a variant on this. Through United Russia's control over the parliament and through a broadly publicly consultative style, Medvedev maintained the inclusive sort of presidency he inherited from Putin. However, he lacked the dominance that Putin was able to exercise both practically and symbolically. In part this is because of the continued presence of Putin in elite councils, but it is also because of the persona that he has projected. While Putin was presented as the action man – hunting tigers, fighting forest fires, driving heavy vehicles in remote locations – Medvedev has appeared as the man in the office giving directions. He presented himself as more "modern" and high-tech savvy than Putin, making wider use of blogging and of video blogging to present himself as in touch with a modern audience.[81] But his presidency lacked the vitality and dynamism that was associated with the early Putin. Nevertheless, like his predecessor, his modus operandi did not provoke conflict or destabilization in the elite as he adhered to the pattern of trying to reinforce elite stability.

But while the focus on elite stability emphasizes the corporate nature of elite rule in Russia, this should not obscure the central and decisive role played by Putin. He is not only the arbiter of elite difference and the fundamental authority figure for the whole structure, but the ultimate source of official policy; most members of the elite tailor their public support for policy positions to what they believe Putin wants. This is so not

[80] Julie A. Cassidy and Emily D. Johnson, "Putin, Putiniana and the Question of a Post-Soviet Cult of Personality," *Slavonic and East European Review* 88 (4), 2010, pp. 681–707. For studies of different forms of cultural representation of Putin, see Helen Goscilo (ed.), *Putin as Celebrity and Cultural Icon* (London: Routledge, 2013).

[81] Natalie Moen-Larsen, "Communicating with the Nation: Russian Politicians Online," *Russian Analytical Digest* 123, February 21, 2013, pp. 10–12.

simply because he is president, but because his own pers
and outlook drive the system. Despite the attempts to stre
tral controls through institutional means, the weakness and
those institutions (reflected inter alia in his criticisms of the p
of government and by implication the power vertical and L
that he has to continue to rely upon his personal associations
tacts to push things through. The framework of his personal a      ...s,
functioning both through and beside the formal structures, reflects not
only the interaction of formal and informal factors, but the continuing
strength of the personalist principle and personal political power. The
importance of such personalist connections is shown in the way in which
so much of the infrastructure and key economic resources have been
placed under the control of long-time Putin allies. This sort of personalism weakens the normative power of the formal institutions and, at lower
levels, undermines the horizontal links between people, who become
united principally through the personalized network. This becomes the
principal vehicle for power and patronage.

One key point at which destabilization could occur within elites is at
the time of succession. The Constitution provides the formal means for
filling the office of president: if the president retired early or was incapable
of fulfilling his functions, his position was taken in an acting capacity by
the prime minister with a new election being held within three months,
and at the end of a presidential term, a new president would be chosen
by popular election. The Constitution also imposed a limit of two consecutive terms on a president. While neither Yeltsin nor Putin sought to
extend their terms in office beyond the two consecutive terms allowed by
the Constitution,[82] both sought to structure the succession in such a way
as to ensure the identity of the new president and thereby avoid change or
disruption. Although Yeltsin carried out this act of political engineering
within the context of his own early retirement while Putin served out
his term, both used the same tactic to shape the succession: nomination
of a trusted subordinate as the preferred presidential candidate.[83] This

[82] This is despite considerable pressure for Putin to do so, either by amending the Constitution or bringing about a real union with Belarus that would involve the elevation of
Putin into a super-presidential position above that of the presidents of the two states.
Some also canvassed the possibility of a new position of senior leader, something like
those adopted by Deng Xiaoping in China or Lee Kuan Yew in Singapore.

[83] Yeltsin was later quite open about this, saying that his "main political goal" was "to
quietly lead the country to 2000 and the presidential elections. Then as I saw it, we
would find a strong, young politician and pass the political baton to him. We would
give him a place at the starting gates and help him develop his potential. Together, we
would help him win the elections." Boris Yeltsin, *Midnight Diaries* (London: Weidenfeld
& Nicolson, 2000), p. 205.

was also the modus operandi of the Medvedev–Putin succession. Yeltsin's shuffling of prime ministers in 1998–9 was part of the process of choosing who to put forward, while Putin seems to have set up a sort of competition between Medvedev and Defense Minister Sergei Ivanov to assist him in making up his mind.[84] In November 2005 Medvedev became first deputy prime minister and acquired responsibility for four national priority areas or projects (health, education, agriculture, and housing) and the enhanced resources required to carry these out. This provided him with a significantly higher public profile. While remaining Defense Minister, Ivanov was made a deputy prime minister and, four months later, head of a commission designed to oversee state military procurement. In any event, Yeltsin, Putin, and Medvedev formally nominated their successors, with their choice ratified by popular election. Elite unity was therefore maintained with the constitutional formalities observed, even if in practice the choice was limited through early presidential intervention. In the case of the Putin succession to Yeltsin, factional considerations within the elite were clearly evident: Yeltsin needed someone to overcome the potential split in the elite posed by the challenge stemming from the emergence of Fatherland-All Russia. In the Medvedev succession to Putin, the latter needed someone who would not upset the broad factional balance within the elite. In both cases, these presidential aims were achieved. In the Medvedev to Putin succession, this was clearly agreed by both parties and seems not to have involved factional concerns, even though significant ranks of officials around Medvedev would have preferred to see him remain as president, but this did not translate into elite tension or conflict. However, the levels of uncertainty about who would be president leading in to the 2008 (Medvedev, Ivanov, or even Putin) and 2012 (Medvedev or Putin) successions did create a degree of paralysis as officials were unwilling to commit to either side until they were sure of the outcome.[85]

## A stable elite?

The Russian political elite has developed from Yeltsin to Putin, and in the process has become more stable and consolidated. It has also retained its autonomy from society at large and, reflecting the changed attitude to the West, also become more insulated from the effects of Western influence. The greater stabilization of the elite under Putin compared with Yeltsin came about because of a number of factors. A chief one was the greater

[84] For one discussion of this, see Sakwa (*Crisis*), pp. 81–3 and Chapters 5 and 6.
[85] Roxburgh (*Strongman*), pp. 208–9.

degree of agreement among the members of the elite about the basic course of development the country should follow. The polarization of the political spectrum under Yeltsin, and the associated conflict and debate generally in the society about where Russia was going, disappeared with Putin's adoption of a range of policy positions that spanned the center of the spectrum and undercut much of the appeal of the communists. With the debate about where the country was going no longer dominating public life, major questions of principle were replaced by those of a nuts and bolts, policy, nature, and this meant that an underlying general consensus could emerge among the elite. Certainly there was discussion of "democracy" and what that meant, but this did not divide the elite into warring clans. Another side to this was the personality of the president. Yeltsin was a divisive figure, because of his personal history, his modus operandi, and the policies with which he was associated. While he was able to compromise and to negotiate, he had a history of adopting the "crash through or crash" approach, which only served to alienate him from many potential supporters and to exacerbate existing differences. In contrast, Putin was seen as an effective manager, someone who took a more low-key approach and sought to include people in the process rather than draw lines between them. He was therefore better able to handle factional tensions and to defuse them when need be.

Putin also sought to regularize elite relations much more than Yeltsin had done. His more consistent working style and his greater capacity to work through existing institutions and processes (e.g., less attempt at a charismatic appeal, more effort to work with the parliament) encouraged the greater regularity of elite relations. Furthermore, he set the tone for this by bringing in lower levels of elite mobility and, through his treatment of most of those defeated in intra-elite struggles, by making elite conflict not a zero-sum game. If defeat did not necessarily mean an end to participation in political life, there was less incentive for conflicts to become deadly and more incentive for people to play by the rules of the elite game. Similarly the regularization of access to material rewards through association with the economic sector provided an incentive for people to play by the rules, so that even if their policy positions did not come out on top, they could still gain some reward.

Crucial to this elite culture was the interaction between formal institutions and informal practices. These intertwined in critical ways to structure the basic course of elite life, crucially in terms of the two chief currencies of elite relations, personal relationships and institutional position. While institutional position provided certain formal rights of access and involvement, it was personal relationships that guaranteed real access to decision-making power. Overwhelmingly, personal relationships with the president were crucial. Those who combined a close personal relationship with the president with high bureaucratic office were best placed to wield influence in this system. But because of the growth over time of institutional norms, institutional position also mattered. If the only thing that was important was a personal relationship with the president, there would have been little need for the office-swapping that accompanied the Putin–Medvedev and Medvedev–Putin successions. So in this elite world, institutions matter; it is not such a personalist system that only the will of the president is important. And it is here that the greater regularity brought to elite processes by Putin has been significant. It has meant a greater sense of security among elites and a propensity to subordinate conflict, so that when there appears to be a potential challenge to the elite, as in 2011–12, that elite does not fracture. It has been this ability to meld the elite together that has enabled Putin to stabilize and consolidate the elite system and, with it, the political system more generally.

The stabilization of the elite reflects in significant measure the greater success of the tripartite strategy pursued by Putin compared with Yeltsin. The first element in this strategy was the appointment of supporters to leading elite positions. Putin was able to call on a much greater reservoir of people with significant career associations with him than Yeltsin was able to do. This was important in the differing contexts in which they found themselves. While Yeltsin as a classic transitional leader had to mold an elite structure out of material comprising the former Soviet elite that he distrusted and inexperienced outsiders, Putin inherited an elite structure in which he felt much more naturally at home. Accordingly while Yeltsin used his appointive powers to promote supporters, they remained in a minority compared with those whose credentials were much more about bureaucratic position and experience than personal loyalty to the president. In contrast, Putin's supporters combined personal loyalty with institutional position, thereby constituting a more secure base for both elite politics and Putin's personal position. This was not altered by the Medvedev interlude.

The second element of this strategy was the prevention of challengers/challenges emerging from within the elite. Putin was much better placed to do this than his predecessor. With his role perceived as a consolidator of the change introduced earlier rather than the initiator of such change, he did not have to confront the major debates about the future trajectory of Russia; communism was no longer seen as a viable option in the way that it was to significant elements in the early 1990s. As a result, Putin's policy positions were much more centrist and embracing of wider sections of the elite than was possible for Yeltsin, whose policies evoked significant opposition. The Putin elite had much greater consistency of outlook and approach than was evident under Yeltsin, while Putin's strategy of generally giving soft landings to elite dissidents acted as a disincentive to become too disruptive. Elite politics was much less of a zero-sum game under Putin than it had been under Yeltsin. Putin's general approach has been much more consensual compared with the divide-and-rule type of strategy that Yeltsin seemed to prefer. Along with acceptance of the right of elites to prosper materially as a result of their high office, which was common to all presidential terms, Putin's strategy was clearly designed to prevent the emergence of elite discontent in a way that Yeltsin's was not.

The third element of elite strategy was for the president to remain continually closely engaged in elite political life. Whereas Yeltsin was frequently absent and his interventions were seen as episodic and idiosyncratic, Putin cultivated a style that relied upon regularity and continual application by the president. This sort of continuing engagement not only enabled him to keep something of a watching brief on the course of elite affairs, but it also enabled him to step in if and when potential difficulties were likely to develop. This involvement rendered him part of the elite in a way that, for Yeltsin, was not always possible.

Through the implementation of this tripartite strategy, Putin has sought to consolidate elite politics and, by so doing, his own position at the top. This was an important step in the process of creating a more consolidated and integrated structure of governmental and administrative machinery of the sort noted at the beginning of this book as necessary to stabilize authoritarian rule. However, it remains unclear whether this arrangement can survive the sort of personalist dominance Putin seems to exercise.

# Conclusion
## The Putin system and the potential for regime change

The political trajectory of post-Soviet Russia was profoundly shaped by a combination of the circumstances of independent Russia's birth and the actions of its two major figures, Boris Yeltsin and Vladimir Putin, in building the new regime. One of the chief legacies of the Soviet period and the way it ended was the weakness of autonomous political forces outside the bounds of the political elite. There had been no room for legitimate autonomous political activity in the USSR, with the only room for political activity being in the official structures of the Soviet system. Accordingly when perestroika created space and impetus for the emergence of autonomous political forces, that emergence was both tentative and fragmented. Civil society forces remained weak and unable to have a major impact on elite politics, so that it was overwhelmingly the latter that shaped the circumstances of the Soviet collapse, albeit assisted materially by social movements in some of the republics (but not Russia). The result was that as the new Russian political system struggled to take form, autonomous social forces were not well placed to exercise substantial influence in it. The weakness of such forces, be they political parties or civil society organizations, left the way clear for the dominating role to be played by political elites, and within this by the dominant figures, Yeltsin and Putin.

As well as this relative absence of opposition to the building of an authoritarian polity, another factor noted in Chapter 1 contributed to the resilience of authoritarian rule: the more authoritarian aspects of Russian culture provided a favorable environment within which authoritarian rule could prosper. For both elite and mass, appeals to Russian tradition could be a potent source of support for authoritarian political arrangements. Other factors too played a part. The initial dispute with the parliament, the Chechen wars, the incidents of terrorist activity (apartment, metro, airport and railway station bombings, the Nord Ost and Beslan sieges), and the growing perception of hostility and challenge on the part of the West were all developments that successive presidents were able to exploit to reduce the scope for opposition and strengthen central control.[1] But it was the drive of the post-Soviet political elite to build an authoritarian system through the structuring of the dimensions of rule in an authoritarian fashion that was central and most important to the emergence of authoritarian rule. Had either president (but especially Yeltsin) been committed to the construction of a democratic political system and sought to structure the opportunities for autonomous political activity and the internal functioning of the regime in different ways consistent with democratic principles, a different outcome may have come about. Instead both presidents and the elites around them sought to constrain and blunt popular involvement in the political system and to centralize the regime and its processes around the presidency. The structure created, especially under Putin, also negated the potential influence from outside that had been so instrumental in the successful challenge to established elites elsewhere. The crucial state-building activities headed by Yeltsin and Putin were therefore the single most important factor in the construction of an authoritarian polity in Russia.

The failure of the democratic potentialities embedded in late perestroika was thus principally a function of elite decisions in post-Soviet Russia. Despite their rhetorical commitment to "democracy," when decisions were made that concerned autonomous political activity or regime structure, those decisions were overwhelmingly of the type that reduced scope for autonomous activity and tightened control around the president. Yeltsin's decisions seem to have been more ad hoc, a function of his fear of political challenge plus his lack of understanding of or commitment to democracy as a principle. Despite the dominant position he seemed to gain from his defeat of the parliamentary opposition in 1993, Yeltsin was never able to exercise the power that seemingly had fallen into his hands. He was always confronted by powerful opposition forces in the parliament that he could neither ignore nor eliminate, and his health remained a clear limitation on his capacity to fulfill his role in a decisive fashion. As a result, from 1992 he was never in a position unilaterally to implement policy. Confronted with this sort of position, he was continually forced to compromise or to seek to get around his opponents, with the result that he was generally more focused on tactical moves to achieve limited ends than upon grander considerations of system construction. His rhetorical commitment to "democracy" waned over the decade in the face of the popular disillusionment that stemmed

---

[1] Indeed some even argue that rather than simply exploiting events over which they had little control that sections within the Russian state may even have been behind some of these actions.

from the association of that "democracy" with the contemporary experience of economic difficulty, crime, and corruption. With the waning of that rhetoric went the strengthening of measures designed to limit opposition, but at the same time there was a weakening of effective central control, reflected most clearly in the substantial autonomy enjoyed by the provinces from Moscow and the perception of widespread growing crime and corruption. The weakness of Yeltsin stemming from the opposition he faced and his own physical frailties meant he could not place a decisive stamp on Russia's future development, except for his choice of Putin as his replacement. But he did also create many of the foundations upon which Putin was to build.

Putin's decisions seem to constitute a more coherent program, developing in response to challenges that emerged, but also reflecting his experience of the Yeltsin years. Putin was in a much stronger position than Yeltsin to shape his country's political trajectory, and he proceeded to do this. He sought to remedy the deficiencies he identified in the Yeltsin legacy, and this took the form overwhelmingly of centralizing control and narrowing the spaces for autonomous political activity. It is not clear whether this reflected an underlying ideological predisposition or not. His enunciation of conservative principles of the strong Russian state and the primacy of Russian tradition, alongside the rejection of Western hegemony, influence, and universal values, were all consistent with an authoritarian style of rule. But his actions could also be seen in terms of a pragmatic (from a conservative viewpoint) reaction to what he saw as the dysfunctional system he had inherited from Yeltsin. While the source of his system-building actions may thus be a matter for dispute, their effect is not: they contributed substantially to the consolidation of the authoritarian regime in Russia.

The system that has emerged is clearly authoritarian rather than totalitarian in scope.[2] The capacity for autonomous political activity has not been totally extinguished, nor the regime permanently unified. Russia under Putin remains a system of limited pluralism, in which there is room for independent action on the part of official institutions (e.g., the courts, provincial administrations), political parties, civil society organizations, and social movements; control from the center remains patchy rather than complete. There is no evidence that Putin ever wanted to extinguish such pluralism entirely; rather he has sought to keep it within acceptable bounds and thereby to manage it. In this sense, his efforts at structuring autonomous political activity and centralizing control within

[2] On the difference, see Juan J. Linz, *Totalitarian and Authoritarian Regimes* (Boulder: Lynne Rienner, 2000).

the political structure were the central means of building an authoritarian polity, but one that retains some scope for autonomous political activity and potentially for change.

The central focus of the system is the personal power and position of Putin himself. Chapter 5 discussed the nature of Putin's personal profile. He is clearly the most important actor in the political system, symbolically dominating the public arena and practically playing a primary role in the processes of politics. However, his dominance should not be exaggerated; his word is not law. He clearly has difficulty getting government ministers and ministries to implement all of his instructions. Regional officials are not the mere ciphers of the president's will. Political parties and civil society organizations do not automatically bend the knee to Putin and his demands, while sections of the populace seem, at least rhetorically, to reject his authority. Thus, while Putin is the dominant figure in the political landscape, he must manage the other actors in that landscape, rather than simply control them. There may also be an increasingly strong sense of the growing normative authority of laws and the Constitution: witness Putin's refusal to alter the Constitution to enable him to run for a third consecutive presidential term. If the law is gaining in normative authority, this too would constitute a potential restriction on presidential power. Russia is clearly a case of limited pluralism, in the sense that autonomous actors continue to function, albeit within general limits set from above. The limits to Putin's personal power and authority, although not precisely identifiable, are real, and they mean that the stability of the system depends in significant measure on his ability to manage the other actors in the system.

Putin's personal power and position reflect a central aspect of the system, the tension between personalism and institutionalism, between a mode of operation in which personal considerations and loyalties are the essence of its functioning and one in which bureaucratic or institutional imperatives and rules are dominant. The coexistence of both of these modes of operation creates considerable ambiguity in the functioning of the system.[3] When the rationalist norms of bureaucracy rub against the personalist principles of patrimonialism, the resulting ambiguity significantly complicates both the stabilization of central control and the institutionalization of bureaucratic bodies, with potential long-term consequences for system development. It also complicates the task

---

[3] This is the actual source of much of what Richard Sakwa refers to as "dualism," which he explains in terms of the "administrative regime" versus the "constitutional state." Richard Sakwa, "The Dual State in Russia," *Post-Soviet Affairs* 26 (3), 2010, pp. 185–206; and Sakwa (*Crisis*).

of managing the public political engagement of other actors in the political system.

The electoral system is a central factor in this management process. It is designed to provide a structured means for the opposition to participate in political life, but without challenging the continued dominance of the president and those around him. It is therefore a means of co-optation of the opposition, as well as demonstrating to potential opponents the strength of popular support the regime enjoys, thereby emphasizing to them the futility of further opposition. To consolidate the regime, that regime needs to dominate the electoral process. But the successful operation of the electoral system in this way requires continued work to ensure that the rules and processes whereby that system functions remain tilted against the opposition, that officials at all levels play their part in producing the required outcome, and that the party that carries the president's banner remains able to generate the level of popular support that is required. As the demonstrations of 2011–12 show, reflecting in a much milder form the lessons of the color revolutions, if these do not work effectively, the potential for such elections to become a destabilizing force rather than one that helps stabilize authoritarian rule can be realized. If the electoral system does not produce the sort of dominance for the ruling group that is expected, or if it does so in such a fashion as to discredit the process in popular eyes (because of popular perceptions of blatant excessive fraud), the result may be a weakening of the regime's popular base and its potential destabilization. In this sense, the difference between stability and a continuation of authoritarian rule relatively untroubled is slight; the effective functioning of the electoral system remains central to continued control over autonomous political activity, and thereby to the continued stability of the regime.

An important product of the dominance the regime can achieve through the electoral system is the neutering of the parliament as an independent force. By gaining a majority (and even better an overwhelming majority) in the legislative chamber, the regime party can prevent the parliament from becoming a site of opposition activity and lock that institution in behind the president. Also by giving opposition parties an arena within which they can play a part, the authorities seek to co-opt such parties and give them a stake in the system that they might otherwise not have. And to the extent that the parliament is an arena in which rent-seeking can be a profitable activity, giving opposition parties some capacity to share in this provides another reason for those parties not to seek to destabilize arrangements. The ability of the regime party to shape the parliament in this way has been a major factor in the stability of the political system under Putin.

Tied in with this is the role of popular pacification in the creation of conditions for stable rule. One aspect of this is the structuring of the activity of civil society groups. Through official channels like laws and regulations, and unofficial channels like the exertion of pressure and the generation of pro-authorities pseudo-autonomous groups, the regime can create an environment within which opposition activity by civil society organizations is both difficult and limited. But in systems that are not classed as totalitarian, this sort of control is always restricted rather than total. There is always some room for such groups to express their discontent and get their message out into the public sphere, even if it is not broadcast widely. This means, again, that the regime must manage a situation of which it is not fully in control; it must deal with other forces, containing their potential dissidence while at the same time allowing them some continuing room for autonomous activity. The continued official adherence to notions of "democracy," however interpreted, compels the maintenance of this sort of space, while the desire to limit opposition demands that this space be managed.

Another aspect of popular pacification is management of the populace as a whole. The structuring of civil society space is important here, in providing a means of regulating the organized involvement of the people in political life. But also important is means to prevent the more spontaneous popular eruption or the mobilization of people outside the institutions the regime provides or allows. The demonstrations of 2011–12 are the best example of the sort of activity the regime seeks to avoid. One potential means of preventing this from happening is coercion, or at least the threat of it. If people know that their involvement in popular mobilization is likely to lead to them facing sanctions, they may be dissuaded from participating in such activity (although the potency of this threat depends upon a range of factors, including judgments about the likelihood of sanctions, the degree of outrage/opposition felt by the would-be demonstrators, and maybe judgments about the number of demonstrators likely to attend). This was one factor in the wide-scale arrests and later trials of leaders and rank-and-file members of the May 6, 2012, demonstration. Coercion, or its threat, is a constant tool of regimes seeking to maintain their dominance.

But also important is another form of pacification, providing the populace with conditions that may dissuade them from opposition to the regime. This is sometimes expressed in terms of a social contract: the populace is given improved living standards and lifestyles, and in exchange surrender the demand for political involvement and offer the regime its support. This has clearly been a strategy for Putin. Between the economic crises of 1998 and 2008 and again following the recovery from

2010 until the setback of 2014, the expanding Russian economy has created greatly improved lifestyles and living conditions for large numbers
of Russian citizens, principally in the big cities and especially in Moscow.
Based primarily on high oil and gas prices (although government policy in other sectors did make some contribution to this), growth rates
were high throughout most of the 2000s and urban living standards rose.
Despite the rhetoric during the Medvedev presidency about the modern-
ization of the economy and the shift to a high-tech economy, the basic
economic model has remained largely unchanged. Heavy income from
reliance upon the sale of natural resources has produced a cash flow that
the government has been able to use to bolster living standards; especially
important has been the state's ability to take resource rents from oil and
gas producers and direct them into the rest of the economy in the form
of investment, subsidies, and welfare payments.[4] The continuing openness to the international market has provided the emergent middle class
(as well as those whose wealth would place them outside the bounds of
that group) with a source of goods and services (including international
travel) previously unavailable. This sort of economic return should have
provided a buffer for the regime as a grateful populace recognized that its
improving position was due to the economic structure and policies that
the regime had set in place.

The sort of economic structure that has emerged under Putin has been
important for regime stability in another way. In practice the economy
has been a hybrid of private and state enterprise. While most small and
medium business has remained in private hands, many large and strategically significant sectors have seen either state domination (e.g., the gas
industry) or an amalgam of state and private activity (e.g., the oil sector).
And where there has been this amalgam, the state has sought to place
itself in a position to shape what happens in that sector of the economy. Major means for the creation of such an amalgam have been the
takeover of private companies by the state and the interlinking of elites,
in particular the placement of state officials in management positions in
companies and the interdependencies created between private owners
and state officials, most particularly Putin and the oligarchs. This sort of
interlinking has obscured the boundaries between state and private such
that the important sectors are best seen as hybrid; for example, the state-
owned Rosneft is listed on the London stock exchange while the private
Lukoil has actively assisted Russian foreign policy in the Caspian area

---

[4] For example, there were significant (>60 percent) increases in pensions between 2007
and 2011, public sector wages increased over the same period, and military and police
salaries doubled.

where the company is active. This hybrid nature of the economy gives the state increased leverage, increasing the capacity not only for more direct running of the economy, but for elite rent-seeking as well. Potentially economically powerful oligarchs[5] may be bought off and thereby effectively co-opted by the regime, while the enhanced state sphere in the economy limits the room for potential opposition to develop an economic base for their activities.

Such rent-seeking is also potentially a mechanism that can assist in attaining and maintaining elite unity. Putin has been very successful in engineering such unity. There have been few defections from within the political elite while economic elites have generally been subservient following the treatment accorded to those deemed to have stepped out of line in the early 2000s. Where there have been policy differences, these have generally been handled either in-house or, when they have escaped into the public arena, they have not resulted in zero-sum conflict. The ability to use political office for economic gain may be one factor behind the continuing elite unity; to defect from the elite could not only deny one continued access to such material rewards, but it could lead to the loss of whatever gains had been achieved in the past. The ability to maintain elite unity has been particularly impressive given that Putin was able to navigate the potentially dangerous situation of his replacement as president and subsequent return to that office. As much of the literature on regime change shows, and the color revolutions affirm, a split in the elite can be fatal for regime survival, and thus far the Putin elite has been able to avoid this.

The stability of the regime has also been buttressed by its ability to minimize the influence of pro-democracy/anti-regime external forces of the type that were present in the color revolutions noted in Chapter 1. The influence that Western governments and NGOs were able to have during the 1990s was dramatically reduced under Putin. This reflects the more assertive stance Russia took internationally, reflected in a foreign policy that sought ostentatiously to pursue Russia's own interests, and to define them in a way that often brought them into tension with the West. Rather than seeming to be kowtowing to the West, as Yeltsin was accused of doing, Russia sought when necessary to openly stand up to the West. This definition of its interests in purely Russian terms was associated with an emphasis on reliance on Russian traditions and values rather than adherence to some nebulous conception of international or universal

---

[5] For one discussion of the role of such economically based oligarchs in authoritarian systems, see Jeffrey A. Winters, *Oligarchy* (Cambridge: Cambridge University Press, 2011).

values, which were increasingly seen as just another name for Western values and a lever for Western influence. This harking back to Russian traditions logically involved a rejection of Western values and the introduction of them into Russia. Accordingly steps were taken to limit such influence. An important part of this was at the ideological level, where Putin's emphasis upon the strong Russian state and reliance on Russian values delegitimized Western influence, but also important were the measures designed to exclude Western influence from the NGO sector. To the extent that the Putinist position was reflected widely within Russian society, the environment for Western influence was unfavorable. This means that the capacity of Western actors to influence the course of Russian developments was more limited after 2000 than it had been between the collapse of the USSR and Putin's accession to the presidency. The important role such actors played in regime change elsewhere and identified in the literature has therefore been much less likely in Putin's Russia. The Ukraine crisis of 2014, which appeared to many in Russia to confirm hostile Western intent, only strengthened this likelihood.

But to show the way in which the regime has been able to stabilize itself is not to suggest that there are not challenges embedded in each of these things. They do include challenges, and the regime will have to meet these satisfactorily if it is to endure.

The first potential challenge stems from Putin's personal role in the system. Given the pivotal part he plays, his disappearance from the scene could have significant consequences for political life. The difference in the way in which the presidency has operated under Putin compared with Yeltsin supports the view building on the work of Richard Neustadt[6] on the US that the presidency is shaped by the way in which the incumbent performs his functions. This is especially the case if the normative authority of the institutions is not firmly consolidated, and therefore the sorts of constraints embedded in those institutions are not sufficiently powerful to restrain a would-be willful incumbent. In the Russian case, where normative authority remains problematic, the personality of the president has increased saliency. If Putin were replaced, the personality, perspectives, and preferences of his successor would be crucial in shaping the course of future development. Should that successor be less inclined to play the sort of activist role Putin has adopted, it may be that power would become more decentralized and frayed, perhaps even leading the system to develop in a more democratic direction. But of course if that successor decided he wanted to strengthen central control, the capacity

---

[6] Richard Neustadt, *Presidential Power. The Politics of Leadership* (New York: John Wiley & Sons, 1960).

to do this would also exist. So given the strength of personalism in the regime, by definition, Putin's departure would be likely to lead to change.

Another potential problem stemming from personalism comes from any substantial decline in Putin's personal approval rating. The high personal approval rating he had during his first two terms as president underpinned the authority he was able to wield at that time. But since the end of his second term, Putin's popularity has been trending down, although it remains at a much higher level than any other Russian political figure, and did pick up considerably at the time of the Ukraine crisis in 2014. However, if it was to decline precipitously, the implications of this would be unclear. It could lead to the erosion of his position within the elite, but whether this will lead to any instability at elite levels is not certain. But given that he has been so closely associated with the regime, dropping popular approval levels could be transferred to the regime as a whole, again with unforeseeable consequences.

The problems highlighted by the 2011 election could potentially be severe, particularly because of the dual nature of the election – means of regime legitimation and consolidation, cf. potentially delegitimation and overthrow. For the regime to overcome this challenge, it needs to restore the election as an event in which overwhelming support for it is demonstrated. Central to this is the state of United Russia (UR). Unless the party can regain its capacity to mobilize popular support on the scale of the mid 2000s, it is unlikely to be able to play the stabilizing role that is needed. This means that it must regain the capacity to both organizationally and ideologically mobilize voter support. The key to this may be ideological. Up until now, the party has basically stood for whatever Putin has said. It has not had an independent policy profile and has been seen widely as standing for nothing except the self-interest of its members, many of whom hold official office in the state structure. As the "officials' party," it is seen as aiding and abetting the corruption that is widely perceived as dogging Russian public life. If it is to overcome this, the party needs to separate itself from Putin, in the sense of showing that it stands for something independent of the president. If it does this, and is able to generate a viable policy platform, and is seen as acting responsibly, it may be able to win back some of the popular support it seems to have lost. And if it does generate its own policy and act responsibly in government, it may be able to solve its organizational problem by reenergizing its own officials and members,[7] including importantly the

---

[7] As one part of this, experiments have been conducted with the establishment of a system of people's primaries to choose candidates. For discussion of such an experiment in

governors, who may then be more effective at getting out the vote than they were in 2011.

However, while this strategy might lead to the party increasing in popularity, it would strike at the heart of the basic dynamic of Russian electoral authoritarianism. The more independent of Putin the party became, the less able it would be to act as his agent in structuring the electoral process. But if it does not change, it is difficult to see it being able to recover its standing among the electorate. Given this paradox, the most sensible solution for Putin could be the creation of another, replacement, party, and his ascension to the leadership of the All-Russian People's Front in mid 2013 may indicate that this strategy was being seriously considered.

But it is not only the performance of the party that needs to be addressed. The demonstrations of 2011–12 were triggered by perceived fraud in the electoral process. As indicated in Chapter 3, in an electoral authoritarian system, there are two aspects to the manipulation of the electoral process: tilting of the electoral arena in favor of the ruling party, and fraud at the time of the election. The more effective the former is, the less need there is for the latter. Of course authoritarian regimes do not always see it this way. Many authoritarian leaders are insufficiently sure of their positions to rely solely on tilting the arena. They seek to burnish their electoral performance by fraud, even when it is unnecessary. Alternatively, even though a central leader may be confident in his position and not seek to use fraud on a wide scale, his subordinates may be motivated by other factors. In particular, where successful tenure of office is defined, in part, in terms of the ability to get out the vote, regional leaders will often be tempted to use fraud even when there is no objective reason to do so. Neither of these two sources of fraud, central uncertainty and regional perception, can be eliminated necessarily by improved tilting of the arena, but such action can relieve the pressure on the part of officials to engage in fraudulent behavior. Thus, if Putin and the people around him wanted to reduce the level of reliance on fraud, they should work at improving the means whereby they tilt the electoral arena as a whole. While such measures may have caused unhappiness among the opposition, they have not generally been the source of popular mobilization to anything like the same extent as fraud has been.

If the deficient performance of the party cannot be addressed, it could have knock-on effects in the parliament. The Duma has a history of opposing the president throughout the 1990s, so the adoption of an oppositionist stance by this body would not be unprecedented. Such a

Moscow, see Andrei Pertsev and Elizabeta Surnacheva, "Moskva – liubitel'skaia," *Vlast'* 19 (1074), May 19, 2014, pp. 32–5.

development might have no immediate substantial effect upon the structure of the system, although it might restore the dysfunctional nature of the president–parliament relationship evident under Yeltsin. However, if the Duma was to seek to act as an independent but constructive check upon the president, a more responsible style of system could emerge. It is also possible that, if it was to act in this way, this could be a stage on the way to a more democratic set of political arrangements.

The structuring of the activity of civil society organizations also holds potential dangers for the regime. The problem here is similar to that of the electoral system. The regime wants to give some room for civil society organizations, yet also to ensure that their activities do not get out of hand. The question for the regime is where to draw the line between what is acceptable and what is not acceptable, and how to avoid making a martyr out of particular organizations. It is not always an easy judgment call to make about what to allow and disallow if you do not want to destroy the whole notion of a sphere of autonomous (or perhaps semi-autonomous) activity. Management of this process is complex and nuanced, and if the regime gets it wrong, it can have significant consequences. This is often a game between authorities and civil society organizations, with some of the latter always testing the boundaries of the permissible, but it is a game that can have serious consequences for both sides. The same applies to popular mobilization. A complete crackdown preventing any form of mobilization or demonstration would seem very heavy-handed and give no outlet for the release of popular tensions. However, where to hold the line and what to allow remain uncertain. The attempt to restrict demonstrations to approved locations, for example, may only encourage further and larger demonstrations. Furthermore, the problem posed by the internet, and in particular the democratizing potential it involves, creates a further challenge to the regime that will not be easy to meet without impinging upon some of the other benefits that an unrestricted internet environment can produce.

The supplement to coercion, buying off through economic performance, also has its limits, especially for an economy like Russia's. Where the economy is so dependent upon one economic sector, natural resource extraction and sale, if that sector suffers a serious setback and popular rewards dry up, the whole equation changes. In Russia's case, the high prices for oil that prevailed over the last fifteen years dramatically fell in the second half of 2014, creating a major problem for the state budget. This problem was exacerbated by the Western sanctions imposed in the wake of the 2014 Ukraine crisis. But there is also a structural problem for the future of Russian energy exports represented by the growth of the exploitation of shale oil outside Russia. The potential of this to displace

Russian energy exports is considerable, especially given the fact that Russia is running out of easily extractable, and therefore cheap, oil.[8] If this were to happen, especially in the absence of economic reform and diversification, the economic consequences for Russia and its people could be disastrous. Furthermore, the increased efforts by the EU to diversify their sources of energy in the wake of the Ukraine crisis poses a significant threat to the continued capacity of Russia to sell large quantities of energy into this major market. Given the weakness of the development of other sectors of the economy, the reliance on natural resources makes the economy vulnerable. And if it is vulnerable, so too is any notion of the regime's social contract with the people.

Such a development could also have implications for the dirigiste nature of the economy. Economic downturn could call into question the whole economic model and create pressures for some form of restructuring. Any breakup of state involvement, such as through privatization, or dramatic expansion of state control would alter the economic structure and change the opportunity structures that existed for various groups, including those benefiting from the current arrangements. A shifting of economic control in either direction would create winners and losers, and would have the potential to create significant tension both in society more broadly and in the elite.

The maintenance of unity within the elite remains central to regime endurance, and there is little reason to expect that this will change in the short term. While Putin retains his personal dominance, elite conflict is likely to be kept within bounds. However, as he approaches the date for the next presidential election, it is likely that uncertainty will increase as the possibility of his departure from the scene becomes more apparent. By 2018 when the election is due, he will be approaching sixty-six, and although at this stage there is no evidence of health problems, it would not be unreasonable to anticipate that he might not go on for another term. The result of such uncertainty would presumably be an outbreak of maneuvering as people seek to position themselves for the approaching succession. This could have a destabilizing effect on the elite. However, the history of the regime since 1991 has been that it has been able to handle such succession issues: the Yeltsin to Putin transition was shaped by Yeltsin, while the choice of Medvedev to succeed Putin was decided by Putin himself after testing out two candidates. And of course Putin's return was arranged, if Medvedev is to be believed, from the time he (Putin) stepped down. So the regime has some experience at handling

---

[8] Gustafson (*Wheel*), p. 5. On Russia's problems not being those of the classic "oil curse," see the discussion on pp. 6–7.

the succession, and even if Putin is no longer personally as powerful when the time comes as he is now, the Yeltsin experience shows that he could still be the deciding factor in determining who is to succeed him. But of course, it might not work out like this. Just because the elite has been able to manage the succession successfully in the past does not mean that it can continue to do so. It may be that elite conflict will break out, and this could lead to some form of regime change. However, it is unlikely to lead to democratization unless that elite conflict is accompanied by mobilization and pressure from below, from civil society organizations pressing for democratic change.

Thus, the survival and stability of the Russian regime depends upon its ability to continue to manage effectively the two tasks central to authoritarian rule: to constrain and channel autonomous political activity and to structure the domestic functioning of the regime effectively. These two components of regime-building are essential to regime survival. This is where the regime is vulnerable to the tension between personal and institutional imperatives that is the chief characteristic of the post-Soviet Russian regime. This tension can only be overcome and authoritarian rule stabilized in the long term if the regime remains as adept at responding to challenges as it has been over the last decade and a half. And what this means is that the sort of state-building engaged in by Yeltsin and, to a greater extent, Putin is a continuing exercise. A successful authoritarian regime is never complete; it is always under construction.

# Bibliography

Almond, Gabriel A. and Sidney Verba, *The Civic Culture. Political Attitudes and Democracy in Five Nations* (Boston: Little, Brown and Company, 1965).

Ambrosio, Thomas, *Authoritarian Backlash. Russian Resistance to Democratization in the Former Soviet Union* (Farnham: Ashgate, 2009).

Applebaum, Anne, "How He and His Cronies Stole Russia," *The New York Review of Books*, December 18, 2014, pp. 26–30.

Aris, Ben, "Russia's Reaction to the Magnitsky Act and Relations with the West," *Russian Analytical Digest* 120 November 23, 2016, pp. 2–5.

Aron, Leon, "Russia's Protesters: The People, Ideals, and Prospects," *Russian Outlook* (Washington, DC: American Enterprise Institute for Public Policy Research, Summer 2012), pp. 1–13.

Ashwin, Sarah and Simon Clark, *Russian Trade Unions and Industrial Relations in Transition* (Basingstoke: Macmillan, 2003).

Balzer, Harley, "Managed Pluralism: Vladimir Putin's Emerging Regime," *Post-Soviet Affairs* 19 (3), 2003, pp. 189–227.

Baturin, Iu.M., A.L. Il'in, V.F. Kadatsky, B.B. Kostikov, M.A. Krasnov, A.Ia. Livshits, K.V. Nikiforov, L.G. Pikhoia, and G.A. Satarov, *Epokha Yeltsina. Ocherki politicheskoi istorii* (Moscow: Vagrius, 2001).

Bechle, Karsten, "Neopatrimonialism in Latin America: Prospects and Promises of a Neglected Concept," GIGA Working Paper No. 153, November 2010.

Beissinger, Mark R., *Nationalist Mobilization and the Collapse of the Soviet State* (Cambridge: Cambridge University Press, 2002).

Berdyaev, Nikolai, *The Russian Idea* (New York: The Macmillan Co., 1948).

Berliand, Irina and Marina Stupakova, *Rzgnevannye nabliudateli. Fal'sifikatsii parlamentskikh vyborov glazami ochevidtsev* (Moscow: Novoe literaturnoe obozrenie, 2012).

Billington, James H., *The Icon and the Axe. An Interpretive History of Russian Culture* (New York: Alfred A. Knopf, 1966).

Birch, Sarah, *Electoral Malpractice* (Oxford: Oxford University Press, 2011).

Bizyukov, Petr, "Labor Protests in Russia, 2008–2011," *Russian Analytical Digest* 104, October 27, 2011, pp. 6–9.

Borogan, Irina and Andrei Soldatov, "The Kremlin versus the Bloggers: The Battle for Cyberspace," *Open Democracy*, March 27, 2012, www.opendemocracy.net.

Braithwaite, Roderic, *Afgantsy. The Russians in Afghanistan 1979–1989* (London: Profile Books, 2011).

Bremmer, Ian and Samuel Charap, "The Siloviki in Putin's Russia: Who They Are and What They Want," *The Washington Quarterly* 30 (1), 2006–7, pp. 83–92.

Breslauer, George W., "Boris Yel'tsin as Patriarch," *Post-Soviet Affairs* 15 (2), 1999, pp. 186–200.

Brownlee, Jason, *Authoritarianism in an Age of Democratization* (Cambridge: Cambridge University Press, 2007).

Buck, Andrew D., "Elite Networks and World Views during the Yel'tsin Years," *Europe-Asia Studies* 59 (4), 2007, pp. 643–61.

Bunce, Valerie J. and Sharon L. Wolchik, *Defeating Authoritarian Leaders in Postcommunist Countries* (Cambridge: Cambridge University Press, 2011).
    "Defeating Dictators. Electoral Change and Stability in Competitive Authoritarian Regimes," *World Politics* 62 (1), 2010, pp. 43–86.

Burlatsky, Fedor, *Mikhail Gorbachev–Boris Yeltsin. Skhvatka* (Moscow: Sobranie, 2008).

Carnaghan, Ellen, "Popular Support for Democracy and Autocracy in Russia," *Russian Analytical Digest* 117, September 19, 2012, pp. 2–4.

Case, William, "Manipulative Skills: How Do Rulers Control the Electoral Arena?," Andreas Schedler (ed.), *Electoral Authoritarianism. The Dynamics of Unfree Competition* (Boulder: Lynne Riener Publishers, 2006), pp. 95–112.

Cassidy, Julie A. and Emily D. Johnson, "Putin, Putiniana and the Question of a Post-Soviet Cult of Personality," *Slavonic and East European Review* 88 (4), 2010, pp. 681–707.

Chaisty, Paul, *Legislative Politics and Economic Power in Russia* (Basingstoke: Palgrave Macmillan, 2006).
    "Majority Control and Executive Dominance: Parliament-President Relations in Putin's Russia", Alex Pravda (ed.), *Leading Russia. Putin in Perspective. Essays in Honour of Archie Brown* (Oxford: Oxford University Press, 2005), pp. 19–137.
    "The Federal Assembly and the Power Vertical," Graeme Gill and James Young (eds), *Routledge Handbook of Russian Politics and Society* (London: Routledge, 2012), pp. 92–101.

Cherniavsky, M., *Tsar and People: Studies in Russian Myths* (New York: Random House, 1969).

Colton, Timothy J., *Yeltsin. A Life* (New York: Basic Books, 2008).

Colton, Timothy J. and Henry E. Hale, "The Putin Vote: Presidential Electorates in a Hybrid Regime," *Slavic Review* 68 (3), 2009, pp. 473–503.

Colton, Timothy J. and Michael McFaul, "Are Russians Undemocratic?," *Post-Soviet Affairs* 18 (2), 2002, pp. 91–121.

Cook, Linda J., "Russian Labour," Graeme Gill and James Young (eds), *Routledge Handbook of Russian Politics and Society* (London: Routledge, 2012), pp. 318–28.
    "Workers in the Russian Federation. Responses to the Post-Communist Transition," *Communist and Post-Communist Studies* 28 (1), 1995, pp. 13–42.

D'Anieri, Paul, "Explaining the Success and Failure of Post-communist Revolutions," *Communist and Post-Communist Studies* 39 (3), 2006, pp. 331–50.

Dawisha, Karen, *Putin's Kleptocracy. Who Owns Russia?* (New York: Simon & Schuster, 2014).

Diamond, Larry, "Thinking about Hybrid Regimes," *Journal of Democracy* 13 (2), 2002, pp. 21–35.

Dicks, H.V., "Some Notes on the Russian National Character," C.E. Black (ed.), *The Transformation of Russian Society* (Cambridge [Mass.]: Harvard University Press, 1960), pp. 558–73.

Dimitrov, Martin K., "Understanding Communist Collapse and Resilience," Martin K. Dimitrov (ed.), *Why Communism Did Not Collapse. Understanding Authoritarian Regime Resilience in Asia and Europe* (Cambridge: Cambridge University Press, 2013), pp. 3–39.

Duhamel, Luc, *The KGB Campaign against Corruption in Moscow, 1982–1987* (Pittsburgh: University of Pittsburgh Press, 2010).

Duncan, Peter J.S., "Russia, the West and the 2007–2008 Electoral Cycle: Did the Kremlin Really Fear a 'Coloured Revolution'?," *Europe-Asia Studies* 65 (1), 2013, pp. 1–25.

Easter, Gerald M., "Preference for Presidentialism. Postcommunist Regime Change in Russia and the NIS," *World Politics* 49 (2), 1997, pp. 184–211.

Eisenstadt, Shmuel, *Traditional Patrimonialism and Modern Neopatrimonialism* (Beverley Hills: Sage, 1973).

Elgie, Robert, *Semi-Presidentialism. Sub-types and Democratic Performance* (Oxford: Oxford University Press, 2011).

European Institute for the Media [EIM], "Monitoring the Media Coverage of the 1995 Russian Parliamentary Election. Final Report," February 15, 1996.

"Monitoring the media coverage of the 1996 Russian presidential election," September 30, 1996.

"Monitoring the Media Coverage of the 1999 Russian Parliamentary Election. Preliminary Findings," March 2000.

"Monitoring the Media Coverage of the March 2000 Presidential Elections in Russia. Final Report," August 2000.

"The Russian Parliamentary Elections: Monitoring of the Election Coverage in the Russian Mass Media. Final Report," February 1, 1994.

Evans, Alfred B. Jr., "The First Steps of Russia's Public Chamber: Representation or Coordination?," *Demokratizatsiya* 16 (4), 2008, pp. 345–62.

Finkel, Evgeny and Yitzhak M. Brudny (eds), "Reassessing Coloured Revolutions and Authoritarian Reactions," *Democratization* 19 (1), 2012, Special issue.

"Russia and the Colour Revolutions," *Democratization* 19 (1), 2012, pp. 18–26.

Fish, M. Steven, *Democracy Derailed in Russia. The Failure of Open Politics* (Cambridge: Cambridge University Press, 2005).

*Democracy from Scratch. Opposition and Regime in the New Russian Revolution* (Princeton: Princeton University Press, 1995).

Flikke, Geir, *The Failure of a Movement: The Rise and Decline of Democratic Russia 1989–1992* (Oslo: Faculty of Humanities, University of Oslo, 2006).

Fortescue, Stephen, *Russia's Oil Barons and Metal Magnates. Oligarchs and the State in Transition* (Basingstoke: Palgrave Macmillan, 2006).

Freedom House, Freedom in the World 2013: Democratic Breakthroughs in the Balance, www.freedomhouse.org/report/freedom-world/freedom-world-2013#.U13eRMcwily.

Freeland, Chrystia, *Sale of the Century. The Inside Story of the Second Russian Revolution* (London: Little, Brown and Company, 2000).

Frye, Timothy, "A Politics of Institutional Choice. Post-Communist Presidencies," *Comparative Political Studies* 30 (5), 1997, pp. 523–52.

Gaidar, Yegor, *Days of Defeat and Victory* (trans. Jane Anne Miller; Seattle: University of Washington Press, 1999).

Gaman-Golutvina, Oxana, "Changes in Elite Patterns," Richard Sakwa (ed.), *Power and Policy in Putin's Russia* (London: Routledge, 2009), pp. 155–72.

Geddes, Barbara, *Paradigms and Sand Castles. Theory Building and Research Design in Comparative Politics* (Ann Arbor: University of Michigan Press, 2003).

"What Do We Know About Democratization after Twenty Years?," *Annual Review of Political Science* 2, 1999, pp. 115–44.

"Why Parties and Elections in Authoritarian Regimes?," unpublished, March 2006, pp. 1–30.

Gel'man, Vladimir, "From 'Feckless Pluralism' to 'Dominant Party Politics'. The Transformation of Russia's Party System," *Democratization* 13 (4), 2006, pp. 545–61.

Gessen, Masha, *The Man without a Face. The Unlikely Rise of Vladimir Putin* (London: Granta, 2012).

Gill, Graeme, *Bourgeoisie, State, and Democracy. Russia, Britain, France, Germany, and the USA* (Oxford: Oxford University Press, 2008).

*Symbolism and Regime Change in Russia* (Cambridge: Cambridge University Press, 2013).

*Symbols and Legitimacy in Soviet Politics* (Cambridge: Cambridge University Press, 2011).

*The Origins of the Stalinist Political System* (Cambridge: Cambridge University Press, 1990).

Gill, Graeme and Roderic Pitty, *Power in the Party. The Organization of Power and Central–Republican Relations in the CPSU* (Basingstoke: Macmillan, 1997).

Gill, Graeme and Roger Markwick, *Russia's Stillborn Democracy? From Gorbachev to Yeltsin* (Oxford: Oxford University Press, 2000).

GOLOS, "Association GOLOS – Domestic Monitoring of Elections of the President of Russian Federation, 4 March 2012: Preliminary Report," *Russian Analytical Digest* 110, March 16, 2012, pp. 8–16.

Goode, J. Paul, "The Revival of Russia's Gubernatorial Elections: Liberalization or Potemkin Reform?," *Russian Analytical Digest* 139, November 18, 2013, pp. 9–11.

Gorer, Geoffrey, "Some Aspects of the Psychology of the People of Great Russia," *The American Slavic and East European Review* 8 (3), 1949, pp. 155–66.

Gorer, Geoffrey and John Rickman, *The People of Great Russia. A Psychological Study* (London: The Cresset Press, 1949).

Gorshkov, M.K., *Gorbachev–Yeltsin: 1500 dnei politicheskogo protivostoianiia* (Moscow: Terra, 1992).

Goscilo, Helen (ed.), *Putin as Celebrity and Cultural Icon* (London: Routledge, 2013).

Gudkov, L.D., B.V. Dubin, N.A. Zorkaia, and M.A. Plotko, *Rossiiskie parlamentskie vybory elektoral'nyi protsess pri avtoritarnom rezhime* (Moscow: Analiticheskiit sentr Iuriia Levady, 2012).

Gustafson, Thane, *Wheel of Fortune. The Battle for Oil and Power in Russia* (Cambridge [Mass.]: The Belknap Press, 2012).

Hahn, Gordon M., *Russia's Revolution from Above 1985–2000: Reform, Transition, and Revolution in the Fall of the Soviet Communist Regime* (New Brunswick: Transaction Publishers, 2002).

Hale, Henry E., "Democracy or Autocracy on the March? The Colored Revolutions as Normal Dynamics of Patronal Presidentialism," *Communist and Post-Communist Studies* 39 (3), 2006, pp. 305–29.

"Eurasian Polities as Hybrid Regimes: The Case of Putin's Russia," *Journal of Eurasian Studies* 1, 2010, pp. 33–41.

"The Myth of Mass Russian Support for Autocracy: Public Opinion Foundations of a Hybrid Regime," *Europe-Asia Studies* 63 (8), 2011, pp. 1357–75.

"Trends in Russian Views on Democracy 2008–12: Has There Been a Russian Democratic Awakening?," *Russian Analytical Digest* 117, September 19, 2012, pp. 9–11.

*Why Not Parties in Russia? Democracy, Federalism, and the State* (Cambridge: Cambridge University Press, 2006).

Hanson, Philip, "The Russian Budget: Why So Much Fuss," *Russian Analytical Digest* 121, December 21, 2012, pp. 2–5.

Hanson, Stephen E., *Post-Imperial Democracies. Ideology and Party Formation in Third Republic France, Weimar Germany, and Post-Soviet Russia* (Cambridge: Cambridge University Press, 2010).

Henderson, Sarah L., *Building Democracy in Contemporary Russia. Western Support for Grassroots Organizations* (Ithaca: Cornell University Press, 2003).

Herron, Erik S., *Elections and Democracy after Communism* (Basingstoke: Palgrave Macmillan, 2009).

Hill, Fiona and Clifford G. Gaddy, *Mr. Putin. Operative in the Kremlin* (Washington, DC: Brookings Institution Press, 2013).

Hoffman, D.E., *The Oligarchs. Wealth and Power in the New Russia* (New York: Public Affairs, 2002).

Horne, Cale, "The Consistency of Policy with Opinion in the Russian Federation, 1996–2006," *Journal of Elections, Public Opinion and Parties* 22 (3), 2012, pp. 214–44.

Horvath, Robert, "Putin's Preventive Counter-Revolution. Post-Soviet Authoritarianism and the Spectre of Velvet Revolution," *Europe-Asia Studies* 63 (1), 2011, pp. 1–25.

*Putin's Preventive Counter-Revolution. Post-Soviet Authoritarianism and the Spectre of Velvet Revolution* (London: Routledge, 2013).

Hough, Jerry F., *The Soviet Prefects. The Local Party Organs in Industrial Decision-Making* (Cambridge [Mass.]: Harvard University Press, 1964).

Huskey, Eugene, "Elite Recruitment and State–Society Relations in Technocratic-Authoritarian Regimes: The Russian Case," *Communist and Post-Communist Studies* 43 (4), 2010, pp. 363–72.

*Presidential Power* (Armonk: M.E. Sharpe, 1999).

"Putin as Patron: Cadres Policy in the Russian Transition," Alex Pravda (ed.), *Leading Russia. Putin in Perspective. Essays in Honour of Archie Brown* (Oxford: Oxford University Press, 2005), pp. 161–78.

"The State-Legal Administration and the Politics of Redundancy," *Post-Soviet Affairs* 11 (2), 1995, pp. 115–43.

*Izmeneniia politicheskikh nastroenii rossiian posle prezidentskikh vyborov. Doklad ekspertov Tsentra strategicheskikh razrabotok Komitety grazhdanskikh initsiativ* Moscow, October 23, 2012.

Javeline, Debra, *Protest and the Politics of Blame: The Russian Response to Unpaid Wages* (Ann Arbor: University of Michigan Press, 2003).

Javeline, Debra and S. Lindemann-Komarova, "A Balanced Assessment of Russian Civil Society," *Journal of International Affairs* 63 (2), 2010, pp. 171–88.

Karlin, Anatoly, "Measuring Churov's Beard. The Mathematics of Russian Election Fraud," www.darussophile.com

Kirschke, Linda, "Semipresidentialism and the Perils of Power-Sharing in Neopatrimonial States," *Comparative Political Studies* 40 (11), 2007, pp. 1372–94.

Knox, Zoe, Peter Lentini, and Brad Williams, "Parties of Power and Russian Politics: A Victory of the State over Civil Society?," *Problems of Post-Communism* 53 (1), 2006, pp. 3–14.

Korzhakov, Aleksandr, *Boris Yeltsin: Ot rassveta do zakata* (Moscow: Interbuk, 1997).

Kostikov, Viacheslav, *Roman c prezidentom. Zapiski press-sekretaria* (Moscow: Vagrius, 1997).

Krashenninikov, Fyodor and Leonid Volkov, "Blue Skies, Clear Thinking: Russian Democracy in the Cloud," *Open Democracy*, November 16, 2012, www.opendemocracy.net.

Kryshtanovskaia, Ol'ga, "Transformatsiia staroi nomenklatury v novuiu rossiiskuiu elitu," *Obshchestvennye nauki i sovremennost'* 1, 1995, pp. 51–65.

Kryshtanovskaia, Olga and Stephen White, "From Soviet *Nomenklatura* to Russian Elite," *Europe-Asia Studies* 48 (5), 1996, pp. 711–33.

"Inside the Putin Court: A Research Note," *Europe-Asia Studies* 57 (7), 2005, pp. 1065–75.

"Putin's Militocracy," *Post-Soviet Affairs* 19 (4), 2003, pp. 289–306.

"The Rise of the Russian Business Elite," *Communist and Post-Communist Studies* 38 (3), 2005, pp. 293–307.

Kryshtanovskaya, Olga & Stephen White, "From Power to Property: The Nomenklatura in Post-Communist Russia," Graeme Gill (ed.), *Elites and Leadership in Russian Politics* (Basingstoke: Macmillan, 1998), pp. 81–105.

"The Formation of Russia's Network Directorate," Vadim Kononenko and Arkady Moshes (eds), *Russia as a Network State. What Works in Russia When State Institutions Do Not?* (Basingstoke: Palgrave Macmillan, 2011).

Lane, David, "Divisions within the Russian Political Elites," *Russian Analytical Digest* 124, March 18, 2013, pp. 2–5.

Lane, David and Cameron Ross, *The Transition from Communism to Capitalism. Ruling Elites from Gorbachev to Yeltsin* (Basingstoke: Macmillan, 1999).

Lane, David and Stephen White (eds), "Rethinking the Coloured Revolutions," *The Journal of Communist Studies and Transition Politics* 25, 2–3, 2009, Special issue.

Laruelle, Marlene, "Anti-Migrant Riots in Russia: The Mobilizing Potential of Xenophobia," *Russian Analytical Digest* 141, December 23, 2013, pp. 2–4.

Ledeneva, Alena, *Can Russia Modernise? Sistema, Power Networks and Informal Governance* (Cambridge: Cambridge University Press, 2013).

     *How Russia Really Works. The Informal Practices That Shaped Post-Soviet Politics and Business* (Ithaca: Cornell University Press, 2006).

     "Informality and Informal Politics," Graeme Gill and James Young (eds), *Routledge Handbook on Russian Politics and Society* (London: Routledge, 2012), pp. 375–85.

     *Russia's Economy of Favours: Blat, Networking, and Informal Exchange* (Cambridge: Cambridge University Press, 1998).

Levada Analytical Center, *Russian Public Opinion 2010–2011. Annual* (Moscow: Levada Center, 2012).

Levada, Iurii, "Segodniashnii vybor: urovni i ramki," *Vestnik obshchestvennogo mneniia. Dannye. Analiz. Diskussi* 2 (76) Mart-aprel' 2005.

Levitsky, Steven and Lucan A. Way, *Competitive Authoritarianism. Hybrid Regimes after the Cold War* (Cambridge: Cambridge University Press, 2010).

Lijphart, Arend (ed.), *Parliamentary versus Presidential Government* (Oxford: Oxford University Press, 1992).

Linz, Juan J., "An Authoritarian Regime: Spain," Erik Allardt and Stein Rokkan (eds), *Mass Politics. Studies in Political Sociology* (New York: The Free Press, 1970), pp. 251–83.

     *Totalitarian and Authoritarian Regimes* (Boulder: Lynne Rienner, 2000).

Linz, Juan J. and Arturo Valenzuela (eds), *The Failure of Presidential Democracy: Comparative Perspectives* (Baltimore: The Johns Hopkins University Press, 1994).

Lonkila, Markku, "Driving at Democracy in Russia: Protest Activities of St Petersburg Car Drivers' Associations," *Europe-Asia Studies* 63 (2), 2011, pp. 291–309.

Lowenhardt, John, James R. Ozinga, and Erik van Ree, *The Rise and Fall of the Soviet Politburo* (New York: St. Martin's Press, 1992).

Lukin, Alexander, *Political Culture of Russian 'Democrats'* (Oxford: Oxford University Press, 2000).

     "Putin's Regime: Restoration or Revolution?," *Problems of Post-Communism* 48 (4), 2001, pp. 38–48.

Magaloni, Beatriz, *Voting for Autocracy. Hegemonic Party Survival and Its Demise in Mexico* (Cambridge: Cambridge University Press, 2006).

Malkin, E. and E. Suchkov, *Politicheskie tekhnologii* (Moscow: Russkaia Panorama, 2008).

Mann, Michael, "The Autonomous Power of the State: Its Origins, Mechanism and Results," John A. Hall (ed.), *States in History* (Oxford: Basil Blackwell, 1986), pp. 109–36.

March, Luke, "Just Russia – From 'Second Leg' to 'Footnote'?," *Russian Analytical Digest* 102, September 26, 2011, pp. 7–10.

"Managing Opposition in a Hybrid Regime: Just Russia and Parastatal Opposition," *Slavic Review* 68 (3), 2009, pp. 504–27.

"Nationalism for Export? The Domestic and Foreign Policy Implications of the New 'Russian Idea'," *Europe-Asia Studies* 64 (3), 2012, pp. 401–25.

Mari, Aburamoto, "Who Takes Care of the Residents? United Russia and the Regions Facing the Monetization of L'goty," *Acta Slavica Japonica* 28, 2010, pp. 101–15.

Matsuzato, Kimitaka, "Elites and the Party System of Zakarpattya Oblast': Relations among Levels of Party Systems in Ukraine," *Europe-Asia Studies* 54 (8), 2002, pp. 1267–99.

McAuley, Alastair, "The Determinants of Russian Federal–Regional Fiscal Relations: Equity or Political Influence?," *Europe-Asia Studies* 49 (3), 1997, pp. 431–44.

McAuley, Mary, "Political Culture and Communist Studies: One Step Forward, Two Steps Back," Archie Brown (ed.), *Political Culture and Communist Studies* (Basingstoke: Macmillan, 1984), pp. 13–39.

McFaul, Michael, *Russia's 1996 Presidential Election: The End of Polarized Politics* (Stanford: Stanford University Press, 1997).

McMann, Kelly M., *Economic Autonomy and Democracy. Hybrid Regimes in Russia and Kyrgyzstan* (Cambridge: Cambridge University Press, 2006).

Mead, Margaret, *Soviet Attitudes toward Authority. An Interdisciplinary Approach to Problems of Soviet Character* (New York: William Morrow, 1955).

Medvedev, Dmitry, "Poslanie Prezidenta Federal'nomu Sobraniiu," December 22, 2011, www.kremlin.ru.

Mendras, Marie, *Russian Politics. The Paradox of a Weak State* (London: Hurst & Co., 2012).

Moen-Larsen, Natalie, "Communicating with the Nation: Russian Politicians Online," *Russian Analytical Digest* 123, February 21, 2013, pp. 10–12.

Moraski, Bryon, *Elections by Design. Parties and Patronage in Russia's Regions* (De Kalb: Northern Illinois University Press, 2006).

Moser, Robert G., *Unexpected Outcomes. Electoral Systems, Political Parties, and Representation in Russia* (Pittsburgh: University of Pittsburgh Press, 2001).

Mukhin, A.A., *Biznes-elita i gosudarstvennaia vlast': Kto vladeet Rossiei na rubezhe vekov?* (Moscow: Tsentr politicheskoi informatsii, 2001).

Myagkov, Mikhail and Peter C. Ordeshook, "The Trail of Votes in Russia's 1999 Duma and 2000 Presidential Elections," *Communist and Post-Communist Studies* 34 (3), 2001, pp. 353–70.

Myagkov, Mikhail, Peter C. Ordeshook, and Dimitri Shakin, *The Forensics of Election Fraud. Russia and Ukraine* (Cambridge: Cambridge University Press, 2009).

Neustadt, Richard, *Presidential Power. The Politics of Leadership* (New York: John Wiley & Sons, 1960).

OSCE Office for Democratic Institutions and Human Rights, "Russian Federation. Elections to the State Duma 19 December 1999. Final Report," February 13, 2000, www.osce.org.

"Russian Federation State Duma Elections 7 December 2003: Statement of Preliminary Findings and Conclusions." www.osce.org.

"Russian Federation. Elections to the State Duma, December 7, 2003," January 27, 2004, www.osce.org.

"Russian Federation Presidential Election 14 March 2004. Election Observation Mission Report," June 2, 2004, www.osce.org.

"Russian Federation. Elections to the State Duma 4 December 2011. OSCE/ODIHR "Election Observation Mission. Final Report" (Warsaw: OSCE/ODIHR, January 12, 2012), http://www.osce.org.

OSCE Parliamentary Assembly, "Russian Duma Elections 'Not Held on Level Playing Field' Say Parliamentary Observers," December 3, 2007, http://www.oscepa.org.

Oates, Sarah, *Revolution Stalled. The Political Limits of the Internet in the Post-Soviet Sphere* (Oxford: Oxford University Press, 2013).

"Television, Voters, and the Development of the 'Broadcast Party,'" Vicki L. Hesli and William M. Reisinger (eds), *The 1999–2000 Elections in Russia: Their Impact and Legacy* (New York: Cambridge University Press, 2003), pp. 29–50.

O'Donnell, Guillermo, "Delegative Democracy," *Journal of Democracy* 5 (1), 1994, pp. 55–69.

Olimpieva, Irina, "'Free' and 'Official' Labor Unions in Russia: Different Modes of Labor Interest Representation," *Russian Analytical Digest* 104, October 27, 2011, pp. 2–6.

Orttung, Robert, "Kremlin Nationalism versus Russia's NGOs," *Russian Analytical Digest* 138, November 8, 2013, pp. 8–11.

Orttung, Robert and Christopher Walker, "Putin and Russia's Crippled Media," *Russian Analytical Digest* 123, February 21, 2013, pp. 2–5.

Ostrow, Joel M., "Procedural Breakdown and Deadlock in the Russian State Duma: The Problems of an Unlimited Dual-Channel Institutional Design," *Europe-Asia Studies* 50 (5), 1998, pp. 793–816.

Ostrow, Joel M., Georgiy A. Satarov, and Irina M. Khakamada, *The Consolidation of Dictatorship in Russia. An Inside View of the Demise of Democracy* (Westport: Praeger, 2007).

Ottaway, Marina, *Democracy Challenged. The Rise of Semi-Authoritarianism* (Washington, DC: Carnegie Endowment for International Peace, 2003).

Oversloot, Hans and Reuben Verheul, "The Party of Power in Russian Politics," *Acta Politica* 35 (2), 2000, pp. 123–45.

Pertsev, Andrei and Elizabeta Surnacheva, "Moskva – liubitel'skaia," *Vlast'* 19 (1074), May 19, 2014, pp. 32–5.

Petro, Nicolai N., *The Rebirth of Russian Democracy. An Interpretation of Political Culture* (Cambridge [Mass.]: Harvard University Press, 1995).

Petrone, Laura, "Pro-Kremlin Youth Movements in Russia and the Idea of Conservative Modernisation," ISPI Analysis (Istituto per gli Studi di Politica Internazionale), No. 46, April 2011.

Pipes, Richard, *Russia under the Old Regime* (London: Weidenfeld & Nicolson, 1974).

Pitcher, Anne, Mary M. Moran, and Michael Johnston, "Rethinking Patrimonialism and Neopatrimonialism in Africa," *African Studies Review* 52 (1), 2009, pp. 125–56.

Ponomareva, Yulia, "Putin's Popular Front to Replace United Russia?," *Russia Beyond the Headlines* June 18, 2013, www.rbt.ru.

"Poslanie Prezidenta Federal'nomu Sobraniiu," December 12, 2012, http://kremlin.ru/transcript/17118.

"Predsedatel' Pravitel'stva Rossiiskoi Federatsii V.V. Putin vystupil v Gosudarstvennoi Dume s otchetom o deiatel'nosti Pravitelstva Rossiiskoi Federatsii za 2011," April 11, 2011, http://premier.gov.ru/events/news/18671/.

"Press konferentsiia Vladimira Putina," December 19, 2013, http://kremlin.ru/news/19859.

Prokhanov, O. (ed.), *Kto est' kto v Rossii. Spravochnoe izdanie* (Moscow: Olimp, 1997).

Putin, V., "'Kakuiu Rossiiu my stroim', Poslanie Prezidenta RF Vladimira Putina Federal'nomu Sobraniiu RF, 8 July 2000" *Ezhegodnye poslaniia prezidenta RF 1994–2005* (Novosibirsk: Sibirskoe universitetskoe izdatel'stvo, 2006), pp. 308–14.

"Poslanie Prezidenta RF Vladimira Putina Federal'nomu Sobraniiu RF, 26 May 2004," *Ezhegodnye poslaniia prezidenta RF 1994–2005* (Novosibirsk: Sibirskoe universitetskoe izdatel'stvo, 2006), pp. 377–93.

Putin, Vladimir, "Poslanie Federal'nomu Sobraniiu Rossiiskoi Federatsii," April 25, 2005, http://archive.kremlin.ru/appears/2005/04/25/1223_type 63372type63374type82634_87049.shtml

"Poslanie Federal'nomu sobraniiu Rossiiskoi federatsii," April 26, 2007, http://archive.kremlin.ru/appears/2007/04/26/1156_type63372type 63374type82634_125339.shtml.

Putin, V.V., "Poslanie Prezidenta Federal'nomu Sobraniiu," December 12, 2013, www.kremlin.ru/news/19825.

"Razgovor s Vladimirom Putinym. Prodolzhenie," December 15, 2001, http://premier.gov.ru/events/news/17409.

Remington, Thomas, "Patronage and the Party of Power: President–Parliament Relations under Vladimir Putin," *Europe-Asia Studies* 60 (6), 2008, pp. 959–87.

Remington, Thomas F. and Stephen S. Smith, "Political Goals, Institutional Context, and the Choice of an Electoral System: The Russian Parliamentary Election Law," *American Journal of Political Science* 40 (4), 1996, pp. 1253–79.

Remnick, David, "How Russia Is Ruled," *The New York Review of Books* April 9, 1998, pp. 10–15.

"The War for the Kremlin," *New Yorker* July 22, 1996, pp. 47–8.

Renz, Bettina, "Putin's Militocracy? An Alternative Interpretation of the Role of Siloviki in Contemporary Russian Politics," *Europe-Asia Studies* 58 (6), 2006, pp. 903–24.

"The Russian Power Ministries and Security Services," Graeme Gill and James Young (eds), *Routledge Handbook on Russian Society and Politics* (London: Routledge, 2012), pp. 209–19.

Reuter, O.J., "The Politics of Dominant Party Formation: United Russia and Russia's Governors," *Europe-Asia Studies* 62 (2), 2010, pp. 293–327.

Reuter, Ora John, "United Russia and the 2011 Elections," *Russian Analytical Digest* 102, September 26, 2011, pp. 2–5.

Reuter, Ora John and Thomas F. Remington, "Dominant Party Regimes and the Commitment Problem. The Case of United Russia," *Comparative Political Studies* 42 (4), 2009, pp. 501–26.

Rivera, Sharon Werning and David W. Rivera, "The Russian Elite under Putin: Militocratic or Bourgeois?," *Post-Soviet Affairs* 22 (2), 2006, pp. 125–44.

Roberts, Sean P., *Putin's United Russia Party* (London: Routledge, 2012).

Robertson, Graeme B., *The Politics of Protest in Hybrid Regimes. Managing Dissent in Post-Communist Russia* (Cambridge: Cambridge University Press, 2011).

Ross, Cameron, "Federalism and Defederalisation in Russia," Graeme Gill and James Young (eds), *Routledge Handbook on Russian Society and Politics* (London: Routledge, 2012), pp. 140–52.

Roth, Guenther, "Personal Rulership, Patrimonialism, and Empire-Building in the New States," *World Politics* xx (2), 1968, pp. 194–206.

Roxburgh, Angus, *The Strongman. Vladimir Putin and the Struggle for Russia* (London: I.B. Tauris, 2012).

"Russian Public Opinion on Migrants," *Russian Analytical Digest* 141, December 23, 2013, pp. 8–12.

Sakwa, Richard, *Putin. Russia's Choice* (London: Routledge, 1st edn., 2004; 2nd edn., 2008).

   *Putin and the Oligarch. The Khodorkovsky–Yukos Affair* (London: I.B. Tauris, 2014).

   *Russian Politics and Society* (London: Routledge, 1st edn., 1993; 2nd edn., 1996; 3rd edn., 2002).

   *The Crisis of Russian Democracy. The Dual State, Factionalism and the Medvedev Succession* (Cambridge: Cambridge University Press, 2011).

   "The Dual State in Russia," *Post-Soviet Affairs* 26 (3), 2010, pp. 185–206.

   *The Quality of Freedom. Khodorkovsky, Putin, and the Yukos Affair* (Oxford: Oxford University Press, 2009).

Sartori, Giovanni, *Parties and Party Systems. A Framework for Analysis* (Cambridge: Cambridge University Press, 1976).

Schedler, Andreas (ed.), *Electoral Authoritarianism. The Dynamics of Unfree Competition* (Boulder: Lynne Riener Publishers, 2006).

Schedler, Andreas, *The Politics of Uncertainty. Sustaining and Subverting Electoral Authoritarianism* (Oxford: Oxford University Press, 2013).

Schröder, H.-H., "El'tsin and the Oligarchs: The Role of Financial Groups in Russian Politics between 1993 and July 1998," *Europe-Asia Studies* 51 (6), 1999, pp. 957–88.

Schröder, Hans-Henning, "Forward to the Past! The President's Message to the Federal Assembly," *Russian Analytical Digest* 124, March 18, 2013, pp. 5–9.

Schwirtz, Michael, "Russia's Political Youths," *Demokratizatsiya* 15 (1), 2007, pp. 73–84.

Shlapentokh, Vladimir, with Joshua Woods, *Contemporary Russia as a Feudal Society. A New Perspective on the Post-Soviet Era* (Basingstoke: Palgrave Macmillan, 2007).

Shugart, M. and A. Carey, *Presidents and Assemblies: Constitutional Design and Electoral Dynamics* (Cambridge: Cambridge University Press, 1992).

Silitski, Vitali, "Contagion Deterred: Preemptive Authoritarianism in the Former Soviet Union (The Case of Belarus)," Valerie Bunce, Michael McFaul, and Kathryn Stoner-Weiss (eds), *Democracy and Authoritarianism in the Postcommunist World* (Cambridge: Cambridge University Press, 2010), pp. 274–99.

"Tools of Autocracy," *Journal of Democracy* 20 (2), 2009, pp. 42–6.

Simis, Konstantin, "Andropov's Anti-Corruption Campaign," *The Washington Quarterly* 6 (3), 1983, pp. 111–21.

Simon, Rick, "Media, Myth and Reality in Russia's State-Managed Democracy," *Parliamentary Affairs* 57 (1), 2004, pp. 169–84.

Slider, Darrell, "How United is United Russia? Regional Sources of Intra-party Conflict," *The Journal of Communist Studies and Transition Politics* 26 (2), 2010, pp. 257–75.

"Regional Governance," Graeme Gill and James Young (eds), *Routledge Handbook of Russian Politics and Society* (London: Routledge, 2012), pp. 153–63.

Smith, Benjamin, "Life of the Party. The Origins of Regime Breakdown and Persistence under Single-Party Rule," *World Politics* 57 (3), 2005, pp. 421–51.

Smith, Kathleen E., *Mythmaking in the New Russia. Politics and Memory during the Yeltsin Era* (Ithaca: Cornell University Press, 2002).

Smyth, Regina, "Building State Capacity from the Inside Out: Parties of Power and the Success of the President's Reform Agenda in Russia," *Politics and Society* 30 (4), 2002, pp. 555–78.

Smyth, Regina, Anna Lowry, and Brandon Wilkening, "Engineering Victory: Institutional Reform, Informal Institutions, and the Formation of a Hegemonic Party Regime in the Russian Federation," *Post-Soviet Affairs* 23 (2), 2007, pp. 118–37.

Soldatov, Andrei and Irina Borogan, *The New Nobility. The Restoration of Russia's Security State and the Enduring Legacy of the KGB* (New York: Public Affairs, 2010).

"Statement of the GOLOS Association on the Results of the Elections of Deputies for the State Duma December 4, 2011," *Russian Analytical Digest* 106, December 21, 2011, pp. 9–10.

Stepan, Alfred and Cindy Skach, "Constitutional Frameworks and Democratic Consolidation: Parliamentarianism and Presidentialism," *World Politics* 46 (1), 1993, pp. 1–22.

Stewart, John Massey, *The Soviet Environment: Problems, Policies and Politics* (Cambridge: Cambridge University Press, 1992).

Stoner-Weiss, Kathryn, "Comparing Oranges and Apples: The Internal and External Dimensions of Russia's Turn Away from Democracy," Valerie Bunce, Michael McFaul, and Kathryn Stoner-Weiss (eds), *Democracy and*

*Authoritarianism in the Postcommunist World* (Cambridge: Cambridge University Press, 2010), pp. 255–69.

*Suverennaia demokratiia: ot idei – k doctrine* (Moscow: Evropa, 2006).

Szamuely, Tibor, *The Russian Tradition* (ed. Robert Conquest; London: Secker & Warburg, 1974).

Taylor, Brian D., *State Building in Putin's Russia. Policing and Coercion after Communism* (Cambridge: Cambridge University Press, 2011).

Theobald, Robin, "Partrimonialism," *World Politics* 34 (4), 1982, pp. 548–59.

Tomasic, D., *The Impact of Russian Culture on Soviet Communism* (Glencoe: The Free Press, 1953).

Tompson, William, "Putin and the 'Oligarchs': A Two-Sided Commitment Problem," Alex Pravda (ed.), *Leading Russia. Putin in Perspective* (Oxford: Oxford University Press, 2005), pp. 179–202.

Treisman, Daniel, *After the Deluge: Regional Crises and Political Consolidation in Russia* (Ann Arbor: University of Michigan Press, 1999).

"Deciphering Russia's Federal Finance: Fiscal Appeasement in 1995 and 1996," *Europe-Asia Studies* 50 (5), 1998, pp. 893–906.

"The Politics of Intergovernmental Transfers in Post-Soviet Russia," *British Journal of Political Science* 26 (3), 1996, pp. 299–335.

Turovsky, Rostislav, "The Mechanism of Representation of Regional Interests at the Federal Level in Russia: Problems and Solutions," *Perspectives on European Politics and Society* 8 (1), 2007, pp. 73–97.

Vakar, Nicholas P., *The Taproot of Soviet Society. The Impact of Russia's Peasant Culture upon the Soviet State* (New York: Harper & Brothers, 1961).

Way, Lucan, "Resistance to Contagion: Sources of Authoritarian Stability in the Former Soviet Union," Valerie Bunce, Michael McFaul, and Kathryn Stoner-Weiss (eds), *Democracy and Authoritarianism in the Postcommunist World* (Cambridge: Cambridge University Press, 2010), pp. 229–52.

"The Sources of Authoritarian Control after the Cold War: East Africa and the Former Soviet Union," *Post-Soviet Affairs* 28 (4), 2012, pp. 424–48.

Weber, Max, *Economy and Society. An Outline of Interpretive Sociology* (eds Guenther Roth and Claus Wittich; Berkeley: University of California Press, 1978).

Wedel, Janine R., *Collision and Collusion. The Strange Case of Western Aid to Eastern Europe 1989–1998* (New York: St. Martin's Press, 1998).

White, Stephen, "'Democratisation' in the USSR," *Soviet Studies* 42 (1), 1990, pp. 3–24.

"Elections Russian Style," *Europe-Asia Studies* 63 (4), 2011, pp. 531–56.

*Political Culture and Soviet Politics* (London: Macmillan, 1979).

"Ten Years On, What Do the Russians Think?," *The Journal of Communist Studies and Transition Politics* 18 (1), 2002, pp. 35–50.

"The USSR: Patterns of Autocracy and Industrialism," Archie Brown and Jack Gray (eds), *Political Culture and Political Change in Communist States* (London: Macmillan, 1977, pp. 25–65.

*Understanding Russian Politics* (Cambridge: Cambridge University Press, 2011).

White, Stephen and Ian McAllister, "Did Russia (Nearly) have a Facebook Revolution in 2011? Social Media's Challenge to Authoritarianism," *Politics* 34 (1), 2014, pp. 72–84.

White, Stephen, Sarah Oates, and Ian McAllister, "Media Effects and Russian Elections, 1999–2000," *British Journal of Political Science* 35 (2), 2005, pp. 191–208.

Whitefield, Stephen, "Russian Citizens and Russian Democracy: Perceptions of State Governance and Democratic Practice, 1993–2007," *Post-Soviet Affairs* 25 (2), 2009, pp. 93–117.

Wilkinson, Cai, "Putting Traditional Values into Practice: Russia's Anti-Gay Laws," *Russian Analytical Digest* 138, November 8, 2013, pp. 5–7.

Willerton, John P., "Post-Soviet Clientelist Norms at the Russian Federal Level," Graeme Gill (ed.), *Elites and Leadership in Russian Politics* (Basingstoke: Macmillan, 1998), pp. 52–80.

"Presidency," Graeme Gill and James Young (eds), *Routledge Handbook of Russian Politics and Society* (London: Routledge, 2012), pp. 81–91.

Wilson, Andrew, *Virtual Politics. Faking Democracy in the Post-Soviet World* (New Haven: Yale University Press, 2005).

Winters, Jeffrey A., *Oligarchy* (Cambridge: Cambridge University Press, 2011).

Yeltsin, Boris, *Midnight Diaries* (London: Weidenfeld & Nicolson, 2000).

Yudina, Natalia, "RuNet, Hate Crime and Soft Targets: How Russia Enforces Its Anti-extremism Law," *Open Democracy*, October 30, 2012, www.opendemocracy.net.

Zuev, Denis, "The Russian March: Investigating the Symbolic Dimension of Political Performance in Modern Russia," *Europe-Asia Studies* 65 (1), 2013, pp. 102–26.

# Index